Challenges and Achievements

OF AMERICAN EDUCATION

1993 Yearbook of the Association for
Supervision and Curriculum Development

D0973845

Editor

Developing Leadership for Quality in Education for All Students

Association for Supervision
and Curriculum Development
1250 N. Pitt Street
Alexandria, VA 22314-1403
   Telephone (703) 549-9110
   FAX (703) 549-3891

Printed in the United States of America by Edwards Brothers, Inc.
Typeset on Xerox™ Ventura Publisher 4.1.0.

Ronald S. Brandt, *Executive Editor*
Nancy Modrak, *Managing Editor, Books*
Carolyn R. Pool, *Associate Editor*
Jennifer Beun, *Editorial Assistant*
Gary Bloom, *Manager, Design and Production Services*
Karen Monaco, *Designer*
Stephanie Kenworthy, *Assistant Manager, Production Services*
Valerie Sprague, *Desktop Publisher*

Price: $19.95
ASCD Stock No.: 610-93000
ISBN: 0-87120-200-X
ISSN: 1042-9018

Challenges and Achievements of American Education

Foreword   v
Stephanie Pace Marshall

Introduction: Change in American Education   1
Gordon Cawelti

1. Equity: A Call to Action   9
Floretta Dukes McKenzie

2. Progress Toward Professionalism in Teaching 19
Linda Darling-Hammond and A. Lin Goodwin

3. The Growth of Assessment 53
George F. Madaus and Ann G.A. Tan

4. Curriculum Reform 80
William H. Schubert

5. Innovation, Reform, and Restructuring Strategies . . 116
Michael Fullan

6. Inventing and Reinventing Ideas: Constructivist
Teaching and Learning in Mathematics 134
Penelope L. Peterson and Nancy F. Knapp

7. Change and Continuity in Supervision
and Leadership 158
Edward Pajak

8. Important Education-Related U.S. Supreme Court
Decisions (1943–1993) 187
Cheryl D. Mills

Conclusion: The Search for a System 193
Gordon Cawelti

About the Authors 203

ASCD 1992–93 Board of Directors 205

    Executive Council 205

    Review Council 205

    Members at Large 206

Affiliate Presidents 207

ASCD Headquarters Staff 209

ASCD Networks and Facilitators, 1992–93 210

Foreword

In 1943, daily life in the United States focused on the nation's extraordinary involvement in the Second World War. While citizens at home struggled with rationing and concern about their loved ones in military service, members of the armed forces risked their lives in another effort to make the world safe for democracy. Few could have foreseen that world leadership by the United States would continue over a half century through the end of the Cold War—and would see democracy emerging throughout the world. Likewise, few could have predicted that the establishment of a new curriculum group in 1943 would create one of the premier leadership organizations in education.

When members of the National Education Association's Department of Supervisors and Directors of Instruction met with members of the Society for Curriculum Study, the result was the new Department of Supervision and Curriculum Development, which marked the birth of the Association for Supervision and Curriculum Development (ASCD). The department's first yearbook was *Leadership at Work*, and ASCD has been working and leading since that time. In this fiftieth year of ASCD, it is most appropriate that the yearbook once again focuses on the challenges of curriculum, instructional supervision, and leadership for education in our nation.

In this retrospective and prospective exploration of the changes that have transpired in education, the authors thoughtfully and persuasively articulate the challenges facing us now and in the future to enhance the systems that affect student learning. The yearbook not only traces the history of curriculum reform, but also provides a perspective on the current debate about providing a national framework for curriculum and assessment. In addition, the authors document how the social forces at work in this country over the years have been reflected not only in our curriculum but in our assessment strategies as well, particularly in the emergence of standardized testing and its profound implications for social policy. The authors address questions of centralization and decentralization and analyze the evolution of teaching and—with John Dewey—the purposes of education in a democracy.

The yearbook contains vital insights about good teaching and learning and the need for all of us to continue our professional growth in these two critical dimensions of the educational enterprise. Borrowing a construct from Peter Senge, the authors of this Golden Anniversary yearbook question whether schools are learning organizations as well as teaching organizations. They also ask us to reflect on the critical attributes of professional practice while concurring with John Goodlad that we lack some of the fully developed components of a profession.

We know that education is often buffeted by the winds of change from other societal forces. The impact of major policy shifts brought about by decisions of the U.S. Supreme Court, as well as the stresses of the Cold War and the bewildering global implications of its end, are synthesized in this yearbook. As we cope with the new technological complexities of the last decade of the 20th century, educators around the world confront new challenges of teaching higher-order learning skills and enabling their students to succeed in a rapidly changing workplace. As the authors of the yearbook emphasize, our belief that *all* students can learn is not just a current fad, but the foundation of all education reform, including recent efforts to restructure schools and effect systemic reform of all services to children and families in our society.

I want to commend all who had a part in the creation and development of this anniversary yearbook. The publication of this milestone in our history required the efforts of numerous contributors. I want to thank them all, especially the editor, Gordon Cawelti; the chapter authors; and the ASCD staff for their important contributions to this historic volume.

For its Fiftieth Anniversary Conference, ASCD chose the theme, "Creating Learning Communities: A Call for Bold Alliances and Commitment." Just as the United States had established alliances with other countries and made lasting commitments in 1943 to bring an end to World War II, we have an opportunity to use the knowledge now available to us to forge new alliances through systems thinking, interdisciplinary teaching, cognitive research, constructivist theory, and other approaches critical to educational redesign and restructuring.

Today ASCD is well positioned to provide international educational leadership. It is most fitting that our fiftieth yearbook recalls the emerging leadership of the United States in the world of 1943, describes the critical alliance that created ASCD, and concludes with the mission we have as an organization to provide educational vision and leadership in a world where democratic forms of government may thrive. I think Thomas Jefferson would have seen it as the opportunity of a lifetime.

STEPHANIE PACE MARSHALL
ASCD President, 1992–93

Introduction: Change in American Education

Gordon Cawelti

It is fitting that on ASCD's Golden Anniversary we take a long look at American education during the past fifty years and try to understand where we are now and where the next fifty years might take us. Ironically, the period 1943–1993 also describes the lifetime of many educators today: according to Linda Darling-Hammond and A. Lin Goodwin in Chapter 2, the average teacher in the United States is about forty years old and has taught for fifteen years. The challenges and achievements described here have been experienced by many teachers, administrators, parents, and professors.

But this yearbook is no walk down memory lane; it could very well have been titled *Change in American Education*, to describe both the changes of the past and the changes needed for the *immediate* future. As Ed Pajak says in Chapter 7, "The world recently crossed the threshold of an era that is as disruptive and full of promise as the Industrial Revolution. Schools are at the forefront of these changes." Think of it: The end of the Cold War. The Technology Revolution. The Global Marketplace. To the infinite implications of these current realities add other disturbing situations: drugs, guns, and our youth; scientific illiteracy among Americans; recession, underemployment, unemployment, and homelessness; poverty levels unseen in twenty-five years; decaying bridges, schools, and social services; single-parent teenagers; continuing discrimination against minorities and people with disabilities; the "glass ceiling" that many women face in pursuit of achievement.

To many of the authors of this yearbook, schools may be at the forefront of the changes needed, but schools alone cannot provide them. Whether or not we embrace the political aims and objectives of President Bush's *America 2000* program to improve the nation's schools, we cannot disagree with one of the goals of the program: Children must come to school *ready to learn*. As Renate Nummela Caine and Geoffrey Caine (1991) emphasize in *Making Connections: Teaching and the*

Human Brain, "If, beginning tomorrow, we did nothing more than protect children from destructive experiences closely linked to some form of abandonment, we would have an emotionally healthier, brighter generation twenty years from now."

Providing equal access to a quality education in a technological society is part of such protection. In the search for excellence in education, **Floretta Dukes McKenzie** reminds us in Chapter 1 of this book that we must not forget the educational equality that Martin Luther King, Jr., and others struggled to gain for students from minority groups, students from economically disadvantaged families, and students with disabilities—as well as students denied opportunities because they were female. McKenzie, a former superintendent of schools in the District of Columbia, endorses the push for higher educational standards evident across the United States—but she emphasizes that such standards should be defined to include an acknowledgement of the multicultural heritage of the diverse groups that are represented by our students. And she implores educators—and communities, businesses, and social service agencies—to come up with creative ways for students at risk of failure to meet those standards. McKenzie reviews recommendations of the Carnegie Corporation Quality Education for Minorities (QEM) Project, including public/private partnerships, parent education, and school/social service centers. Our motivation for such systemic change may no longer be the noble ideals of equity and equality, but of economic survival in a global, technological society. As the QEM Project found, we suffer from dangerous myths in education today. Myth Number 1: "We can be competitive and have a world class country with an educated elite while most of the country remains uneducated." McKenzie flatly refutes those holding to this view—and makes the issue intensely personal by showing that our own retirement income depends on the educational outcomes of *all* of today's students.

The preparation of teachers and the conditions of their employment are critical to the improvement of educational opportunities for our students, as **Linda Darling-Hammond** and **A. Lin Goodwin** state in Chapter 2. Unfortunately, teaching is still a "not-quite" profession, and the second-class status of most teaching jobs does not attract the best and the brightest. The authors examine the background of these limitations, including public regulations, hierarchical bureaucracies, standardized testing and "teaching to the test," and teaching shortages that lead to emergency certification. The authors state: "Paradoxically, numerous reforms intended to 'professionalize' teaching have included measures that further control and regularize teaching (e.g., externally developed curriculum mandates and tests, regulation of teaching methods, and routinized prescriptions for the curriculum of teacher preparation programs)."

Meanwhile, fewer and fewer college students are showing an interest in teaching as a career (though there has been a recent, slight, upward swing), and about one-third of the current teaching force faces retirement in the '90s. How do we attract *and retain* bright new teachers? Darling-Hammond and Goodwin examine new and proposed policies that could contribute to the professionalism of teaching—including salary structures that are competitive with other professions; partnerships between schools of education and practitioners, including mentoring and peer-coaching programs that help support new teachers; a grounding of teacher education programs in cognitive psychology, developmental psychology, learning theory and pedagogy, and professional ethics; and the creation of professional standards boards for teacher licensing. Research has shown that better prepared teachers produce better education for our children. As the authors state, teachers have made much progress over the past fifty years; but the challenges facing teachers today require vast changes of our educational institutions, including "fundamental restructuring of schools—the ways in which they make decisions, organize instruction, provide for collaborative planning and assessment of outcomes, and allocate authority for tasks ranging from personnel selection to program development and student assessment."

In Chapter 3, **George F. Madaus** and **Ann G.A. Tan** explore the issue of student—and teacher—assessment as it has developed in the past fifty years. The predominance of standardized testing and the proposals for a national assessment of student achievement affect every aspect of U.S. education. How do we reconcile the need for accountability on a mass scale with calls for higher-order learning, critical thinking skills, and authentic assessment? How do we justify reliance on multiple-choice tests and fill-in-the-bubble exams in a world where complexity is the rule and flexibility is the norm? In a standardized testing environment in which every community is "above average," how do we find out what students really know and can do?

Madaus and Tan trace the development of standardized testing in the United States, particularly following the invention of the optical scanning device that makes scoring the bubbles cheap and easy, as well as the development of ability and intelligence tests that are used to stratify and classify students. These developments have often obscured the older American belief that all children could learn if properly taught.

Often children are tracked, through test results, into subgroups that are not expected to learn as much as other, "better" students. As the authors state, "Curriculum became differentiated according to student 'ability' level, often with disastrous consequences for minorities and non-English speakers." The cycles of educational reform that have swept the United States in the past fifty years have, ironically, often included testing as one of the remedies for the deficiencies that testing has uncovered. The most recent wave of reform includes national assessments and authentic assessments as guarantors of student success; but the authors remind us that because assessment drives curriculum, we need to carefully consider our accountability measures.

Chapter 4, by **William H. Schubert**, continues our exploration of the reform cycles in American education, focusing on curriculum. As the author states, generations of American educators have quarreled and wrangled over even the *definition* of curriculum; and as of the publication of this yearbook, there is still no agreement, except to say that curriculum is whatever is taught. Schubert describes the different camps of educational curricular theorists, including the "intellectual traditionalists," the "social behaviorists," the "experientialists"—and a fourth, exemplified over the years by ASCD, the "conciliators." What should be the *Content of the Curriculum*? (This, indeed, was the title of ASCD's 1988 best-selling yearbook, edited by Ron Brandt.) Should we emphasize the great works and ideas of Western culture, with a focus on learning all the information possible during our school years? Should we try to change students' behavior through manipulatives, carefully planning objectives and measuring results as scientifically as possible? Should we provide a range of meaningful experiences for our students, so that they learn by doing?

American educators have tried all these approaches, and an infinite number of blends, throughout the fifty years of ASCD's existence. Indeed, many an inservice session has been greeted with skepticism by teachers who wonder what bandwagon they will be asked to board next. First new math, then thinking skills. Now cooperative learning, then global education. As Darling-Hammond and Goodwin advocate in Chapter 2, Schubert insists that teachers learn about the theoretical foundations of each educational reform movement. Was Dewey right? Why was Alfred North Whitehead so up-to-date (measured in our time) in 1928? Was Skinner wrong? Should we go back to the basics? What *are* the basics in a globally competitive, technological society? Schooling in the next century may well have to be completely different from what we know today. Will we be ready?

Schubert provides a decade-by-decade survey of curriculum in the United States, from mid-World War II to the present, with ample references to both curriculum scholars and well-known education writers. He discusses current attempts at curricular reform, including collaboration, interdisciplinary education, and action research; and he reminds us that we can learn much from these scholars and writers—we don't have to reinvent the wheel. Schubert states: "Too many who do collaborative action research are virtually unaware of the heritage of similar work at their disposal. If collaborative researchers of today immersed themselves in similar work of the progressive education era, they might well determine more ways to involve not only teachers, administrators, and scholar-researchers, but students and parents as well."

It is this possibility for *systemic* change that intrigues **Michael Fullan** in Chapter 5. To Fullan, much of the past fifty years in education has demonstrated failed reforms, innovations that were not implemented, and restructuring that had no effect on instructional strategies or on student learning. American systems of education have proved to be incredibly resistant to change—despite influential works like *A Nation at Risk* and innumerable state and district mandates, as well as the grass roots movement for school-based management. Fullan explores the issue of top-down mandates versus bottom-up initiatives, citing studies of state-level reforms over a three-year period. Results varied widely. Why? "Aggressive state leadership that coupled comprehensive focus with local district and school development did have an impact . . . . The key variable seemed to be local district capacity." Fullan stresses the importance of both leadership and local change, and he presents "Eight Lessons of Change" that reflect the dynamic nature of change, the constant tension between what's "out there" and what's "in here." Fullan calls for a culture of change, a "reculturing" to go with restructuring. Drawing on the works of current reform experts such as Miles, Goodlad, Odden, Marsh, Sarason, and Senge, Fullan defines this new culture within the framework of his eight lessons.

To Fullan (and others in this yearbook), the future of American education is threatened by unparalleled concerns: lopped-off budgets in recessionary times; the decay and violence of our cities; teacher burnout and public criticism of schools; and the quasi-public/private school and the growing movement for choice in education. How will we accomplish *systemic* reforms if school *cultures* don't change? In our complex age, we unquestionably need better schools. But Lesson 1, according to Fullan, is "You Can't Mandate What Matters." We need to connect with each other and with our local communities, always re-membering Lesson 8, "Every Person Is a Change Agent." Then we will see *real* improvements in the teaching and learning process.

In Chapter 6, **Penelope L. Peterson** and **Nancy F. Knapp** use results of action-research projects to provide a remarkable look at how students construct knowledge and how teachers facilitate their work. This process, known as the almost unpronounceable "constructivist" approach to learning, has its roots in Deweyan experiential theory and its branches in social behaviorist theory, in a way. For teachers guide and encourage, plan and test; but they let their students discover things, find importance, learn how to learn. The authors transcribe scenes from two classrooms engaged in mathematics lessons. In one classroom, a student, "Sean," disputes with the teacher and many of the students over what's odd and what's even, and ends up discovering a new type of number, which the teacher respectfully calls "Sean numbers." Turns out that Sean had rediscovered one of Euclid's definitions of odd/even numbers, which everyone else had forgotten.

In another classroom, the teacher gently nudges an unwilling student to make his own discoveries, while encouraging another student to go beyond what the group is discussing and apply what he has learned to other situations. This teacher had been math phobic herself until she participated in a math workshop based on cognitive learning theory, the foundation of constructivism. As Peterson and Knapp state, "The major thesis of [Cognitively Guided Instruction] is that children enter school with a great deal of informal, intuitive knowledge of mathematics that can serve as the basis for developing much of the formal mathematics of the primary school curriculum." The authors describe classrooms where children use their own prior experiences with, say, parallel lines, to develop their own problems and come up with their own applications to mathematics, learning addition, subtrac-tion, and geometry along the way—as well as learning that they are competent, skilled human beings. In these classrooms, "Students . . . 'ask hard questions' because 'they really want to know things.'"

Are our schools learning environments? That is one question raised by **Edward Pajak** in Chapter 7. In our current bureaucracy-laden school systems, supervision too often assumes an inspectorial role, not the facilitative, collaborative leadership role required of supervisors in changing schools. Indeed, the concept of "supervision" is changing as a result of school-based management, school-community partnerships, and the increasing professionalism of teaching. As Pajak states, the collaborative view of supervision is not new to ASCD: The 1943 Yearbook, *Leadership at Work*, urged educational leaders (in incredibly straightforward, clear language) to solicit ideas from other people, work on real problems, and plan cooperatively.

Pajak traces fifty years of supervisory thought in roughly four categories: the supervisor as the "democratic educator," the "organizational change agent," the "corporate visionary," and the "leader as teacher." Today the teaching and learning aspects of supervision are becoming more important, as people in supervisory roles help "transform" education through empowerment of themselves and others; systemic solutions involving the entire community; inquiry, reflection, and innovation; and collaborative, moral vision.

Though, as the old saying goes, you can't legislate morality, the U.S. Supreme Court has served in the past fifty years as the conscience of the nation, particularly concerning issues of equity and access to quality education. As well, according to **Cheryl D. Mills** in Chapter 8, the Supreme Court has ruled on educational issues related to the Bill of Rights—such as free speech and free exercise of religion. Mills provides a concise description of education-related Supreme Court decisions, from *Brown v. Board of Education* (1954), which overturned the "separate but equal" doctrine, to the recent *Board of Education of Westside Community Schools v. Mergens* (1990), which guaranteed students the right to hold religious group meetings in public schools if other non-curriculum-related groups were allowed such access.

Other Supreme Court decisions address teachers' rights and authority, such as the right to conduct "legally justifiable" searches of students (e.g., for drugs or cigarettes), the right to prohibit vulgar language in school, and the right to "reasonably" censor school-sponsored student newspapers. Other cases extended students' rights to free political expression and guaranteed due process in cases of misconduct.

A decision related to the freedom of religion—but with much broader implications—is *Mueller v. Allen* (1983), which allowed deductions from state taxes for tuition at any elementary or secondary school. Because this decision laid the groundwork for a "voucher" or choice program in public education, Mills states that this decision has "perhaps the most far-reaching effects."

* * *

In the 1992 ASCD Yearbook, *Supervision in Transition*, the editor, Carl D. Glickman, made a concerted effort to obtain the views of practitioners (teachers), supervisors (administrators), and "experts" (professors). Many of the chapters are relevant to the change process taking place in schools across the United States today. For example, in Chaska, Minnesota, the school renewal team emphasized three lessons they had learned from their change process:

1. Create a shared vision of the desired outcome.
2. Create a climate for collaboration.
3. Take the long view and hold the course.

Many schools and districts are working today to develop new structures (even, literally, to come up with new architectural designs for more effective schools); invent new curricular frameworks that support global student outcomes; implement more balanced assessment programs; provide more equitable access to quality instruction through untracking, nongrading, mainstreaming, cooperative learning, and attention to learning styles; prepare students for a technologically demanding work environment; provide advanced staff development and mentoring opportunities for teachers and administrators; work with communities and social service agencies—and come up with creative funding. As Schubert says in Chapter 4, educators need a deep knowledge base in education—they don't have to start from scratch in innovation. Read. Talk. Gather. And—today—learn about the bar code, conquer the mysteries of the VCR, and fire up that modem.

References

Brandt, R. (1988). *Content of the Curriculum.* 1988 Yearbook of the Association for Supervision and Curriculum Development. Alexandria, Va.: ASCD.

Caine, R.N., and G. Caine. (1991). *Making Connections: Teaching and the Human Brain.* Alexandria, Va.: ASCD.

Glickman, C. (1992). *Supervision in Transition.* 1992 Yearbook of the Association for Supervision and Curriculum Development. Alexandria, Va.: ASCD.

1

Equity: A Call to Action

Floretta Dukes McKenzie

> *Through education we seek to change attitudes; through legislation and court orders we seek to regulate behavior. Through education we seek to change internal feelings (prejudice, hate, etc.); through legislation and court orders we seek to control the external effects of those feelings . . . . One method is not a substitute for the other, but a meaningful and necessary supplement.*
>
> *Martin Luther King, Jr.*

Over twenty years ago, Martin Luther King, Jr., spoke of his belief in the interrelationships among educators, the courts, and legislators as the major forces for overcoming racial prejudice. This initial focus on equal access has since evolved into a focus on equity. Moreover, the interrelationship between education and legislative policy has evolved—and continues to evolve—into a partnership to remove obstacles that now prevent many members of society—especially minorities—from striving for and achieving success through educational excellence. Although we have come a long way since the days of Martin Luther King, Jr., we face a growing need to find new approaches to achieving the educational equality that King thought would come once the physical barriers were removed. Educators and policymakers must join forces with other government agencies to bridge the gap between the haves and have-nots. This gap threatens the safety of our cities today, as well as the economic survival of our society into the next century.

For many students, the gap has been narrowed through programs and policies legislated over the past twenty years. Such programs have enhanced educational opportunities for racial minorities, people with disabilities, and students from low-socioeconomic status families. For example, the rights of students with disabilities have been communicated widely so that parents can advocate the educational supports students need. For students from poor families, many states are attempting to distribute state education funds so that districts affected by poverty are able to give their schools the same levels of resources found in richer districts.

As well, girls and women today have more access to traditionally male occupations and educational pathways. In the past twenty years, we have seen progress in opportunities for women students in athletic activities, in career counseling, and in mathematics and science enrollments.

Despite all these gains, equity in the schoolhouse, particularly for minorities, continues to be a critical issue that must be addressed.

Definitions and Clarifications

What does *equity* mean? Differences in definition—for terms like *equal access, equity, equality,* and *excellence*—have implications for policy development. Unfortunately, these terms have been used in association with education so frequently that often they are thought to be interchangeable.

One dictionary defines equity as "conformity to accepted standards of natural right, law and justice *without prejudice, favoritism, or fraud or without rigor entailing undue hardship*" (emphasis added). The same dictionary defines equality as "the quality or state of being equal as likeness or sameness in quality in spite of physical inequality." In layman's terms, *equity* usually means fairness and justice or impartiality, whereas *equality* refers to sameness of status or competency.

Equity does *not* mean lowering of standards for minorities but rather raising the abilities of all students to meet existing standards. Further, the "sameness in quality or status," which defines equality, does not imply that the goal of equality is to enable minorities to achieve success by the standards of the majority culture, but that new standards should emerge for minorities and nonminorities alike.

Though not as easily defined, *equal access* traditionally means impartiality in opportunity. Equal access and equal opportunity are usually applied only to physical and legal barriers and, therefore, can be achieved by removing those barriers—and by providing adequate support for those who have traditionally been "locked out."

Excellence, a popular buzzword, unfortunately has been translated into a preoccupation with toughening standards. Examples of excellence—by way of the standards route—are increased graduation requirements, the obsession with test scores, and competency exams as a prerequisite for granting diplomas. One of the most troubling trends today is that legislators—and even educators—have embraced the notion of excellence and turned a rather cold shoulder to an earlier emphasis on equity. Unfortunately, when people push to raise standards, they sometimes overlook the need for coupling higher standards with the means of enabling students to reach those standards. The "C-average standard" for extracurricular and athletic participation is a classic example of how a "positive trend" can potentially become harmful if imposed without adequate support for those failing to meet the standard. Excellence without attention to adequate support and assistance has emerged as another obstacle "entailing undue hardship" and, therefore, is in opposition to equity.

Educators are in the business of nurturing, developing, and producing student success. The real task is to do it as equitably as possible, opening the doors of educational opportunity for educational excellence to all students. The real measure of excellence is in what we do for all students to help them rise to those expectations of performance—and that is also a measure of equity. Equity means fairness; and any proposal for educational excellence that fails to address the question of "What is fair?" falls short of the mark. Any school district's strategy for achieving educational excellence must reexamine its courses of study, its curriculums, its promotion standards and graduation requirements, its teacher certification and recertification standards, and its employment practices.

Excellence with equality is the goal of education; equal access, with equity, is the means for achieving that goal. Excellence and equity represent ideal values, to be sure, but we must not for this reason slacken our pursuit of them.

Motivations for the Pursuit of Equity

It would be somewhat naive to believe that the motivation for pursuing educational excellence through equity is grounded solely in the constitutional guarantees that underpin our society. Appeals for "fairness" and "inalienable rights" have little impact in the political climate that has emerged during the 1980s and early 1990s. Excellence in schools and schooling has not always been inspired by noble considerations of equity. Large segments of our population—black and white, yellow and brown, male and female—have been systematically excluded from opportunities to pursue or achieve educational excellence or to secure a place in the larger society. It is difficult for women and racial minorities to secure equally fair and just treatment if the power group (composed overwhelmingly of white men) does not admit them to equality of opportunities in the economic structure.

Some very compelling motives exist for pursuing educational equity. These motives are based on changing societal and economic conditions and the growing failure of the current educational structure to adapt to these changes. In fact, a greater understanding and acknowledgment of these motives may provide a better rationale for policymakers than any of the more noble reasons pursued by King. The evolution of American society and the work force into a multicultural environment and the growing influence of international trade on the economy are more than enough justification. Indeed, economic necessity is becoming the key to increasing our commitment to educational equity. Minorities compose an increasing proportion of our population and work force.

The problems with which public educators are grappling reflect the broader society. The disenfranchisement of minority youth (especially males) has resulted in an epidemic of drug abuse and drug-related violence, as well as the attraction of drug sales as a viable career option. Equity should be about raising aspirations for success for all students. We need to view educational equity in terms of economic equity: investments in educational equity are more profitable than investments in penal institutions.

From a global perspective, the majority of the U.S. population is a minority of the world population. With an increasing global and international social and economic interdependence, it is self-defeating for the United States to continue to attempt to dominate through its elite rather than building on the strengths of its ethnic and racial diversity.

From a purely economic point of view, failure to pursue educational equity for minority youth is a form of slow suicide. The internationalization of the economy will require an increasing economic competitiveness. The U.S. lead in this area continues to diminish as we lose ground in technology and manufacturing and in the development of a competent and competitive work force. Just as twenty-five years ago no one could have projected the diversity of the computer-related careers that exist today, it is impossible to project the diversity of careers that will be available during the 21st century. We must transcend the common practices of focusing on basic skills and marketable skills for minority students without providing the thinking and learning skills that will help them adapt to the 21st-century career environment. The continued development and use of leading-edge technology will require a high-quality work force.

On a more selfish note, the next generation of workers will require three workers to support each person on Social Security—and two of those three workers will be minorities. Whether politically liberal, conservative, or middle-of-the-road, today's older workers must maximize the learning skills and, therefore, the earning skills of tomorrow's minority workers, on whom they will rely for their retirement incomes.

It is clear that the shaping of educational policy must include a reshaping of schools and community colleges to better equip them to meet the challenge of providing educational equity. In this literacy-intensive society, when we need basic reading and writing skills more than ever before, our education system is turning out an increasingly inferior product. The overstated emphasis on test scores and the use of these scores as an indication of success by school districts often hinders innovative instruction and affects minority and low-income students more negatively than others. Current trends, such as basic skills, life skills, and competency-based education, can be dangerous if we view these approaches as the primary methods for achieving equity. We must pay increased attention to the development of higher level thinking skills.

According to testimony provided before the Carnegie Corporation Quality Education for Minorities (QEM) Project National Resource Group, educational institutions have much to do with why minorities do not stay in school. Factors cited during this testimony include:

- Differential tracking
- Segregation into minority schools
- Lack of identification with counselors and teachers
- Poor attitudes and low expectations from teachers
- Lack of support systems
- Unclear goals
- Feelings of failure
- Undefined values
- Problems at home
- Lack of parental involvement
- Curriculum that does not include minority perspectives

Although none of these factors breaks new ground in identifying new approaches for addressing the equity issue, each factor indicates the broad spectrum of problems that must be addressed before any change can be made.

The reshaping of educational institutions must also include higher education. Colleges and universities, as well, have failed in their mission to better promote educational equity. This failure is particularly evident at the community and junior college level, on which many minority students must rely to pursue higher education degrees. As these institutions, perennially subject to funding shortages, take on new functions to meet the needs of their students, they assign less emphasis on the transfer function and, thereby, inadvertently block their students from gaining entrance to universities and four-year colleges.

Education Myths

Before looking at some suggested solutions for shaping educational policy to promote equity, we should analyze frequently mentioned myths that stand in the way of any significant progress. The Carnegie Corporation QEM Project identified some of the more common myths:

• *"We can be competitive and have a world class country with an educated elite while most of the country remains uneducated."* This dangerous myth not only perpetuates past inequities but also seriously undermines our ability to remain internationally competitive.

• *"The growth of services will reduce the need for well-educated workers."* The growth of leading-edge technology in even the service industries clearly contradicts this myth.

• *"Learning is due to innate ability."* Past successes in Head Start programs have proven this myth false and have demonstrated that a healthy and enriched environment is more influential on learning than innate ability.

• *"It costs too much to provide quality eduction to all people."* Numerous studies have indicated that proactive intervention is more cost effective than either social services support or incarceration.

• *"We cannot have equity and excellence in education systems."* This myth assumes that equity implies the lowering of standards and, therefore, compromises excellence. A system with equal educational opportunity is more likely to achieve a higher average level of excellence and have a larger number of outstanding performances than one based on extremes in opportunity.

• *"We need only make marginal changes to our educational systems in order to restore them to the 'golden age.' "* This myth is usually repeated by people whose educational experiences were filtered through the rose-colored glasses of their youth. Return to the "good old days" is a return to elitism, tracking, and sex stereotyping.

- *"School reform is a passing fad."* Thomas Dewey did not consider school reform to be a passing fad at the turn of the century, and many of his recommendations remain valid almost 100 years later.
- *"The problems are so deeply entrenched that there is nothing we can do about them."* Although it is true that many problems are deeply entrenched, the very worst thing we can do about them is to continue to ignore them in the hopes that they will just go away.

Proposed Solutions

In good conscience, we cannot speak of the need for a greater emphasis on educational equity by educators and policymakers without proposing some solutions. If the solutions were easy, the problems would already be solved. The need still remains for a strong commitment of fiscal and human resources. Most effective solutions will require more effective funding—and this means better use of existing and additional resources. Educators and policymakers must use their creativity to develop new ideas. The policy challenge is to approach education with a holistic view.

Fortunately, some recent approaches and new ideas can produce results and are easy to replicate, as the QEM Project has made clear. The following solutions are not meant to be all inclusive, but rather the catalyst for further discussions.

Public/Private Partnerships

Public and private partnerships have arisen during the past decade to fill the void caused by funding cutbacks. Though originally perceived as more charitable than cost effective, these unique working relationships among schools, private industry, and public agencies are proving their benefit on many levels. A surprising outcome is the high degree of personal satisfaction for those employees from the private and government sector who are involved in the partnerships.

People form partnerships to minimize costs and reap mutual gains, not to subsidize one another. Many private partners are willing to make substantial contributions for economic incentives other than tax write-offs or public relations. U.S. businesses spend an estimated $60 billion annually on training employees, and a large part of that money is spent to upgrade employees' basic skills. An active role in the development of future workers, as well as the opportunity for preferential recruitment from a dwindling labor force, are proving to be adequate incentives for an increasing role by industry in the public education process.

Leadership Development

Leadership development through special institutes, programs, and clubs is an emerging alternative to the lure of the world outside the school. The leadership abilities demonstrated by minority male youths on the streets need to be developed and positively channeled within the educational environment. Positive minority male and female role models are taking an active role in this area.

We also need to pay greater attention to equity in leadership at the employee level. In 1982, 241 of 13,715 superintendents were women—only 1.8 percent. This is indicative of the fact that public education is staffed by women but controlled by men. There is a desperate need for more minority teachers and administrators. The industry lure of the best and the brightest to meet racial quotas, which took place during the late '60s and the '70s, must now be reversed by luring the best and the brightest back to education as a profession.

Year-Round Schooling and Saturday/Summer Academies

Basic-skills instruction, tutoring, and other similar remediation strategies usually rely on pullout or special grouping approaches that conflict with regular classroom instructional time designated for all students and, therefore, perpetuate the need for remediation. The problem is exacerbated by the fact that pullout often occurs either during enrichment activities that promote higher level thinking skills or during grade-level reading and mathematics instruction, possibly the most important time for remedial students to be regular classroom participants. It is clear that the only viable opportunity to provide *extra* instruction is after students receive the same instruction as their peers. Therefore, additional instructional time should be accomplished through extended days, Saturday and summer academies, or other scheduling options. Neighborhood learning or homework centers should be located within the community to provide enriched environments conducive to better achievement.

Transition Transfer Colleges

At the postsecondary level, two types of educational institutions need to be created in place of the current community and junior colleges. The transition college, using the most advanced educational technology available to diagnose and deliver individualized instruction, would be responsible for providing whatever necessary instructional support is required for young adults who wish to continue their education yet lack the necessary skills. Writing, research, and reasoning skills would be a normal part of the curriculum, in addition to basic skills remediation. Students exiting the transition colleges would be able to enroll into transfer colleges and directly into four-year colleges or universities. Transfer colleges would concentrate solely on those courses required for an associate of arts degree, which may then be used for transfer of credits and completion of studies at regular four-year colleges or universities. Transfer colleges would work closely with these institutions to ensure the validity of their course offerings and the acceptance of their transfer credits.

Parent Education and Early Intervention

Enriching the environment of babies through early intervention and parental education will dispel the notion that learning results from innate abilities and not from environmental influences. Teenage parents without adequate learning skills, thinking skills, and self-actualization skills cannot be expected to create the appropriate environment for their children to obtain these skills without adequate assistance and support. Transition colleges could also serve a role in this endeavor by providing a daytime educational environment for young parents who are too old for public school and too involved with familial responsibilities for evening schools. A time bomb waiting to explode is the growing number of children whose parents have used drugs, alcohol, and cigarettes during pregnancy and who are suffering learning and behavioral problems as a result. Increased prenatal services must be provided as an educational investment in these future students.

Professionalism and Alternative Hiring Practices

While looking at new and improved instructional delivery systems, we must also concentrate on the development of personnel involved in that process. In addition to raising the level of pay and, therefore, the quality of the teaching and administration in our schools, we must develop fair methods for rewarding the efforts of exceptional employees, as in the private sector. Additional resources must be used to attract the best teachers into working with students most in need of remediation and support and to reward those who achieve accelerated growth among their students. The issue of merit pay must not be abandoned, but further negotiated until both administrative and teaching staff can find a fair way of determining and rewarding instructional success.

In addition, alternative hiring practices need to be explored that would allow retirees, part-time employees, college professors, non-working mothers with professional degrees, and other personnel with skills in such areas as science, mathematics, and computers to augment the full-time teaching staff without denigrating existing certification requirements. Surely the increasing teacher shortages in these critical areas are motivation enough to pursue this alternative.

Combined School/Social Service Delivery Institutions

Many urban schools sit like oases in the center of the community (locked up during evenings, weekends, holidays, and summers) with laboratories full of computers; libraries full of books; and classrooms full of math, science, and reading instructional materials while students play on the asphalt surfaces among the syringes and other drug paraphernalia. Unlocking these doors will do more to unlock the barriers toward achieving equity for all students than any other investment. The growing failure of traditional social support structures (family, church, mental health units, etc.) and the proliferation of negative factors (drugs, crime, etc.) that affect our minority youth require that the schools go beyond their traditional roles to address these problems before they can proceed with the business of education.

Although educators have traditionally frowned on these new responsibilities, it is increasingly clear that the school must emerge as the center of community life and support just as the church filled this role in earlier generations. Extended day care, health care, and combined social service and educational delivery institutions would provide the necessary services while freeing educators to do what they do best.

* * *

We have seen some progress in the struggle to remove many physical barriers to equality in education since Martin Luther King, Jr.'s, call to action twenty years ago. Now, all citizens must echo King's call to action by pressuring our legislators and the leaders of our educational institutions to remove the other barriers (status and economic inequities) to educational equity. The solutions described here would help remove these barriers and move us toward our goal of excellence and equity in education; and these are only a few of many possible proposals that offer that promise for our schools in the future.

Our nation's economic survival and the personal future of each citizen depend on a strengthened educational experience for *all* students. Through dialogue and problem solving, our legislators and educational leaders can produce the changes in schools needed to revitalize the future for all U.S. citizens.

2

Progress Toward Professionalism in Teaching

Linda Darling-Hammond and A. Lin Goodwin

> *Teaching has long been numbered among the profes-*
> *sional occupations. . . . [Yet] teaching has developed the*
> *characteristic features of a profession very slowly and*
> *is still in the process of achieving equal status with other*
> *professions (Anderson 1962, p. 140).*

The quasi-professional status of teaching has long been noted by scholars of the professions. Three decades after Anderson's tenuous prognosis was published in *Education for the Professions*, the professionalism of teaching continues to constitute a major dilemma for educators. It is also a critical issue in the reform of American education, featured prominently in the public and professional debates of the 1980s.

In the past five years, the focus of these debates has shifted attention from curricular mandates (National Commission on Excellence in Education 1983) to an examination of the ways in which teachers are, or should be, prepared (Carnegie Forum on Education and the Economy 1986, The Holmes Group 1986). Embedded in the debate about teacher preparation are deeper questions involving teacher quality, the nature of teaching, and governance and decision making in education.

In this chapter, we examine the evolution of teaching in terms of the many dimensions of professional work:

- The nature of preparation
- Standards for entry
- The nature of the work

• The responsibilities assumed by members of the occupation for defining and enforcing professional practice

We begin with an analysis that evaluates teaching against broad definitions of a profession: Does teaching yet exhibit the hallmarks of a profession? This analysis serves as a backdrop for an examination of the current status of teaching as an occupation and the evolution of teaching as a professional activity. We then explore why teaching continues to be perceived as "the not-quite profession" (Goodlad 1990a, p. 71), and we suggest which of many current initiatives might further teaching as a profession. Finally, we discuss the implications for practice associated with the continued pursuit of policies that enhance teaching as a profession.

The Question of Teaching as a Profession

Many different models for professionalism have evolved in technical fields, such as architecture, engineering, and accounting, and human service fields, such as medicine, social work, and the clergy. These models demonstrate both common features of professions and differences in how they incorporate professional goals. The differences are related to their diverse missions in society, their occupational status, and their authority for self-governance and control over membership. The progress of teaching toward professionalism should be evaluated both according to the common goals of professions and the unique role that education plays in society.

Definitions of Professionalism

Becoming a profession is neither a dichotomous event nor a state of grace clearly granted to an occupation. Rather, it describes points along a continuum representing the extent to which members of an occupation share a common body of knowledge and use shared standards of practice in exercising that knowledge on behalf of clients. A profession incorporates specialized knowledge, self-regulation, special attention to the unique need of clients, autonomous performance, and responsibility for client welfare (Darling-Hammond 1990a).

Although the term *professionalism* "is a collective symbol . . . not a neutral and scientific concept" (Becker 1962, p. 33), a common set of beliefs and behavior is associated with the notion of professionalism:

1. The work of professionals relies on a codified body of knowledge, which is not applied routinely but rather according to the individual needs of each case.

2. Entry to the profession must be strictly controlled by members within the profession through internally structured mechanisms that regulate recruitment, training, licensure, and standards for appropriate and ethical practice.

3. Professionals owe their primary responsibility to the needs of clients; this ethical commitment should override secondary imperatives, such as personal gain, political exigencies, or simple expedience (Becker 1962, Darling-Hammond 1990a, Goodlad 1990a).

Thus, issues like money, status, and autonomy, though often thought to indicate professional status, are not the primary definers of a profession; nor are they the primary impetus for seeking professional status. Rather, professional practice is distinguished by its efforts to become *client oriented* and *knowledge based* (Darling-Hammond 1990a). Professionals aim to improve practice and enhance accountability by creating means for ensuring that practitioners will be competent and committed. Professionals undergo rigorous preparation and socialization so that the public can have high levels of confidence that professionals will behave in knowledgeable and ethical ways.

Professionalism is not an end state for an occupation; rather, it is a continual process of reaching for this set of goals, differently realized in various kinds of work. Occupations that are in various stages of being "professionalized" (and, often simultaneously, "deprofessionalized") are dealing in many different ways with the dilemmas of regulating occupational governance, membership, work structure, and knowledge acquisition. Such regulation must serve the public's interest in accessible, high-quality services, while enhancing the professionwide knowledge base and the competence of members of the profession.

Many tensions exist between costs and quality; between public regulation and professional self-governance; between controls that ensure competence among practitioners and those that create self-interested monopolies. Reconciling all these tensions—which manifest themselves in different ways at different times for various occupations—is part of the challenge facing professionals as they seek to serve social goals and the needs of their clients.

Teaching is certainly susceptible to these tensions. In fact, given its special character in a system providing compulsory education to serve society's political, economic, and social needs, teaching is more heavily buffeted by these cross-currents than most other occupations seeking to assume the mantle of professionalism. It is partly for these reasons that teaching, by almost any definition, is still not quite a profession.

Professionalism and Teaching

Progress toward professionalism can be recognized by (1) the requirements for training and entry into an occupation, (2) the nature of the work and the structure of the job, (3) the authority relations that govern these things, and (4) the bases for accountability, including the relationship that exists between practitioners and their clients and between practitioners and the society at large. On several of these dimensions, teaching has made considerable progress toward professionalism over the past century—especially in the past two decades—but on none of them has teaching attained the goals of a profession.

Although requirements for training have increased, standards for entry remain violable when classrooms must be staffed in the face of shortages. And shortages in various fields have been nearly perpetual in American schools for more than a century (Sedlak and Schlossman 1986). Teaching remains the only licensed occupation—including many that are not considered professions, such as cosmetology or plumbing—in which licensing standards are routinely waived to fill employment vacancies.

And though effective teaching requires a great deal of discretion and flexibility, the structure of teaching jobs in bureaucratized schools presses for routine implementation of standardized procedures. This contradiction frequently places teachers in the nonprofessional position of having to treat diverse students uniformly, even when the standardized practice required for bureaucratic accountability would be viewed as malpractice if evaluated by the standards of professional accountability.

Whereas professions assume responsibility for defining, transmitting, and enforcing standards of practice, teachers currently have little or no control over most of the mechanisms that determine professional standards. Instead, in most states, authority for determining the nature of teacher preparation, the types and content of tests used for licensure, and the regulations that govern practice rests with governmental bodies (legislatures and school boards) and with administrative agencies (state departments of education and central offices). These authority relations ultimately tend to produce bureaucratic rather than professional controls over the content and structure of the work. Finally, there is not yet a highly developed professional accountability structure in teaching. No professional organization, such as the American Bar Association or the National Architectural Registration Board, exists to represent the professional views of all members of the occupation. State professional practice boards, such as those that set licensing standards and provide oversight of practice in all other professions, are still relatively rare in teaching. Educators have not yet been able to establish the kinds of peer review and other accountability mechanisms that will guarantee that only those who can meet acceptable standards of practice will be admitted, graduated, licensed, hired, and retained in the profession. This kind of self-regulation is required of legitimate professions.

Despite this rather gloomy analysis of the current status of teaching as a profession, important progress has been made in each of these areas in recent years; and developments on the horizon hold great promise. The ultimate outcome of current initiatives to professionalize teaching will largely depend on how well teachers articulate and justify a more professional conception of teaching than has been common until now, and the extent to which teachers accept responsibility for more professional accountability structures to support this view.

Conceptions of Teaching

Clearly, teachers play many different roles and undertake an extraordinary range of tasks (Anderson 1962). One way to examine conceptions of teaching is to look at how teachers' work is viewed and structured. Mitchell and Kerchner (1983) suggest that the work of teachers may be conceptualized as labor, craft, art, or profession, depending on how tasks are organized.

Teaching as Labor

A view of teaching as labor suggests work that is preplanned, highly structured and routinized, and closely supervised. Tasks are generally defined by those not directly engaged in the work: "It is the manager, not the laborer, who must decide when, how, and for what purposes work effort should be directed" (Mitchell and Kerchner 1983, p. 217).

In our hierarchical systems of schooling, many people at the top view the teacher as technician or laborer. In their view, learning is predictable; and student learning depends on strategies predetermined by the administration and passed on for implementation by teachers. The "separation of conception from execution" (Apple 1987, p. 68) places the teacher in the role of technician. In this role, the teacher is charged with implementing "a defined set of skills, knowledge, and attitudes which lead to predetermined learning outcomes" (Zumwalt 1988, p. 153). This image continues to dominate educational reform legislation, as well as popular views of how educational change occurs (Apple 1988, Duke 1984, Gitlin and Smyth 1989, McCutcheon 1988).

Teaching as a Craft

Teaching as a craft connotes greater responsibility for "selecting and applying appropriate specialized techniques in order to realize . . . specific objectives" (Mitchell and Kerchner 1983, p. 217). Work is not directly supervised but is evaluated for competence and precision. Craft workers are more likely to be licensed to ensure minimum standards of quality and to protect the public. Though craft workers exhibit specialized knowledge, their decisions are based on the application of standardized modes of practice.

The notion of teacher as craft worker can be seen in training programs that emphasize "tricks of the trade" over theory and reflection, and that rely on formulas for action over contingent uses of knowledge. Craft conceptions of teaching undergird many "research-based" approaches to teacher education and teacher evaluation that impart or assess a set of basic techniques, usually derived from correlational studies, as a basis for routine practice. These approaches are fairly circumscribed and do not encourage investigation into techniques that might be more appropriate for diverse circumstances and goals (Darling-Hammond, Wise, and Pease 1983).

Teaching as an Art

Teaching as an art emphasizes personal creativity and adaptability. Because artistry depends on the marriage between innate talent and a codified knowledge base or a delineated set of skills, artists are "granted a great deal of autonomy in order to allow for the exercise of this artistic sensitivity" (Mitchell and Kerchner 1983, p. 218). The act of teaching is artful in that teachers must display creativity and initiative in their work with students. Greatness as a teacher is often characterized by immeasurable qualities that extend beyond content knowledge or specific technique—intuition, personality or individual dynamism, a sixth sense that "reads" students' needs.

Though teaching does rely on a foundation of knowledge as well as on technique, many people who consider teaching as an art might believe that teachers are born rather than developed; some fear that teaching practice conceived this way could become so individual as to be idiosyncratic. However, teachers who conceive of their work as art can incorporate standards shared by peers as the foundation for more personalized interpretations or performances.

Teaching as a Profession

When teaching is seen as a profession, teachers are "expected to analyze or diagnose situational factors and adapt working strategies to the true needs . . . of their clients" (Mitchell and Kerchner 1983, p. 218). The deliberative teacher engages in self-reflection and analysis, makes carefully considered choices about instruction based on the needs of students, and assumes responsibility for the curriculum (Zumwalt 1988).

Like craft workers, professionals depend on specific knowledge and skills. The difference lies in a mode of "thinking or reflectiveness that is very different from the predictive or calculative" (Greene 1987, p. 183). Professionals not only know whether and when to choose particular courses of action according to general principles, but they can also evaluate multifaceted situations in which many variables intersect. Practice is monitored by peers according to standards of the profession; and the standards reflect the interactive, complex nature of the work.

These four conceptions of teaching are not mutually exclusive; teaching encompasses elements of each. Some teaching tasks are appropriately routine, such as taking attendance or handing out materials. Many others, such as planning a lesson, managing classroom activities, or giving a lecture, require more specialized skills. Some, such as inspiring and motivating students, may rely on artistry. Still others, such as evaluating student learning, designing learning opportunities to meet the needs of individual children, or diagnosing interpersonal problems, require substantial judgment and analysis.

Problems with nonprofessional conceptions of teaching arise when they create constraints on the acquisition of knowledge or the use of judgment in circumstances where these are necessary for success. And recent research on teaching suggests that requirements for substantial knowledge and judgment are more often present than not, given the differences in student learning modes and the complexities of teacher decision making. Effective teaching techniques vary by subject area, grade level, the goals of instruction, and the characteristics of students—their learning styles, stages of development, interests, aptitudes, prior experiences, and motivations (Darling-Hammond et al. 1983).

Because student needs vary, most teaching work cannot be effectively routinized; thus, the standard methods for managing nonprofessional work cannot be applied without jeopardizing the success of the work. Since the knowledge base in professions is indeterminate—that is, it cannot be reduced to rules or prescriptions for practice—professionals must have autonomy in determining their occupational tasks and must evaluate performance by expert peer review rather than by bureaucratic procedures.

"Knowledge-based work," says Friedson, "the work of professionals, is by its very nature not amenable to mechanization and rationalization" (1973, p. 55). Judgment and nonroutine skill define the work of professionals. By this standard, teaching ought to be both considered and managed as a profession. As Benveniste explains:

> Professionalization . . . is the substitution of discretionary roles for routinized roles. Professional roles rely on a knowledge base and discretion within the limited domain of that base . . . . These roles depend more on peer evaluation than on line-management evaluation . . . . They also imply greater interaction with other professionals and greater discretion in designing and carrying out tasks (1987, p. 23).

Quite often, however, nonprofessional conceptions of teaching, though they are not consciously held, determine the structure of the occupation and the design of teaching tasks. Paradoxically, numerous reforms intended to "professionalize" teaching have included measures that further control and regularize teaching (e.g., externally developed curriculum mandates and tests, regulation of teaching methods, and routinized prescriptions for the curriculum of teacher preparation programs). The persistence of nonprofessional conceptions of teaching largely rests in the evolution of teaching as an occupation, and in the characteristics of those who serve within its ranks.

The Evolution of Teaching as an Occupation

As in other professions, the educational requirements for entering teaching have increased over time. One hundred years ago, teachers needed no more than a grammar school education to teach; fifty years ago, a college education was desirable but not mandatory. Today, most teachers have at least a master's degree, and members of the Holmes Group and others are discussing whether teacher education should be moved to the graduate level. Meanwhile, the focus of regulatory measures has shifted from restrictions on teachers' *personal* lives to stricter controls over what teachers need to know to practice—their *professional* qualifications. Since the 1940s, virtually all states have "raised" standards for entry by regulating teacher education offerings and, more recently, requiring licensing tests.

Yet, as we discuss later, these efforts to raise entry requirements for teaching have often provided the trappings of professionalism without the substance. There are three reasons for this. First, the nature of the standards adopted has been largely outside the control of the profession. Thus, the standards represent screens to entry, but not a professional consensus about knowledge, standards of practice, or appropriate forms of regulation.

Second, the standards are waived or diluted whenever the supply of teachers fails to meet demand. Thus, because they are not standards that function to guarantee some level of knowledge on the part of all practitioners, they cannot claim to protect the public interest.

Finally, the social and economic features of teaching as an occupation have maintained shortages and impeded self-governance.

Teacher Education and the Social Status of Teaching

Horace Mann initiated American reforms to professionalize teaching in 1839 by establishing the first publicly supported "normal" (or model) school for preparing teachers. Others soon followed suit, so that by 1900 most urban elementary teachers had attended normal school (Woodring 1975, p. 3). However, normal schools offered "little more than helpful hints on controlling and managing children, handling classroom routines and the like" (Goodlad 1990a, p. 71).

Because most American communities in the late 1800s hired only unmarried females, these normal schools were attended primarily by single, middle-class women and by those who did not intend to teach but were attracted by the opportunity to receive inexpensive schooling. The feminization of teaching throughout the last part of the 19th century helped local communities keep salaries for teachers low and controls over teachers high (Sedlak and Schlossman 1986). Teachers were typically expected to perform all teaching and custodial chores for schools, to board with local citizens, to remain unmarried, and to restrict their personal and social activities in many ways. They could be dismissed at will.

At the turn of the century, the progressives began pressing for professional schools of education analogous to those being established in law, medicine, and the applied sciences. Their establishment in many universities, albeit with lower status than those they sought to emulate, is, according to Cremin (1965, p. 104), "one of the leading educational developments of the twentieth century. . . . But," he notes, "they have always been under attack from faculties of arts and sciences, and in recent years that attack has grown sharper."

After World War II, rapid expansion and prosperity encouraged many more Americans, including teachers, to attend and complete college. State teachers colleges became part of multipurpose state colleges and universities. By 1961, 85 percent of all teachers possessed bachelor's degrees (Sedlak and Schlossman 1986).

Ironically, the "baby boom" of the '50s and '60s precipitated another teacher shortage, which resulted in the issuance of thousands of emergency teaching licenses to fill the gap, once again setting back efforts to professionalize teaching. With another round of temporary salary increases to counteract these shortages, teaching became an upwardly mobile route for individuals from modest circumstances who took advantage of increased educational opportunities and G.I. Bill support. This changed the social and gender composition of the teaching force, attracting more poor and working-class males (30 percent by 1970) and members of minority groups (Sedlak and Schlossman 1986).

By the 1970s, with declining school enrollment, the country experienced its first short-lived teacher glut. Enrollment in teacher preparation programs plummeted, forcing numerous colleges to close or scale back their teacher education programs. Between 1972 and 1987, the number of bachelor's degrees awarded in education fell from more than 194,000 to about 87,000 (Darling-Hammond 1990b). For most of the '70s and into the '80s, teaching was seen as an undesirable pursuit, the choice of last resort. Fewer of the students attracted to teacher education programs had strong academic records, as reflected by college entrance examinations and academic work in high school (Darling-Hammond 1990b, Galambos 1985, Garibaldi 1987).

Only in the past few years has interest in teaching risen somewhat, spurred by reports of a growing teacher shortage, rises in compensation, and educational reform initiatives. After a long decline, interest in teaching among college freshmen has recently nosed slightly upward (Astin, Green, and Korn 1987). Nonetheless, teaching has clearly been substantially replaced by other professions as a career interest for young women. Whereas education was by far the number one choice in 1966, attracting nearly 35 percent of freshmen women, it now ranks far behind business and other professions, such as law, medicine, and engineering. Together these fields attract the 35 percent once pledged to education, while teaching is interesting to only about 8 percent (Astin et al. 1987). The same patterns are true for minority college freshmen as well. Between 1976 and 1985, education degrees earned by minority candidates declined by more than half, with the greatest decreases evidenced by African-American graduates (Darling-Hammond 1990b). Current debates about professionalizing teaching stem partly from the need to entice new entrants to teaching now that women and minorities, once a "captive labor pool" for the teaching profession, have a wider selection of professional options.

The Current Status of Teaching

In 1987–88, the average teacher was likely to be a white female just over 40 years of age with a graduate degree and 15 years of service, earning about $32,000 a year (National Center for Education Statistics 1991). Compared with the general population of college-educated workers, teachers are older, have completed more years of college, earn less, and are more likely to be female (Darling-Hammond 1990c). Most public school teachers come from working-class backgrounds (60 percent) and are first-generation college graduates (80 percent), proportions that have remained fairly constant since 1961 (NEA 1981, 1987).

About one-third of the current teaching force is expected to retire during the 1990s. These pending retirements are the major source of the growing demand for teachers throughout the 1990s and into the 21st century. An overall increase in the size of the teaching force (from 2.2 million to about 2.6 million) will be propelled by enrollment increases (higher birth rates plus immigration) and curriculum reforms. Meanwhile, the replacement of older teachers by younger teachers, who traditionally have very high attrition rates, will increase turnover throughout the decade, unless changes occur in the capacity of the profession to retain beginning teachers (Darling-Hammond 1990b).

The dwindling supply of teachers noted earlier stands in startling contrast to estimates that place the total demand for new teachers at around 2.5 million between 1990 and 2000, averaging about 250,000 entrants annually (NCES 1991). Given current trends, colleges will graduate no more than two-thirds of the number needed (Darling-Hammond 1990b). Teacher shortages grew throughout the 1980s in fields such as bilingual education, special education, physics and chemistry, mathematics, and computer science. Emerging shortages have been reported for teachers of the gifted, biology and general science, industrial arts, and foreign languages, along with school psychologists, elementary guidance counselors, and librarians (Akin 1989).

Although college students have recently shown a renewed interest in teaching, because of another brief rise in salaries, more aggressive recruiting, and improved job opportunities, the supply of qualified teachers is inadequate in relation to projected needs. Without further substantial boosts in both the financial and nonmaterial attractions to teaching, it is likely that teaching will have difficulty competing in the increasingly intense contest for college-educated workers over the coming years. In the long run, much depends on policies currently being proposed, or yet to be formulated, in response to emerging teacher shortages.

Salaries, Supply, and Standards

Though professionalism is not measured in terms of compensation, the issue of salaries has had important implications for who enters and remains in teaching. Teacher salaries have continually lagged behind the salaries of other professions requiring similar educational qualifications. Consequently, "despite brief periods of surplus, there has always been a shortage of willing and qualified teachers" (Sedlak and Schlossman 1986, p. vii). Thus, a constant tension develops between raising standards of practice and keeping pace with the need for teachers.

> The states . . . [have] found themselves with a set of internally conflicting demands: Improve quality, but guarantee a body in every public classroom. Periodic severe shortages of teachers are much more obvious and compelling than the need for higher quality . . . . Temporary and emergency certificates ease the shortage in times of undersupply; while in times of oversupply, a glut of teachers removes any rising interest in providing incentives for the improvement of quality. The call for higher salaries is muted when many of those teaching have done little to be temporarily certified, just as it is muted when there are dozens of applicants for each vacancy (Goodlad 1990a, pp. 94–95).

Apple (1987, p. 73) suggests, "We have built whatever excellence we have in schools on the backs of the low-paid labor of a largely women's work force." In a society that continues to measure status according to compensation, teaching as a meagerly paid, predominantly female occupation has had low prestige. Until the '60s, teaching was an "in and out" career (Lortie 1975); women continually entered and left the profession for child-rearing purposes, and many men and women stayed only a short time before leaving for other pursuits. These patterns further depressed teaching salaries by ensuring a continuous cycling into the profession of new or untenured educators with little power to demand more competitive wages. Attempts to increase teacher salaries have done little to change the high turnover rate of the beginning teaching force, nearly half of whom leave within 5 to 7 years of entry (Vance and Schlechty 1982, Grissmer and Kirby 1987), in part because salary schedules are "front-loaded" and flat, with teachers experiencing diminishing returns the longer they are in the field.

Recent efforts to address shortages have included modest increases in teacher salaries. However, the wage increases throughout the 1980s have just returned average teachers' salaries to the level they had reached in 1972, before the declines in purchasing power throughout that decade (Darling-Hammond and Berry 1988). They have not eliminated the 25–30-percent gap between beginning teacher salaries and those of college graduates in other fields, and they do not provide professionally meaningful incentives for exemplary career service.

As the 1990s unfold, salary increases for teachers have once again slowed nearly to a halt, leaving teaching in a still noncompetitive position compared with most other professional occupations. Meanwhile, vacancies for teachers in a growing number of fields continue to be filled by emergency hires and the use of substandard forms of certification. In the midst of a rhetorical renaissance of professionalism, teaching remains poised on the not-quite-profession brink.

Dimensions of Professionalism

Earlier we suggested that progress toward professionalism can be recognized in several aspects of an occupation: the ways in which members are prepared and admitted; the ways in which work is structured; and the accountability systems established to transmit and maintain professional standards. Next we examine the status of teaching in each of these areas, the implications of new initiatives, and the prognosis for the future.

Teacher Preparation

Professionalism starts from the proposition that knowledge must inform practice; its major goal is to ensure that all individuals permitted to practice are adequately prepared. Yet school reform has rarely focused on the support and improvement of teacher education programs. In most universities, colleges of education receive the fewest resources; and teacher training is the least well funded activity within the school of education. Even during those periods of interest in educational reform that seem to occur about once a generation, neither federal or state governments nor colleges or school systems seem inclined to spend much money on the education of teachers.

One reason for this lack of support may be that policymakers are ambivalent about whether a knowledge base for teaching exists or whether its acquisition would improve teaching. This ambivalence is most obvious in the recent enactment of alternative routes to teacher certification in more than thirty states. Some of these alternatives are managed outside of teacher education institutions altogether—and they require little more than a few weeks of preparation before entry into the classroom, where on-the-job learning is supposed to occur (Darling-Hammond unpublished manuscript). These alternatives "reflect unbelief in a knowledge base in teaching . . . a lack of respect for schools of education . . . and mitigate against professional teaching" (Schwartz 1988, p. 37).

Often loopholes to certification are justified by reference to the presumed inadequacies of teacher preparation programs, although shortages are always an underlying concern. Yet the presumption that flaws in teacher education should justify its avoidance is unfounded. The weight of research indicates that fully prepared teachers are in fact more highly rated and more successful with students than are teachers without full preparation for licensure (Darling-Hammond in press; Evertson, Hawley, and Zlotnik 1985; Hawk, Coble, and Swanson 1985; Ashton and Crocker 1986; Ashton and Crocker 1987; Greenberg 1983; Haberman 1984; Olsen 1985). As Evertson and colleagues conclude in their research review:

> The available research suggests that among students who become teachers, those enrolled in formal preservice preparation programs are more likely to be effective than those who do not have such training. Moreover, almost all well planned and executed efforts within teacher preparation programs to teach students specific knowledge or skills seem to succeed.

Studies of teachers admitted through quick-entry alternate routes frequently note that the candidates have difficulty with curriculum development, pedagogical content knowledge, attending to students' differing learning styles and levels, classroom management, and student motivation (Lenk 1989; Feiman-Nemser and Parker 1990; Grossman 1989; Mitchell 1987). In comparison to beginners who have completed a teacher education program, novice teachers without full preparation are less sensitive to students, less able to plan and redirect instruction to meet students' needs (and less aware of the need to do so), and less skilled in implementing instruction (Rottenberg and Berliner 1990; Bents and Bents 1990; Grossman 1988; Bledsoe, Cox, and Burnham 1967; Copley 1974). They are less able to anticipate students' potential difficulties and less likely to see it as their job to do so, often blaming the students if their teaching is not successful.

The shortcomings of unprepared teachers, however, cannot still the widespread criticisms of teacher education programs raised even by those who firmly believe in the importance of teacher preparation. The approximately 1,300 institutions of higher education that offer teacher preparation have been characterized as fragmented, incoherent, and lacking in vision or purpose (Goodlad 1990a, Zeichner 1986). Researchers have found "loose linkages" among the three components of teacher preparation programs—liberal arts education, "professional" study, and practical experience. Because these elements often are unconnected, there are also loose connections among subject matter content, educational theory, and practical application (Goodlad 1990a, b; Schwartz 1988; Zeichner 1986). This fragmentation may reinforce teachers' conceptions that content and theory have little utility in the "real world" of the classroom.

Some observers claim that much of the instruction in schools of education is based primarily on past experience, intuition, or opinion, rather than something that might be viewed as a teaching knowledge base (Goodlad 1990a, Griffin 1986, Schwartz 1988). In addition, the conception of knowledge is often technological rather than scientific, that is, oriented toward formulaic approaches rather than complex analysis. This conception results in training in "how to do it, rather than why to teach in a given way—the 'technification' of teacher education" (Goodlad 1990a, p. 234).

Colleges of teacher education also frequently exert little influence over practicum placements; these are often chosen by principals based on administrative convenience rather than educational value to the student teacher, or are assigned to whichever cooperating teachers are willing to volunteer. This practice provides haphazard and idiosyncratic student-teaching experiences. Divorced from other aspects of the teacher education program, these clinical experiences may meet some immediate classroom needs but often pay scant attention to the deeper, more substantive issues teachers must wrestle with.

After new teachers complete their formal preservice courses, most find that supervised induction to teaching is ad hoc or nonexistent (Borko 1986, Lortie 1975). Typically, administrators make little distinction between novice and veteran teachers except that they often give new teachers the most difficult assignments—the ones that senior teachers have "earned" the right to avoid (Darling-Hammond 1990c). Senior teachers also tend to transfer out of the least desirable schools, often those in impoverished areas serving the neediest students, leaving these schools to hire disproportionate numbers of new and inexperienced teachers. Even when new teachers are offered some kind of induction, this assistance generally emphasizes evaluation over support (Darling-Hammond and Berry 1988) or is provided by untrained mentors (Huling-Austin 1990).

Thus beginning teachers face the most challenging educational problems with little assistance. For people entering teaching with little or no preservice preparation, the situation is more grave. Allowing unprepared and unsupervised teachers to practice on clients, something unheard of in other professions, demonstrates how far teaching deviates from a profession's pledge to safeguard the welfare of clients.

A profession is formed when members of an occupation agree that they have a knowledge base, that what they know relates directly to effective practice, that being prepared is essential to being a responsible practitioner. Until teachers and teacher educators band together as members of the profession to articulate and enforce their own standards, professionalism will remain just beyond reach.

In the fifty years following the 1910 Flexner Report, a "scholarly and devastating analysis of educational facilities and offerings in the 150 medical schools then operating," medical education in America transformed from, "its worst . . . [which] had been training for a trade . . . [and] became universally what it had rarely been at its best, sound preparation for a scientific profession" (Miller 1962, p. 104). No such wholesale transformation has yet occurred for teacher education. "Schools of education are in limbo, waiting for directional signals" (Goodlad 1990b, p. 19), pulled about by competing political and accrediting demands and suffering from internal ambivalence.

A professional approach to teacher education will be based on a view of teaching knowledge as complex and contingent, rooted in an understanding of learning and the many different paths it takes. It will include an appreciation for human motivation, multiple intelligences, and diverse modes of performance. Such a view will ultimately require that teachers have rigorous grounding in the following:

- Cognitive psychology, so that they understand how people learn.
- Developmental psychology, so that they understand when children are ready to learn particular things in particular ways.
- Learning theory and pedagogy, so that they can teach in developmentally and cognitively appropriate ways.
- Professional ethics, so that they can manage schools' competing agendas in ways that keep the best interests of students at the forefront of their actions.

Furthermore, teachers must understand the structure of knowledge within disciplines, so that they can develop methods that allow students to understand fundamental concepts and to acquire conceptual frameworks that are the basis for disciplinary learning. They will need to know about the assessment of learning, not simply to interpret scores on existing tests, but to critically examine and construct instruments for evaluating students' knowledge. Teachers need to learn these things in application as well as in theory, in programs that allow for the integration of subject-matter and pedagogical study, and for the study of learners and learning in clinical as well as didactic settings.

Teaching as a profession will demand universal standards for entry to be applied to all prospective teachers. Such standards will shift teacher-supply issues away from dependence on market conditions to a focus on quality and professional preparedness. The socialization of teachers will include formalized induction systems that emphasize growth rather than remediation (Borko 1986), including supervised internships for new teachers and teacher-to-teacher support systems. Professional internship models will use classroom data as a basis for analysis and discussion; rely on inquiry and problem solving; and rest on an awareness of student learning (Cook, cited in Borko 1986, p. 59).

Many believe that transforming teacher education will require reshaping both education courses and the structure of teacher education programs. The Holmes Group (1991) urges the creation of professional development schools—school-university partnerships in which expert teachers join with university faculty to provide carefully structured practicum and internship experiences for prospective teachers. More than 100 such schools have been created in the past few years, based on the premise that the education of teachers must occur in an atmosphere where theory *and* practice jointly inform their work.

Other recent changes in teacher education include efforts to characterize and codify the knowledge base for teaching (AACTE 1990, Shulman 1987). The faculties of many schools of education are rethinking their programs and practices, reshaping coursework, designing internship programs, and creating professional development schools as part of these and other professionwide activities.

Unfortunately, many of these initiatives are undermined by the resurgence of licensing practices aimed at putting teachers in classrooms quickly and cheaply. The extent and quality of preparation that states are willing to require of teachers is directly related to the level of investment they are willing to make in teacher knowledge (Darling-Hammond in press). Until the profession can control standards for preparation and licensing, it will suffer from an inability to assure the public that all teachers have encountered and mastered a common knowledge base.

In the current policy environment, the efforts of many colleges are constrained by the traditional approach to teacher licensing, which heavily relies on state prescriptions of course offerings and regulation of teacher education programs. The National Council for the Accreditation of Teacher Education (NCATE) has offered promising and more rigorous professional alternatives to state regulations. NCATE has undertaken changes to raise its standards and to encourage states to accept NCATE accreditation as the benchmark of professional education quality. In addition, some states, such as Minnesota, are replacing course-counting approaches with licensing standards that articulate the types of knowledge and skill needed to teach. Finally, a few states, including Minnesota, New York, and California, are anticipating the creation of internship programs as a prerequisite to licensure. These initiatives could professionalize entry into teaching.

Entry into Teaching

Until recently, teaching has not had a body governing professional certification analogous to those in medicine, architecture, accounting, or other professions. Professional certification performs a different function from state licensing. Members of all professions and many other occupations (e.g., contractors, plumbers, and barbers) must be licensed by the states in which they wish to practice, meeting standards of minimal competence established by the state. In the case of professions, these standards are typically developed by professional standards boards to which the state delegates this function. Professional certification often reflects even more advanced or exacting standards established by the profession—sometimes through a national organization—for designating a high level of competence and skill. Thus, certified public accountants, board-certified physicians, and registered architects have met professional standards that exceed those demanded by most states for licensure.

The new National Board for Professional Teaching Standards will soon begin to assume some of the functions of other professions' organizations by certifying teachers who demonstrate advanced levels of knowledge and skill. Initial entry into teaching continues to be regulated differently from entry into other professional occupations. In other professions, states delegate responsibility for licensing functions to professional standards boards comprised of members of the profession who are charged with establishing and enforcing standards. About a dozen states have created professional standards boards for teaching that have some authority for these functions. Most, however, regulate entry into teaching through state departments of education, which set licensure rules and program approval standards.

The ability to set and enforce standards for entry—and thereby to protect the public welfare by establishing protection from incompetence—is a critical attribute of a profession not yet fully attained by teaching. As Benveniste explains:

> The professions are organized, and they are able to express responsibility for knowledge and technique collectively. The professions—alone or with the assistance of the state—are able to erect machinery to determine whether would-be practitioners are competent to practice. It is not sufficient to be able to convince clients that one can perform services. It is necessary to convince an organization that represents all or most practitioners that one has acquired the necessary skills . . . . The fact that clients cannot readily recognize charlatans and are, to some extent, at the mercy of the professionals, defines the need for a professional organization, one of whose missions will be to protect clients from potential abuses (1987, pp. 30–31).

Despite the general lack of professional control over licensing standards, many states have tried to create the trappings of professionalism by requiring tests for entry into teaching. During the 1980s, at least forty-six states adopted teacher testing as part of teacher training or licensure, and many mandated changes in teacher preparation curricula (Darling-Hammond and Berry 1988).

Theoretically, professional requirements like teaching tests serve two important functions—sorting and screening candidates, and defining the knowledge base for defensible practice. Current teacher tests perform the first function, but not the second. Most of the mandated tests are basic skills examinations and thus are not in the realm of professional testing. Furthermore, existing tests of general and professional knowledge assess little of what might be considered a knowledge base for teaching (Darling-Hammond 1989, Shulman 1987).

Most current teacher examinations eschew a contextual understanding of teaching and learning in favor of items requiring the recognition of facts within subject areas, knowledge of school law and bureaucratic procedures, and recognition of the "correct" teaching behavior in a situation described in a short scenario of only one or two sentences. The tests currently used do not allow for demonstrations of teacher knowledge, judgment, and skills in the kinds of complex settings that characterize real teaching. Furthermore, these tests may discourage the use of such knowledge by positing a unidimensional philosophy of teaching that test takers must consistently apply if they are to find the "best" answers to poorly defined questions (Darling-Hammond

1986a, Shulman 1987). A recent review concluded that the paucity of research confirming the predictive and construct validity of the National Teachers Examination and the fact that it correlates only with other standardized test scores suggest it measures general aptitude and test-taking skills rather than mastery of professional knowledge (Haney, Madaus, and Kreitzer 1987).

Teaching tests that rely on a simplistic view of teaching not only inadequately assess what knowledgeable teachers know, but eliminate many candidates from teaching on grounds that are tenuous. Thus, shortages are exacerbated, and pressures to create loopholes increase, while the capacities of those who enter teaching are not clearly improved (Darling-Hammond 1989). To compound the problem, recently mandated teacher-licensing tests have become barriers to entry for minorities who pass at significantly lower rates than whites (Garibaldi 1987, Goertz and Pitcher 1985, Graham 1987, Haney et al. 1987). While reducing the supply of minority candidates, the tests fail to heighten the profession's claim to meaningful standards.

Paradoxically, in the midst of initiatives to revise admissions and exit criteria for teacher education, states continue to issue tens of thousands of emergency, provisional, temporary, and alternative certificates (Darling-Hammond 1990b). In teaching, strategies for regulating the labor market have created a dual credentialing system that simultaneously appears to support and retard teacher professionalism. If wages do not rise sufficiently to ensure an adequate supply of entrants at a given level of quality, standards are lowered to produce a larger supply at a lower level of quality.

Regardless of whether standards are being ostensibly raised or lowered, though, the substance of standards—that is, the extent and kind of knowledge they reflect—remains outside the hands of the profession. Because tests "[transfer] control over the curriculum to the agency which sets or controls the exam" (Madaus 1988, p. 97), and certification loopholes are created by state legislators, both the content of teacher education curricula and the endorsement of teachers are removed from the hands of the profession.

The process used to assess and license members of other professions (e.g., doctors, architects, and engineers) differs markedly from the process now used to assess and license teachers. Rather than being determined by state agencies or external testing agencies, testing in other professions is managed by members of the profession, who are charged with developing and scoring the examinations as well as defining the standards for internships and other entry requirements.

Candidates who seek admission to these professions must demonstrate their understanding of professional knowledge and their ability to apply this information in a variety of settings. Thus, candidates in psychology, engineering, medicine, and architecture are required to serve a supervised internship before they are eligible to sit for the final assessment of professional competence (Wise and Darling-Hammond 1987).

Progress in establishing meaningful professional standards for teaching is very slow. A few states, like New York, have made a commitment to eliminate substandard licensing for teachers or to require all entrants to meet the same rigorous entry standards. A number have recently established professional standards boards for teaching, and several others are considering doing so. The newly created National Board for Professional Teaching Standards, composed of a majority of practicing teachers, will use peer evaluation and performance-based assessments as part of its advanced certification examinations. The National Board, however, currently lacks a means of connecting to state boards or otherwise influencing preparation in the ways that other professional certifying bodies do. Until these linkages are established, its influence on entry standards is likely to be weak.

The transformation of teacher licensing tests into more adequate and thoughtful representations of teaching knowledge may be spurred by an exercise launched by the Council for Chief State School Officers' Interstate Teacher Assessment Consortium. This consortium will work with state members to develop licensing standards compatible with the emerging standards of the National Board. Several states (e.g., Connecticut, New York, Texas, and California) have recently begun to try to revamp their teacher licensing tests to represent more authentic and complex understandings of teaching knowledge and skill. Meanwhile, the Educational Testing Service is developing an entirely new version of the National Teacher Examinations. Whether any of these efforts will provide an adequate standard-setting role for the profession remains to be seen. In combination, however, these changes represent a convergence of developments that could launch an era of teacher professionalism.

Teaching Roles and Conditions of Work

There is little use in demanding that members of an occupation acquire and demonstrate high levels of knowledge and expertise if they are not permitted to use this knowledge in their work. The approach to teaching implicit in a factory model of schooling both constrains the use of teacher judgment and fails to address the differential needs of students. Viewing the teacher as a semiskilled laborer in the school assembly line has led to reform based on the notion that students will automatically learn if teachers' activities are highly prescribed (Darling-Hammond 1985). However, prescriptive policies limit teachers' actions in ways that they find distressing and antiprofessional. Standardized curricular and testing mandates limit their choices of strategies and materials that might better meet diverse student needs while making them feel pressured to use methods that, though not conducive to higher order learning, are compatible with standardized testing requirements. Forty-five percent of the teachers in one study reported that the only policy that would make them leave teaching was "the increased prescriptiveness of teaching content and methods—in short, the continued deprofessionalization of teaching" (Darling-Hammond 1985, p. 209).

The bureaucratization of teaching, rooted in the "scientific management principles" outlined by Franklin Bobbitt in 1913, emphasizes conformity and uniformity to facilitate hierarchical decision making and efficiency. In fact, since the early 1970s, state governments have exerted more and more control over the form, substance, and conduct of schooling (Darling-Hammond 1990a). Centralized planning and stifling of diversity are predictable outcomes of bureaucratization (Sizer 1984). "Treating all clients similarly . . . lies at the heart of bureaucratic practice. It is one of the features distinguishing the behavior of bureaucrats from that of professionals" (Duke 1984, p. 27).

The bureaucratic structure of teaching works against many professional prerequisites—professional preparation, knowledge for decision making, ethical and codified standards of practice, attention to the unique needs of clients. In a bureaucracy, key decisions are made outside the purview of practitioners, and practice is governed by rules and procedures. As information descends from individuals at the pinnacle of the hierarchical pyramid, far removed from schools, and slowly makes its way down to teachers at the implementation level, practitioners are limited to formulaic approaches that cannot possibly attend to the myriad needs of individual students.

Teachers' working conditions support this top-down organization of schooling. The assembly-line approach to teaching isolates teachers in egg-crate classrooms with packed teaching schedules that hinder professional consultation among teachers and the sharing of knowledge or experience (Goodwin 1987, Lortie 1975, Lieberman and Miller 1984, Sarason 1982). The segmentation of school schedules into subject-specific fragments further denies the complexity of teaching and the integrated nature of learning. Meanwhile, teachers are rarely involved in making decisions about those matters that deeply affect their work and students' learning opportunities—decisions about curriculum, teaching materials, standards for student assessment, the organization of the school and the ways it structures learning opportunities, and the selection of other teachers and administrators.

Schools thus treat teachers more as bureaucrats than as professionals. In contrast, if treated as professionals who understand both the principles of learning and the specific needs of their students, teachers would determine the content and structure of teaching tasks. As a professional activity, teaching would be distinguished by "the kind of praxis in which specialized practitioners and their clients . . . [are] involved in a dialogical determination of the course of action to be followed" (Beyer, Feinberg, Pagano, and Whitson 1989, p. 71). Teachers' work would be structured so that they could devote personal attention to the needs of students and time to collegial planning and inquiry toward the improvement of practice.

Reshaping teachers' roles, responsibilities, and teaching conditions will ultimately require fundamental restructuring of schools—the ways in which they make decisions, organize instruction, provide for collaborative planning and assessment of outcomes, and allocate authority for tasks ranging from personnel selection to program development and student assessment (Darling-Hammond 1990a). Many school reform efforts have sought to include teachers, along with parents, in school decision making. These include school-based management and shared-decision-making initiatives in San Diego, California; Salt Lake City, Utah; Dade County, Florida; Rochester, New York; and New York City, among many others. Other collaborative efforts include the involvement of teachers in developing curriculum and student performance assessments in states such as Vermont and California.

A growing consortium of schools belonging to the Coalition of Essential Schools has embraced a comprehensive conception of learner-centered education based on professional structures for teaching. In these schools, curriculum, instruction, the organization of teaching and learning, administration, professional development, and evaluation are all structured to allow teaching that is student centered and knowledge based. These schools organize time so that teachers can jointly develop curriculum, invent authentic assessments of learning, discuss student progress, and evaluate school functioning. Team teaching in interdisciplinary core courses allows teachers to integrate content and to teach fewer students for longer periods of time, thus coming to know the minds of students well. Teachers treat students as coworkers who have a voice in their own education. Accountability results from the connections that school staff develop with students, parents, and each other through frequent consultation and cooperation toward shared goals (Brandt 1988, Meier 1987). In this context, teachers are professionals, guided by the needs of their students and the depth of their shared understanding.

Changes such as these may eventually reshape the occupational structure of teaching, allowing for more professional forms of practice in schools, as well as attracting and retaining a greater number of talented teachers. The prognosis for school restructuring is uncertain, but there is a growing consensus among policymakers and the public that schools require fundamental rather than superficial reform. This consensus may bode well for the kinds of changes needed to produce more learner-centered schools.

Certainly, school restructuring and teacher professionalism are closely interdependent. Teachers cannot practice in professional ways without fundamental changes in the organization and management of schools. Neither can schools be restructured in ways that attend to the diverse needs of learners without relying on a strong professional structure for teaching—one that ensures that teachers are prepared to teach in the more complex ways required for learner-centered practice and are able to responsibly exercise their new decision-making opportunities.

Professional Development for the Development of a Profession

The strength and legitimacy of any profession depends on the continued growth and development of its members. Because competence and caring are the foundations of professional accountability, professional organizations must have effective mechanisms that help inform practitioners about their work and provide opportunity for consultation, reflection, self-assessment, and continued improvement.

In most school districts, however, teacher evaluation is a perfunctory, routine exercise of little utility to teachers or school districts. As it is currently structured—a one-on-one exercise in which principals inspect the work of all teachers, give advice, and file reports—meaningful learning from evaluation is rare. The evaluator's span of control is too large, the number of observations too small, the expertise of a single evaluator too limited, and the process too standardized to allow for the kind of intensive, highly specific dialogue about real problems of practice that would make a substantial difference in the perspectives and knowledge of most teachers (Darling-Hammond 1986b).

Several features of evaluation are constant across most school districts:

- A single process is intended to serve all purposes, for example, individual and collective improvement goals, as well as accountability goals.
- Assessment criteria are generic and are employed and weighted in the same way for all teachers.
- The process generally relies on one or two observations.
- The principal is the primary and often sole evaluator.
- The outcome is a rating of the teacher, on a 3- or 5-point scale.

Consequently, teacher evaluations often focus on generic indicators of performance (Does the teacher plan? set objectives? follow the curriculum?) oriented toward the evaluation of minimal competence, with little attention paid to the appropriateness or effect of these actions, to long-term results, or to the specific context being observed. "Most teacher evaluation schemes assess teachers' performance against minimum standards. This makes evaluation an irrelevant exercise for the 90–95 percent of the 'satisfactory' teachers in the district" (McLaughlin and Pfeifer 1988, p. 83).

> Furthermore, observations framed in this way reveal little about the coherence of the curriculum, the depth and breadth of content covered, the range of teaching techniques used, the quality and variety of materials employed, the types and frequency of student assignments, the quality of instruments (tests, papers, projects) used for student assessment, the kinds of feedback students receive on their work, or the appropriateness of any of these things for the classroom context (Darling-Hammond 1986b, p. 534).

Conceptions of teaching as a technical endeavor drive evaluation that is close-ended, providing only brief snapshots of what is occurring in the classroom. The approach does not seek to evaluate performance over time or in a variety of circumstances. It does not assume that evaluators must have special expertise in subject matter or pedagogy to judge the appropriateness of different classroom decisions. In an attempt to design reliable, generic evaluation instruments without incorporating professional judgments about context and content, some systems have sought to create "evaluator-proof" instruments that preclude any assessment of teaching appropriateness.

A rather extreme example of an attempt to implement context- and content-free teacher evaluation is the Florida Performance Measurement System, which has also been adopted in several other states. The FPMS is an observation-based behavioral tally that observers use to record frequencies of "effective" and "ineffective" behavior. Observers do not record any other behavior, any information about contextual variables, student behavior, or that of other individuals in the classroom—nor does any interpretive narrative accompany the tally. Even though the research used to justify this system acknowledges that many of the types of behavior listed on the instrument are differentially effective with different students under different circumstances, the instrument does not allow these considerations to be taken into account, having arbitrarily assigned different kinds of behavior to one category or the other. Thus, the system "consciously conveys to teachers that their use of pedagogically acceptable practices is not acceptable, and they should ignore research that suggests they adjust their behaviors to different student responses or circumstances" (Darling-Hammond 1992, p. 22). This kind of evaluation system is fundamentally antiprofessional.

Professional evaluation, on the other hand, involves much different processes (Darling-Hammond 1990a):

• Teachers are involved in developing and implementing the evaluation process.

• Evaluation is based on professional standards of practice that are client oriented.

• Multiple teaching strategies and student learning outcomes are recognized.

• The importance of teaching context and content is acknowledged, including teachers' assignments, stages of development, and classroom goals.

More professional conceptions of teaching are reflected in approaches to evaluation in some states. For example, Minnesota's standards for evaluating prospective teachers are grounded in a view of teachers as "thoughtful, creative persons who use a set of principles and strategies derived from an informed personal philosophy of education and the multiple demands of learning contexts" (Minnesota Board of Teaching 1986). Minnesota's system of evaluation for beginning teachers will require them to examine different needs and contexts, to question their teaching strategies, and to apply wide-ranging sources of knowledge to the complex problems of practice they face. Evaluation will be based on their ability to exhibit professional modes of thinking and judgment, as assessed by master teachers and teacher educators whose judgment in turn can be trusted because they have been chosen for their professional expertise (Darling-Hammond 1992).

Minnesota's approach acknowledges that professionalism requires peer control over decisions that define acceptable practice, as well as peer assessment of individual practitioners. Peer review in teaching is in its infancy. Ultimately, the development of a strong peer review structure in teaching will require major changes in conceptions of evaluation, as well as designations of who participates in evaluation.

An example of promising practice can be found in Toledo, Ohio, where the teachers' union initiated changes in teacher evaluation to engage teachers in mentoring beginners, providing consultation to each other, and policing their own ranks. The Toledo model for peer assistance and review has since been adopted by several other districts, including Cincinnati, Ohio, and Rochester, New York. These districts have moved beyond the predominant labor conception of teaching that is reflected in contracts in which teacher evaluation has become more and more rule bound.

Over the past two decades, collective bargaining has tended to increase bureaucratic approaches to teaching in its quest for procedures that could ensure equal treatment, job specification (in terms of hours, workday, and duties), and links between evaluation and personnel decisions (Mitchell and Kerchner 1983). Thus, measures of teacher competence have been defined in terms of teachers' adherence to minimum work standards or the demonstration of technical competence, allowing schools to give the appearance of successful evaluation by simply declaring that teachers meet minimum, though often educationally irrelevant, standards. In contrast, professional negotiations emphasize control over who should be allowed to engage in teaching and the evaluation of teaching based on knowledge and expertise.

Toledo's teacher evaluation plan represents a collaborative attempt between the union and the board of education to move away from labor conceptions of teaching and define teacher evaluation as the cornerstone of a profession. The intern program, launched in 1981, places first-year teachers under the supervision of expert consulting teachers in their grade level or subject area. The consulting teachers are released from their own classroom duties to work intensively with interns on all aspects of teaching and build a well-documented foundation on which to base their evaluations. Consulting teachers' recommendations regarding future employment of novice teachers are reported twice a year to an intern review board composed of teachers and administrators who vote on the consultants' recommendations (Darling-Hammond 1986b).

A companion "intervention" program provides intensive assistance from "master" teachers to veteran teachers who have had serious difficulty and have been placed on probation. The same board reviews consulting teachers' recommendations about probation removal or dismissal. The central role of peer review by master teachers in the evaluation process is one element of a professional conception of teaching; the model is an important step toward the professionalization of teaching.

Professional control of an occupation—who enters, what constitutes good practice, who remains—is central to any discussion of teacher professionalism. In most professions, peer review of *practice* is at least as important as the involvement of peers in the formal evaluation of *practitioners*. Peer review of practice occurs when professionals consult regularly with each other about particular problems (e.g., in staff reviews about individual students), as well as more general problem solving. Peer review also routinely engages professionals in evaluating the ongoing activities of their organization, diagnosing what is working well and what needs rethinking, and proposing solutions that will promote more effective practices.

Peer review of practice includes growth-oriented forms of evaluation featuring personal goal setting and peer-mediated self-evaluation (Barber 1984, Darling-Hammond 1986b), as well as activities in which teachers engage in school needs assessment and problem solving (Darling-Hammond 1990a). As teaching becomes professionalized, "monological" forms of teacher evaluation, featuring one-way conversations between evaluators and teachers, should give way to "dialogical" exchanges among teachers. These peer exchanges empower teachers to think more broadly and richly about their practice (Gitlin and Smyth 1989, p. 4).

New forms of professional development are also beginning to abandon traditional models of one-shot staff development. These older models featured an emphasis on information transfer and remediation rather than collaboration as a basis for teacher growth; a lack of continuity and coordination among school, district, state and federal efforts; and an absence of feedback to teachers (Howey and Vaughn 1983). Rather than inservice courses on such things as specific classroom management techniques, professional development should occur in forums in which teachers interact with other educators, exchange ideas, and critically examine their own practice (Goodwin 1987). This is beginning to happen in many restructuring schools. Increasingly, such schools have assumed responsibility for determining and shaping ongoing staff development, along with other school decisions.

Finally, peer review is evident in teacher leadership programs emerging in districts like Rochester, New York (Murray 1991, Urbanski 1988), and states with career ladders or mentorship programs like Arizona and California (McDonnell 1989). These programs engage the talents of teachers in improving teaching practice. As mentors, peer coaches, staff developers, and curriculum makers, teachers can use their cumulative wisdom to guide and shape the mission of the school while their new roles position them as critical and strategic decision makers. These kinds of initiatives can provide the necessary leadership for envisioning, and eventually actualizing, professional development that can support a developing profession.

Implications of Professionalism for Teaching

The preceding analysis suggests why teaching remains the "not quite" profession. Achieving the goals of professionalism in teaching will require major changes on several fronts—teacher preparation, licensing and certification, school structure, teacher evaluation, and professional development.

The education of teachers must reflect a professional vision of teaching—one in which highly developed judgment grounded in knowledge of learners, learning, and teaching is used in a variety of contexts to meet the diverse needs of students. Teacher education should enable novice teachers to experiment and question, to make connections, to become "students of teaching" (Perrone 1991, Schwartz 1988). Teacher preparation should emphasize deliberation rather than teaching tricks; should provide opportunities to put theory into practice—and practice into theory—and should engage prospective teachers in constant reflective analysis.

Licensing and certification standards for teachers must become both educationally meaningful and inviolable, and they must be defined and enforced by the profession itself. The newly established National Board of Professional Teaching Standards, along with some state professional standards boards, will seek to employ more authentic forms of assessment to evaluate teacher competence. This board also proposes to provide national certification, endorsement by the profession that board-certified practitioners are qualified to teach anywhere in the country. Meanwhile, NCATE is moving to establishing national professional standards for approving teacher preparation programs. The actions of these national organizations to create unified standards approved by the profession could be an important step toward teacher professionalism. Their influence will be far reaching if they occur alongside the development of professional standards boards in the states and are linked to state licensure standards that incorporate completion of an accredited teacher education program as part of their requirements.

School structure cannot remain static if teachers are to take on new roles as deliberative practitioners. The hierarchical organization of schools must make way for more inclusive, decision-making structures. The work of teachers must be structured to allow for integrated and personalized teaching, as well as continuous, ongoing opportunities for collegial consultation, planning, and evaluation of practice.

Teacher evaluation needs to change in corresponding ways to include both a complex, context-dependent view of practice and appropriate peer-review mechanisms for providing expert advice on problems of practice. New forms of evaluation, coupled with mechanisms allowing regular review of practice, will reduce the burden on principals for inspecting classrooms and induce teachers to assume major responsibility for professional behavior. These changes could help make evaluation a supportive, collegial process as teacher discussion of professional issues is fostered, rather than a process that enforces only minimum standards.

Professionalizing teaching involves attending to all facets of the teaching enterprise. Reforms to professionalize teaching are likely to be more productive if they are based on an understanding of how teaching has evolved and has been conceptualized. Deliberate reconstruction of all aspects of teaching—as an occupation, a form of work, a job, and a career—is necessary if teaching is to move from "not quite" to a true profession.

References

Akin, J.N. (1989). *Teacher Supply and Demand in the United States: 1989 Report*. ASCUS Research Report. Addison, Ill.: Association for School, College, and University Staffing.

American Association of Colleges for Teacher Education. (1990). *Advancing the Agenda for Teacher Education in a Democracy* (Vols. 1–4). Washington, D.C.: American Association of Colleges for Teacher Education.

Anderson, A.W. (1962). "The Teaching Profession: An Example of Diversity in Training and Function." In *Education for the Professions*, The Sixty-First

Yearbook of the National Society for the Study of Education (pp. 140–167), edited by N.B. Henry. Chicago: University of Chicago Press.

Apple, M.W. (1987). "The De-skilling of Teaching." In *Teacher Renewal* (pp. 59–75), edited by F.S. Bolin and J.M. Falk. New York: Teachers College Press.

Apple, M.W. (1988). "Social Evaluation of Curriculum." In *The Curriculum; Problems, Politics and Possibilities* (pp. 334–350), edited by L.E. Beyer and M.W. Apple. Albany: State University of New York Press.

Ashton, P., and L. Crocker. (1986). "Does Teacher Certification Make a Difference?" *Florida Journal of Teacher Education* 3: 73–83.

Ashton, P., and L. Crocker. (May/June 1987). "Systematic Study of Planned Variations: The Essential Focus of Teacher Education Reform." *Journal of Teacher Education* 38,3: 2–8.

Astin, A.W., K.C. Green, and W.S. Korn. (1987). *The American Freshman: Twenty Year Trends*. Los Angeles: Cooperative Institutional Research Program.

Barber, L.W. (1984). *Teacher Evaluation and Merit Pay: Background Papers for the Task Force on Education for Economic Growth*. Working Paper No. TF-83-5. Denver: Education Commission of the States.

Becker, H.S. (1962). "The Nature of a Profession." In *Education for the Professions*, The Sixty-First Yearbook of the National Society for the Study of Education (pp. 27–46), edited by N.B. Henry. Chicago: University of Chicago Press.

Bents, M., and R. Bents. (1990). "Perceptions of Good Teaching Among Novice, Advanced Beginner and Expert Teachers." Paper presented at the Annual Meeting of the American Educational Research Association, Boston.

Benveniste, G. (1987). *Professionalizing the Organization: Reducing Bureaucracy to Enhance Effectiveness*. San Francisco: Jossey-Bass.

Beyer, L.E., W. Feinberg, J.A. Pagano, and J.A. Whitson. (1989). *Preparing Teachers as Professionals*. New York: Teachers College Press.

Bledsoe, J.C., J.V. Cox, and R. Burnham. (1967). *Comparison Between Selected Characteristics and Performance of Provisionally and Professionally Certified Beginning Teachers in Georgia*. Washington, D.C.: U.S. Department of Health, Education, and Welfare.

Borko, H. (1986). "Clinical Teacher Education: The Induction Years." In *Reality and Reform in Clinical Teacher Education* (pp. 1–24), edited by J.V. Hoffman and S.A. Edwards. New York: Random House.

Brandt, R. (1988). "On Changing Secondary Schools: A Conversation with Ted Sizer." *Educational Leadership* 45, 5: 30–36.

Carnegie Forum on Education and the Economy. (1986). *A Nation Prepared: Teachers for the 21st Century*. New York: Carnegie Forum on Education and the Economy.

Copley, P.O. (1974). *A Study of the Effect of Professional Education Courses on Beginning Teachers*. Springfield, Mo.: Southwest Missouri State University. ERIC Document No. ED 098 147.

Corwin, R.G. (1975). "The New Teaching Profession." In *Teacher Education*, The Seventy-Fifth Yearbook of the National Society for the Study of Education (pp. 230–264), edited by K. Ryan. Chicago: University of Chicago Press.

Cremin, L.A. (1965). *The Genius of American Education*. New York: Vintage Books.

Darling-Hammond, L. (1985). "Valuing Teachers: The Making of a Profession." *Teachers College Record* 87, 2: 205–218.

Darling-Hammond, L. (1986a). "Teaching Knowledge: How Do We Test It?" *American Educator* 10, 3: 18–21.

Darling-Hammond, L. (1986b). "A Proposal for Evaluation in the Teaching Profession." *The Elementary School Journal* 86, 4: 531–551.

Darling-Hammond, L. (1989). "Teacher Supply, Demand and Standards." *Edu-*

cational Policy 3, 1: 1–17.

Darling-Hammond, L. (1990a). "Teacher Professionalism: Why and How?" In *Schools as Collaborative Cultures: Creating the Future Now* (pp. 25–50), edited by A. Lieberman. New York: The Falmer Press.

Darling-Hammond, L. (1990b). "Teacher Supply, Demand and Quality: A Mandate for the National Board." Paper prepared for the National Board for Professional Teaching Standards.

Darling-Hammond, L. (1990c). "Teachers and Teaching: Signs of a Changing Profession." In *Handbook of Research on Teacher Education* (pp. 267–290), edited by W.R. Houston. New York: MacMillan.

Darling-Hammond, L. (1992). "Policy and Supervision." In *Supervision in Transition*. Yearbook of the Association for Supervision and Curriculum Development, edited by C. Glickman. Alexandria, Va.: ASCD.

Darling-Hammond, L. (in press). "Teaching and Knowledge: The Policy Implications of Alterative Teacher Certification." *Peabody Journal of Education*.

Darling-Hammond, L., and B. Berry. (1988). *The Evolution of Teacher Policy* (JRE–01). Santa Monica, Calif.: The RAND Corporation.

Darling-Hammond, L., A.E. Wise, and S.R. Pease. (1983). "Teacher Evaluation in the Organizational Context: A Review of the Literature." *Review of Educational Research* 53, 3: 285–328.

Duke, D.L. (1984). *Teaching: The Imperiled Profession*. Albany: State University of New York Press.

Evertson, C., W. Hawley, and M. Zlotnik. (1985). "Making a Difference in Educational Quality Through Teacher Education." *Journal of Teacher Education* 36, 3: 2–12.

Feiman-Nemser, S., and M.B. Parker. (1990). *Making Subject Matter Part of the Conversation or Helping Beginning Teachers Learn to Teach*. East Lansing, Mich.: National Center for Research on Teacher Education.

Friedson, E. (1973). "Professionalization and the Organization of Middle Class Labour in Postindustrial Society." In *Professionalization and Social Change* (Sociological Review Monograph 20), edited by P. Halmas. Keele, England: University of Keele.

Galambos, E.C. (1985). *Teacher Preparation: The Anatomy of a College Degree*. Atlanta: Southern Regional Educatin Board.

Garibaldi, A.M. (1987). *Quality and Diversity in Schools: The Case for an Expanded Pool of Minority Teachers*. Racine, Wisc.: American Association of Colleges for Teacher Education.

Gitlin, A., and J. Smyth. (1989). *Teacher Evaluation: Educative Alternatives*. New York: The Falmer Press.

Goertz, M.E., and B. Pitcher. (1985). *The Impact of NTE Use by States on Teacher Selection*. Princeton, N.J.: Educational Testing Service.

Goodlad, J.I. (1990a). *Teachers for Our Nation's Schools*. San Francisco: Jossey-Bass.

Goodlad, J.I. (1990b). "Connecting the Present to the Past." In *Places Where Teachers Are Taught* (pp. 3–39), edited by J.I. Goodlad, R. Soder, and K.A. Sirotnik. San Francisco: Jossey-Bass.

Goodwin, A.L. (1987). "Vocational Choices and the Realities of Teaching." In *Teacher Renewal* (pp. 30–36), edited by F.S. Bolin and J.M. Falk. New York: Teachers College Press.

Graham, P.A. (April 1987). "Black Teachers: A Drastically Scarce Resource." *Phi Delta Kappan* 68, 8: 598–605.

Greenberg, J.D. (1983). "The Case for Teacher Education: Open and Shut." *Journal of Teacher Education* 34, 4: 2–5.

Greene, M. (1987). "Teaching as Project: Choice, Perspective, and the Public Space." In *Teacher Renewal* (pp. 178–189), edited by F.S. Bolin and J.M. Falk. New York: Teachers College Press.

Griffin, G.A. (1986). "Clinical Teacher Education." In *Reality and Reform in Clinical Teacher Education* (pp. 1–24), edited by J.V. Hoffman and S.A. Edwards. New York: Random House.

Grissmer, D., and S.A. Kirby. (1987). *Understanding Teacher Attrition: The Uphill Climb to Staff the Nation's Schools*. Santa Monica, Calif.: The RAND Corporation.

Grossman, P.L. (1988). "A Study in Contrast: Sources of Pedagogical Content Knowledge for Secondary English." Doctoral diss., Stanford University.

Grossman, P.L. (1989). "Learning to Teach Without Teacher Education." *Teachers College Record* 91, 2: 191–208.

Haberman, M. (September 1984). "An Evaluation of the Rationale for Required Teacher Education: Beginning Teachers with or Without Teacher Preparation." Paper prepared for the National Commission on Excellence in Teacher Education, University of Wisconsin-Milwaukee.

Haney, W., G. Madaus, and A. Kreitzer. (1987). "Charms Talismanic: Testing Teachers for the Improvement of American Education." *Review of Research in Education* 14: 169–238.

Hawk, P., C.R. Coble, and M. Swanson. (1985). "Certification: It Does Matter." *Journal of Teacher Education* 36, 3: 13–15.

The Holmes Group. (1986). *Tomorrow's Teachers*. East Lansing, Mich.: The Holmes Group.

The Holmes Group. (1991). *Tomorrow's Schools*. East Lansing, Mich.: The Holmes Group.

Howey, K.R., and J.C. Vaughn. (1983). "Current Patterns of Staff Development." In *Staff Development*, The Eighty-Second Yearbook of the National Society for the Study of Education (pp. 92–117), edited by G. Griffin. Chicago: University of Chicago Press.

Huling-Austin, L. (1990). "Teacher Induction Programs and Internships." In *Handbook of Research on Teacher Education* (pp. 535–548), edited by W.R. Houston. New York: MacMillan.

Lenk, H.A. (1989). "A Case Study: The Induction of Two Alternate Route Social Studies Teachers." Doctoral diss., Teachers College, Columbia University.

Lieberman, A., and L. Miller. (1984). *Teachers, Their World and Their Work*. Alexandria, Va.: ASCD.

Lortie, D. (1975). *Schoolteacher: A Sociological Study*. Chicago: University of Chicago Press.

Madaus, G.F. (1988). "The Influence of Testing on the Curriculum." In *Critical Issues in Curriculum*, The Eighty-Seventh Yearbook of the National Society for the Study of Education (pp. 83–121), edited by L.N. Tanner. Chicago: University of Chicago Press.

McCutcheon, G. (1988). "Curriculum and the Work of Teachers." In *The Curriculum: Problems, Politics and Possibilities* (pp. 191–203), edited by L.E. Beyer and M.W. Apple. Albany: State University of New York Press.

McDonnell, L.M. (1989). *The Dilemma of Teacher Policy*. Santa Monica, Calif.: The RAND Corporation.

McLaughlin, M.W., and R.S. Pfeifer. (1988). *Teacher Evaluation: Improvement, Accountability and Effective Learning*. New York: Teachers College Press.

Meier, D. (Fall 1987). "Success in East Harlem." *American Educator* 11, 3: 34–39.

Miller, G.E. (1962). "Medicine." In *Education for the Professions*, The Sixty-First Yearbook of the National Society for the Study of Education (pp. 103–119), edited by N.B. Henry. Chicago: University of Chicago Press.

Minnesota Board of Teaching. (1986). *Minnesota's Vision for Teacher Education: Stronger Standards, New Partnerships*. Minneapolis: Task Force on Teacher Education, Minnesota Higher Education Coordinating Board.

Mitchell, D.E., and C.T. Kerchner. (1983). "Labor Relations and Teacher Policy." In *Handbook of Teaching and Policy* (pp. 214–238), edited by L.S. Shulman and G. Sykes. New York: Longman.

Mitchell, N. (1987). *Interim Evaluation Report of the Alternative Certification Program* (REA87-027-2). Dallas: DISD Department of Planning, Evaluation, and Testing.

Murray, C. (1991). "Rochester's Reforms: The Teachers' Perspective." Paper presented at the annual meeting of the American Educational Research Association, Chicago.

National Center for Education Statistics. (1991). *The Condition of Education 1991. Vol. 1. Elementary and Secondary Education.* Washington, D.C.: U.S. Department of Education.

National Commission on Excellence in Education. (1983). *A Nation at Risk.* Washington, D.C.: U.S. Government Printing Office.

National Education Association. (1981). *Status of the American Public School Teacher, 1980–81.* Washington, D.C.: National Education Association.

National Education Association. (1987). *Status of the American Public School Teacher, 1985–86.* Washington, D.C.: National Education Association.

Olsen, D.G. (1985). "The Quality of Prospective Teachers: Education vs. Noneducation Graduates." *Journal of Teacher Education* 36, 5: 56–59.

Opp, R.D. (1989). "Freshman Interest in Teaching: Recent Trends." *Journal of Teacher Education* 40, 4: 43–48.

Perrone, V. (1991). *A Letter to Teachers.* San Francisco: Jossey-Bass.

Rottenberg, C.J., and D.C. Berliner. (1990). "Expert and Novice Teachers' Conceptions of Common Classroom Activities." Paper presented at the Annual Meeting of the American Educational Research Association, Boston.

Sarason, S.B. (1982). *The Culture of School and the Problem of Change*, 2nd ed. Boston: Allyn and Bacon.

Schwartz, H. (1988). "Unapplied Curriculum Knowledge." In *Critical Issues in Curriculum*, The Eighty-Seventh Yearbook of the National Society for the Study of Education (pp. 35–59), edited by L. N. Tanner. Chicago: University of Chicago Press.

Sedlak, M., and S. Schlossman. (1986). *Who Will Teach? Historical Perspectives on the Changing Appeal of Teaching as a Profession* (R-3472). Santa Monica, Calif.: The RAND Corporation.

Shulman, L. (1987). "Knowledge and Teaching: Foundations of the New Reform." *Harvard Educational Review* 57, 1: 1–22.

Sizer, T.R. (1984). *Horace's Compromise: The Dilemma of the American High School.* Boston: Houghton Mifflin.

Urbanski, A. (1988). "The Rochester Contract: A Status Report." *Educational Leadership* 46, 3: 48–52.

U.S. Bureau of the Census. (1984). *1984 Current Population Survey.* Washington, D.C.: U.S. Government Printing Office.

Vance, V., and P. Schlechty. (1982). "The Distribution of Academic Ability in the Teaching Force: Policy Implications." *Phi Delta Kappan* 64, 1: 22–27.

Wise, A., and L. Darling-Hammond. (1987). *Licensing Teachers: Design for a Teaching Profession* (R-3576-CSTP). Santa Monica, Calif.: The RAND Corporation.

Woodring, P. (1975). "The Development of Teacher Education." In *Teacher Education*, The Seventy-Fifth Yearbook of the National Society for the Study of Education (pp. 1–24), edited by K. Ryan. Chicago: University of Chicago Press.

Zeichner, K.M. (1986). "Social and Ethical Dimensions of Reform in Teacher Education." In *Reality and Reform in Clinical Teacher Education* (pp. 87–108), edited by J.V. Hoffman and S.A. Edwards. New York: Random House.

Zumwalt, K.K. (1988). "Are We Undermining or Improving Teaching?" In *Critical Issues in Curriculum*, The Eighty-Seventh Yearbook of the National Society for the Study of Education (pp. 148–176), edited by L.N. Tanner. Chicago: University of Chicago Press.

3

The Growth of Assessment

George F. Madaus and Ann G.A. Tan

Education in the United States has undergone extraordinary changes during ASCD's first half-century. Arguably, one of the most radical and influential changes concerns the role of standardized tests. In 1943, when ASCD was new, most teachers and children considered standardized achievement tests innocuous. As one observer put it:

> [Everyone] knew virtually nothing was ever done with the results. When the teacher spent the morning giving a [standardized] test, it was an easy morning for him or her, and a not unpleasant one for most of the pupils. Such tests were much less threatening to the children than a test prepared by the teacher on which a grade might depend (Travers 1983, p. 145).

Although testing had been used as a policy tool in American education at the local level since at least the 1840s (Tyack and Hansot 1982, Massachusetts Historical Society Documents 1845–46, White 1888, Madaus and Kellaghan 1992) and in New York with its Regents Examination since the 1870s, the nature and magnitude of test use changed dramatically after World War II. Each succeeding decade witnessed an inexorable shift—at first subtle, then dramatic—in the importance of testing as a major tool of educational policy.

The passage in 1958 of the National Defense Education Act (NDEA) marks the emergence of testing as a tool in the national policy arena. By the late '60s, as one key observer stated, standardized test results were "employed to make keep-or-kill decisions about educational programs. Big dollars were riding on the results of achievement tests . . . . The days of penny-ante assessment were over" (Popham 1983, p. 23). A decade later, many states discovered the policy potential of testing and linked standardized test performance to decisions about student graduation, promotion, and placement (Madaus and McDonagh 1979, Madaus 1983). In the 1980s, states expanded the use of student test results in several ways: evaluating teacher and school effectiveness, putting school systems into receivership, and allocating resources to schools and districts (Haertel 1989; Madaus 1985, 1988). And in this, the last decade of the 20th century, clarion calls are heard from many, including President Bush, to create a national testing system, geared to "world class standards." In its seminal report, the National Council on Education Standards and Testing (NCEST) argued that "standards and assessments linked to the standards can become *the cornerstone of the fundamental, systemic reform necessary to improve schools*" (NCEST 1992, p. 5; emphasis added).

Over the past fifty years, we have seen U.S. educational testing proliferate into many important, interesting applications—test use in the guidance movement, creativity testing, the development of test standards and codes of testing by professional organizations, the establishment of the National Merit Scholarship Corporation, test use in mastery learning, school effectiveness indicators, and criterion/curriculum-referenced testing. On the technical front, we witnessed the development and use of normal curve equivalents (NCEs), National Assessment of Educational Progress (NAEP) scaling, and item response theory (IRT). As well, we have seen declines in the scores of U.S. students on the Scholastic Aptitude Test (SAT). Testing has also been part of important debates in education, such as the IQ controversy, the influence of teachers' expectations (known as "Pygmalion in the classroom"), and "Truth in Testing" legislation. More recently, we have seen the emergence of new developments, such as the theory of multiple intelligences and "authentic" assessment. However, we believe that the main testing story of the past fifty years is its evolution as a social technology, first to inform, and eventually to implement national educational reform policy. This chapter documents and describes the extraordinary growth of standardized testing as a policy mechanism and the reasons behind this growth, from 1943 through the present.

We first present a brief history of how changes in the technology of testing and beliefs about teaching and learning before the 1950s influenced testing after World War II. Next, we describe some indicators of the growth of testing over the past fifty years and offer an explanation for this remarkable growth. We then describe the present status of testing and the rise of the assessment movement. Finally, we attempt to predict the future of standardized testing in American education.

Changes in the Technology of Testing Before 1943

Testing was first introduced as a policy mechanism in China in 210 BC to select virtuous men for civil service positions. Since then, there have been only three ways to test or examine people—by requiring them to:

1. Supply an oral or written answer to a series of questions (e.g., essay or short-answer questions or the oral disputation), or to produce a product (e.g., a portfolio of artwork, a research paper, or an object, such as a chair or a piece of cut glass).

2. Perform an act to be evaluated against certain criteria (e.g., conduct a chemistry experiment, read aloud from a book, repair a carburetor).

3. Select an answer to a question or posed problem from among several options (e.g., the multiple-choice or true-false item).

Each testing method has built-in constraints inherent in its design. Over the centuries, test users have had to grapple with these constraints, and their solutions help explain the evolution of standardized testing as a major social technology in the educational policy arena in the United States. An apt metaphor to use in problem solving in any technological area comes from the military: *the reverse salient in an expanding military front*. In World War I, advances along the battle line were often uneven. Before a general advance could continue, any reverse bulge or "salient" in the front line had to be eliminated. Technological systems, like an advancing military front, also develop unevenly. Some components of the system fall behind others, acting as a drag on the entire system by functioning inefficiently, malfunctioning, or adding disproportionately to costs. Inventors such as Edison, the Wright brothers, Bell, and Sperry concentrated their efforts on eliminating "reverse salients" impeding the advance of already existing technologies (Hughes 1989). Similar changes have occurred in the technology of testing over the centuries.

The history of testing in Europe and the United States shows that changes or adaptations in testing technology were directed at making testing more efficient, manageable, standardized, objective, easier to administer, and less costly in the face of increasing numbers of examinees. For example:

• In the 18th century, the oral disputation—the predominant assessment technology of the time—aimed at assessing universal rhetorical skills that could be brought to bear on any subject, was supplemented by the written exam to more *efficiently* assess mathematics, a new curricular offering in the university (Hoskins 1968, Montgomery 1967, Madaus and Kellaghan 1992).

• The same century saw the innovation of assigning quantitative marks to performance, because examiners tended to be subjective and partial in their *qualitative* judgments of students' oral disputations and written examinations. This shift permitted the seemingly more "objective" ranking of examinees and the averaging and aggregating of test scores (Hoskins 1968, Madaus and Kellaghan 1992).

• In 1845 Horace Mann supplanted the oral exam in the Boston Public Schools with the written essay exam. Although Mann had political reasons for making the change, he also recognized that written examinations allowed examiners to administer *uniform* examinations to a rapidly expanding student body in much *less time*, producing *comparable results* across students that were not previously possible with oral examinations (Madaus 1990).

• In the first decade of the 20th century, the short-answer-supply mode appeared. Samelson (1987) named Fredrick Kelly as the inventor of the multiple-choice item in 1914 (though Thorndike and Lohman 1990 credit the Chinese with the development and use of the selection/multiple-choice test). The development of short, easily scored test items occurred partially in response to the Starch and Elliott (1912, 1913) studies, which showed that the marks assigned to essay questions were highly unreliable, and partly in response to the growth of the scientific management movement's adaptation to education, which required that growing numbers of children be tested to measure a district's efficiency (Callahan 1962).

• In 1917, Otis's development of a group-administered IQ test, the Army Alpha, overcame the administrative, scoring, and cost limitations associated with the individually administered Binet. Once again the sheer number of examinees that needed to be tested—almost 2 million recruits—demanded a technology that was more efficient, cheaper, more manageable, and easier to score and record (Sokal 1987).

• In 1926, the College Entrance Examination Board adopted the multiple-choice format and dropped the writing component of the SAT in 1937, partly because of the cost of scoring and to permit greater variety of test content (Angoff and Dyer 1971).

One important post-World War II technological development—the invention by Lindquist of the high-speed optical scanner—further facilitated the deployment of the large-scale, low-cost, multiple-choice testing programs of the '60s, '70s, and '80s. (At the beginning of the 1990s, a reaction against these cheap, efficient, administratively convenient, multiple-choice testing programs set in—a development we discuss later in this chapter.)

Before leaving this pre-1950 history of testing, we should mention a widely held belief and a momentous technical development that became closely related: the recurring, strong, traditional notion that all students could learn if properly taught and the invention of *ability* or *intelligence* tests in the late 19th century.

The Belief That All Children Can Learn

Since at least the 15th century, many people have believed that if teachers taught correctly, pupils would surely learn. Coupled with this belief was the practice of using examination results as a mechanism for holding teachers accountable to ensure that students obtained certain educational outcomes. For example, a 1444 contract between the town fathers of Treviso and its schoolmaster stipulated that the schoolmaster's salary would be linked to the pupils' level of attainment—measured by a *viva voce* examination—on the grammar curriculum of the time (Aries 1962). This "payment by results" provision of the Treviso contract is one of the earliest examples—predated perhaps only by the Chinese mandarin civil service examinations—of the use of the technology of testing as a form of centralized, hierarchical, managerial control. Indeed, much of the mandated standardized testing that goes on today is essentially bureaucratic rather than educational in its sponsorship, character, and use (Madaus and Kellaghan 1992).

The assumption that all students would learn if properly taught continued to be common both in Britain and America, at least through the first half of the 19th century, when schools dealt with small numbers of pupils. For example, consider this 1845 letter from Horace Mann to Samuel Gridley Howe on how to use results from the newly introduced, printed, written examination in the Boston public schools:

> Some pieces should be immediately written for the papers, containing so much of an analysis of the answers, as will show that the pupils answered common and memoriter questions far better than they did questions involving a principle; and it should be set forth most pointedly, that in the former case, the merit belongs to the scholars, in the latter the demerit belongs to the master. All those abominable blunders which are even more to be condemned for their numbers than for their enormity: orthography, punctuation, capitalizing and grammar are the direct result of imperfect teaching. *Children will not learn such*

things by instinct. They will not fail to learn them, under proper instruc-tion . . . . One very important and pervading fact in proof of this view of the case, is the great difference existing between schools, on the same subject, showing that children could learn, if teachers had taught (Massachusetts Historical Society Documents 1845–46; emphasis added).

This remarkable quote has a distinctly contemporary ring to it: the publication in the newspapers of test results for political and bureaucratic purposes; the use of test results to describe curricular outcomes and to hold teachers and school accountable for poor results; and the distinction between lower and higher order thinking skills in the curriculum and examinations.

The belief that all students could learn if properly taught, however, was seriously eroded in the face of poor student performance when compulsory attendance, new immigration, and the abolition of child labor in the latter part of the 19th century forced educators to deal for the first time with a large and very diverse population of students.

The Development of Intelligence and Ability Tests

Until the end of the 19th century, tests or examinations were what we now call "achievement" tests. They concentrated on a syllabus, curriculum, or craft. The advent of the IQ testing movement in the latter part of that century altered testing forever. Proponents of mental testing claimed, and it was widely believed, that testing could do more than assess what people learned: it could now measure their underlying mental ability or intelligence (Madaus 1990). This development had profound effects on the ways in which educators came to view school organization, classroom grouping, and the capacity of individual students to learn and profit from instruction.

Thus, by 1918 the ability level of students was used to "explain" why many students could not be expected to do well. For example, one prominent educator of the time argued that "unsatisfactory school results is [sic] to be traced to the native limitations in the ability of the child or to the home atmosphere in which the child grows up" (Judd 1918, p. 152). "Scientific" tests of both achievement and "intelligence" quickly began to serve as selection devices to identify talent and to place students in the "proper" curriculum for their ability level. Curriculum became differentiated according to student "ability" level, often with disastrous consequences for minorities and non-English speakers.

The interpretation of "intelligence" test scores as reflecting some sort of innate ability overlooked the fact that Binet's original intent was to identify persons in need of specialized instruction. Binet's tests were samples of ability, and "to interpret them as measures of 'general intelligence' was a flagrant overgeneralization" (Snow and Yalow 1982, p. 505). Nonetheless, such overgeneralizations have been made repeatedly over the decades. It reemerged with a vengeance in the 1960s with the publication of Arthur Jensen's (1969) controversial article, "How Much Can We Boost IQ and Scholastic Achievement?" Jensen argued that "genetic factors are strongly implicated in the average Negro-white intelligence difference" (p. 82). Another controversial article along the same lines of Jensen's was Richard Herrnstein's "IQ." Rebuttals and counter arguments to Jensen's thesis quickly followed and continued into the 1980s (see Block and Dworkin 1976). Stephen Jay Gould, for example, in *The Mismeasure of Man* (1981), addressed what he saw as the twin fallacies underlying Jensen's hereditarian IQ argument: "reification"—the assumption that test scores represent a single, scalable thing called general intelligence; and "hereditarianism"—equating "heritable" with "inevitable" and the confusion of within- and between-group heredity.

In the 1980s, Carroll raised a variation on the controversy when he pointed out that many of the more difficult tasks used in the NAEP reading assessment—tasks measuring so-called higher-order thinking—resemble tasks found on tests of verbal and scholastic aptitude. While he recognizes the argument might be unpopular, he wondered if those NAEP exercises were a measure of national verbal ability, and if they were, then he worried that the research literature did not hold out much hope of improvement given present educational methods (Carroll 1987).

The School Effectiveness Movement

The idea that all students could learn if properly taught lay dormant from the first decade of this century until Jerome Bruner (1966), John Carroll (1963), and Benjamin Bloom (1968) revived the idea in the 1960s. Beginning in the late '70s, the school effectiveness movement linked the reemergence of the idea that all students could learn with another popular development of the mid-'60s related to testing: the expectancy, self-fulfilling prophecy or "Pygmalion" effect (Rosenthal and Jacobson 1968). In one of the most oft-cited works in education (Wineburg 1987), Rosenthal and Jacobson concluded that the provision of *false ability*-test information to teachers had led to an improvement in pupils' measured scholastic *ability*. Despite being strongly criticized on statistical and design grounds, and years of failure on the part of hosts of researchers to demonstrate a similar effect, Rosenthal and Jacobson's Pygmalion effect nonetheless became widely accepted as a social truth (Kellaghan, Madaus, and Airasian 1982; Wineburg 1987). A central tenet of the school effectiveness movement was that effective schools made it clear to both teachers and students that all students could and were expected to learn (e.g., Edmonds 1980). As Wineburg (1987) observed, the road to academic success "was paved with the power of positive thinking" (p. 35).

A similar belief in the power of positive expectation can be found in the rhetoric of the 1990s reform movement, with the assertion that all students can attain "world class standards" in the five curricular areas covered by the National Goals—math, science, English, history, and geography (Madaus and Kellaghan 1991, U.S. Department of Education 1991). This expectation would be backed up by a high-stakes accountability system that would monitor the progress of schools and individuals toward the attainment of these world class standards.

Let us turn now to the phenomenal growth of testing over the past fifty years.

The Growth in Testing, 1950 to 1990

In 1930, an estimated 5 million standardized educational tests were administered annually (Strenio 1981. Unfortunately, there is little documentation on Strenio's growth estimates.) By 1990, it was conservatively estimated that each year elementary and secondary students take 127 million separate tests as part of standardized test batteries mandated by states and districts [National Commission on Testing and Public Policy (NCTPP) 1990]. At some grade levels, a student might have to sit for 7 to 12 such tests a year.

The commission found that testing was generally heavier for students in special education or bilingual programs. Many indicators show the enormous growth of testing over the past fifty years: the growth in the number of state testing programs from 1960 onward; sales of tests and scoring services; citations in *Education Index*; and citations in *Educational Leadership*. Incidentally, growth in U.S. testing programs is also shown by changes in the *Mental Measurement Yearbooks*, from the first edition in 1938 to the tenth edition in 1989 (Buros 1938, Conoley 1989).

Growth in State-Mandated Testing Programs

Figure 3.1 shows a steady rise in numbers of state-mandated *assessment programs*, from one in 1960 to thirty-two by 1985. The rise in numbers of *minimum competency testing programs* at the state level

Figure 3.1
States Authorizing Minimum
Competency and Assessment Programs

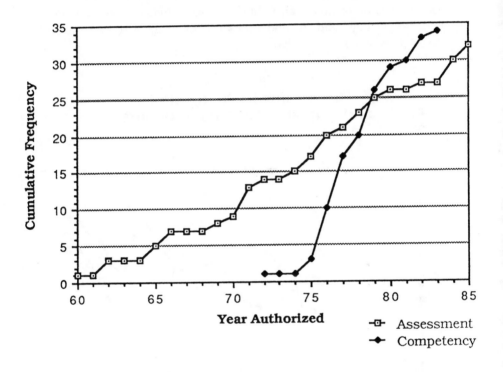

Source: Office of Technology Assessment; U.S. Congress (1987).

has been even more dramatic: from one such program in 1972 to thirty-four programs by 1985. By 1990, every state had some kind of mandated testing program. Naturally, with every state mandate, the number of students tested—and hence the number of tests administered—increased (NCTPP 1990).

Growth in Test Sales

The second growth indicator is that of the increase in the *reported* dollar volume of sales of tests and testing services at the elementary and secondary levels (referred to in the industry as the Elhi market). Figure 3.2 shows the sales figures for standardized tests for the Elhi market, from 1955 through 1986, and those sales adjusted for inflation using the 1988 Consumer Price Index (NCTPP 1990). These data were taken from *The Bowker Annual* (1970–1987). *Bowker* gets its sales figures from the Association of American Publishers' (AAP) *Industry Statistics Report*. See Haney, Madaus, and Lyons (in press) for a more detailed description of the *Bowker* figures.

Figure 3.2
Test Sales in Unadjusted
and Adjusted Millions of Dollars

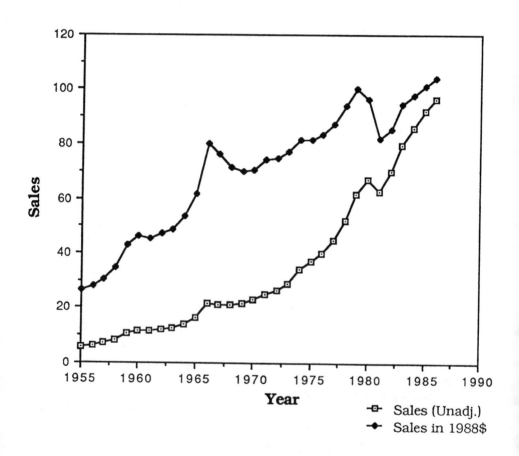

Source: *The Bowker Annual*, 1970–1987

Figure 3.2 shows a dramatic growth rate since 1955, of almost 400 percent, in the real dollar volume of sales of tests and testing services. Sales rose from less than $30 million in 1955 to more than $100 million by 1986 (1988 dollars). Actual revenues from sales of tests and related testing services may be as much as four or five times higher than those reported in *Bowker*—somewhere on the order of half a billion dollars (not shown in Figure 3.2). Further, the increased revenues of the testing industry are due more to the increased volume of testing than to increases in the costs of tests or test-scoring services (Haney, Madaus, and Lyons in press).

Growth as Reflected in the Education Index

An indirect indicator of the growth in testing developed by Haney and Madaus (1986) charts the number of citations in the *Education Index* under the rubric "tests and scales" (as indicated by number of column inches) from 1930 onward. For comparative purposes, and of interest to ASCD members, Haney and Madaus also charted the citations under the "curriculum" rubric.

In terms of the sheer *numbers* of articles under the various testing rubrics found in *Education Index*, there were 179 articles in the edition covering the years 1941–44; by the 1990–91 edition, the number had swelled to 728; the number of articles peaked between July 1984 and June 1985 at 1,154 titles.

Figure 3.3 shows that the average annual number of column inches devoted to citations concerning *curriculum* increased only modestly over the past sixty-one years—from 50 to 100 inches per year in the 1930s and 1940s to only 100 to 150 in recent years. In contrast, column inches devoted to *tests and scales* have increased dramatically, from only 10 to 30 in the 1930s and 1940s to well over 300 in 1990–91. (The correlation between column inches devoted to testing and year is a whopping 0.91.) This index is admittedly crude; but the data certainly indicate that the prominence of testing, as represented in the education literature, has increased dramatically, particularly since the mid-1960s.

Growth as Reflected in Educational Leadership

In the decade of the '40s, *Educational Leadership* published a total of five articles with the rubrics "evaluation," "test," or "measurement" in the title. The number of articles, as well as the rubrics relating to testing, grew to more than ninety articles during the decade of the '80s. The first two years of the '90s have already seen thirteen such articles.

Figure 3.3
Education Index Listings
Under Testing and Curriculum

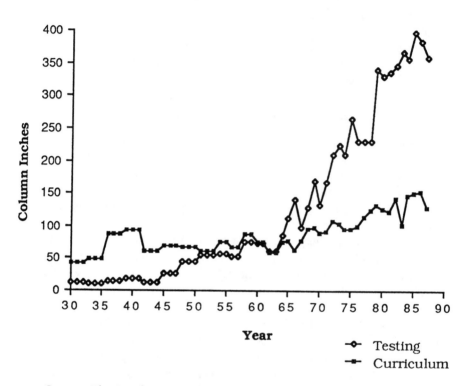

Source: *The Bowker Annual,* 1970–1987

The phenomenal growth of minimum competency testing (MCT) is clearly documented by coverage in *Educational Leadership.* For example, the cover of a 1977 issue had two maps of the United States, the first showing states that had MCT programs in January, the second showing that ten additional states had programs the following September. Between October 1978 and May 1979, *Educational Leadership* published eleven articles dealing with MCT, compared to one article between the same months for 1976 to 1977.

Changes in Test Use

The conclusion seems inescapable: educational testing has expanded dramatically over the life of ASCD, in terms of both volume and societal importance. But growth is only part of the story; the uses to which test results were put also have changed dramatically. The NCTPP (1990) noted that dramatic growth in testing since the 1950s was coupled with the trend of greater reliance on test results to make critical decisions about children, such as:

- Entry to and exit from kindergarten
- Promotion from grade to grade
- Placement in remedial programs
- Graduation from high school

Further, there was a dramatic increase in the use of students' scores to hold school systems, administrators, and teachers accountable.

In 1992, as previously noted, the NCEST endorsed the use of assessments to monitor individual and system progress toward the national education standards and:

- to exemplify for students, parents, and teachers the kinds and levels of achievement that should be expected;
- to improve classroom instruction and improve the learning outcomes for all students;
- to inform students, parents, and teachers about student progress toward the standards;
- to measure and hold students, schools, districts, states, and the Nation accountable for educational performance; and
- to assist in education program decisions to be made by policy makers (NCEST 1992).

Thus, not only has the volume of testing increased, but testing has become a high-stakes policy tool looming ominously over the lives of many educators and children, influencing what is taught and how, and what is learned and how (NCTPP 1990).

In addition, the costs to taxpayers for state and local testing have also increased. The NCTPP estimates annual costs of between $725 and $915 million, and points out that classroom time taken to prepare students specifically for mandated tests could be put to any number of alternative instructional uses. For example, one study of "opportunity costs" in mathematics concluded that teachers who spend the bulk of their effort teaching to the yardstick of present standardized tests sacrifice the intellectual engagement that students need to develop the kind of mathematical abilities recommended by the National Council of Teachers of Mathematics (Romberg, Zarinnia, and Williams 1989).

Reasons for the Growth in Testing

What caused the rapid growth in testing and the attendant shift to high-stakes policy uses of test results? Four broad social forces at work during the past fifty years help explain the transformation of testing today (Haney, Madaus, and Lyons in press).

• Recurring public dissatisfaction with the quality of education in the United States and efforts to reform education.

• A broad shift in attention from focusing on the inputs or resources devoted to education toward emphasizing the outputs or results of our educational institutions.

• An array of legislation, at both federal and state levels, promoting or explicitly mandating standardized testing programs.

• Bureaucratization of education and schooling.

These broad forces are by no means independent. For example, a specific episode of public dissatisfaction with education often leads to legislation mandating new tests, which in turn focuses public attention on outcomes of schooling, or at least on test scores; and legislation and testing are implicated in the increased bureaucratization of education. Despite such interdependencies, for ease of discussion we treat these forces separately.

Dissatisfaction with Education and Efforts at Reform

Over the past fifty years, there have been at least six major cycles of educational dissatisfaction and reform, each of which has contributed to the growth of standardized testing either by using test results to inform policymakers about the state of education or as a mechanism of policy aimed at transforming education.

The first cycle began with the Sputnik launching in 1957, which sparked national concern about U.S. science, math, and technical education in general and our military and technological competitiveness with the Soviet Union in particular. In response, the U.S. Congress passed the National Defense Education Act.

The second cycle of dissatisfaction and reform began with the compensatory education and civil rights movements of the 1960s. First, advocacy groups seeking aid for their constituents pointed to glaring disparities between the standardized test performance of their constituents and that of middle-class students. Second, in the early 1960s, with the publication of the famous *Coleman Report* (Coleman et al. 1966), policymakers began to use standardized test results not only for information about the condition of American education in general, but also eventually as the yardstick against which to judge the impact of compensatory programs, such as Head Start and Title I (Madaus 1985). These movements also led to important legislation, which had a serious impact on testing and the testing industry.

The third cycle was marked by the furor in the 1970s over national declines in SAT scores. These declines raised great concern over the quality of education in the United States and contributed to the rise of the MCT movement.

The 1980s saw the next wave of reform reports, the most famous of which was *A Nation at Risk* (National Commission on Excellence in Education 1983a). This cycle of dissatisfaction and reform efforts rekindled concerns over U.S. competitiveness, now economic rather than military. All of the reform reports used test score data to argue that the nation's schools were failing. (See Stedman and Smith 1983 for an excellent analysis of the 1980s reform reports.) Most of the reports also saw testing as a policy mechanism that would remedy the ills disclosed by testing in the first place. For example, a follow-up study to *A Nation at Risk* found that thirty-five states had enacted testing requirements and forty-four had strengthened graduation requirements (National Commission on Excellence in Education 1983b).

In the late 1980s, John Jacob Cannell found that all states, and the vast majority of school systems, scored above average on standardized achievement tests (dubbed the Lake Wobegone phenomenon). This finding called into question the efficacy of the mandated-measurement-driven instruction programs of the '70s and '80s (Cannell 1987, 1988). Cannell's work paved the way for calls in the 1990s for new forms of assessment.

Finally, the reform movement of the 1990s saw a reemphasis of concern over U.S. economic competitiveness and what was perceived to be the poor performance in math and science of our students compared to students in other countries. In response, the President and the nation's governors agreed on six goals for the reform of U.S. education. America 2000 incorporated those goals and called for the establishment of "world class standards" and a national testing program to monitor progress toward the goals and the attainment of those standards (U.S. Department of Education 1991).

The idea that the United States needs to create a "national" test or testing system has appeal. Advocates argue that the creation of such a test or system is essential if the United States is to develop a world class education system, one that will motivate the unmotivated, lift all students to world class standards, increase our nation's productivity, and restore our global competitiveness. The NCEST was created by Public Law 102-62 on June 27, 1991, to provide Congress with advice on the desirability and feasibility of national standards and testing in education. It can be argued that the feasibility of creating a national testing system was never adequately addressed by NCEST (Koretz, Madaus, Haertel, and Beaton 1992). Nonetheless, the NCEST report argued that "standards and assessments linked to world class standards can become the cornerstone of the fundamental, systemic reform necessary to improve schools" (NCEST 1992, p. 5). Testing, albeit referred to by the new buzzword "authentic" assessment, was once again touted as the policy tool of choice to hold schools and individuals accountable and reenergize American schools.

We would be remiss if we failed to point out that while testing played an important role in informing educational critics from the 1950s onward, testing itself was also the subject of intense criticism during the same period (see Haney 1981; Haney, Madaus, and Lyons in press; and Kellaghan, Madaus, and Airasian 1982 for reviews of literature critical of testing from 1950 to 1990). Consider, for example, the following sampling of books critical of the role of testing in our society:

- Martin Gross's *The Brain Watchers* (1962)
- Banish Hoffman's *The Tyranny of Testing* (1962)
- Hillel Black's *They Shall Not Pass* (1963)
- Vance Packard's *The Naked Society* (1964)
- Brian Simon's *Intelligence, Psychology and Education* (1971)
- Leon Kamin's *The Science and Politics of IQ* (1974)
- Joel Spring's *The Sorting Machine* (1976)
- Block and Dworkin's *The IQ Controversy* (1976)
- Paul Houts's *The Myth of Measurability* (1977)
- J. Lawler's *IQ, Heritability, and Racism* (1978)
- Allan Nairn and associates' *The Reign of ETS: The Corporation That Makes Up Minds* (1980)
- Mitch Lazarus's *Good-bye to Excellence: A Critical Look at the Minimum Competency Testing Movement* (1981)
- George Madaus's *The Courts, Validity, and Minimum Competency Testing* (1982)
- Stephen Jay Gould's *The Mismeasure of Man* (1981)
- Andrew Strenio's *The Testing Trap* (1981)
- David Owen's *None of the Above* (1985)
- James Crouse and Dale Trusheim's *The Case Against the SAT* (1988)

Most of these books dealt with the IQ controversy or the use of the SAT. However, Hoffman (1962) and Houts (1977) remarkably foreshadowed the criticism of multiple-choice testing and the move to alternative assessment techniques that broke through in the 1990s.

The Focus on Outcomes of Schooling

The last fifty years have seen a fundamental shift in the way in which people perceived the quality of schools. Reformers through the early '60s focused on *inputs*, such as the quality of the physical plant, characteristics of teachers, and school finance, as measures of school quality (e.g., Conant 1961). In 1966, the *Equality of Education Opportunity Report* (EEOR), or *Coleman Report*, found that "schools bring little to bear on a child's achievement that is independent of his background and general social context." This widely publicized finding shifted the focus of discussion about equality of opportunity away from inputs to the *outcomes* of schooling (Coleman et al. 1966). (The EEOR's major finding was widely debated, and the data were reanalyzed. For a discussion of that literature, see Madaus, Airasian, and Kellaghan 1980.)

The shift away from school resources toward school outputs measured by tests of academic achievement clearly contributed to the prominence of testing as a policy tool of accountability from the '40s to the present.

Legislation

Whereas state-mandated testing programs contributed to the increase in testing (see Figure 3.1), major pieces of federal legislation enacted between 1957 and 1990 reinforced the upsurge in testing documented in Figures 3.2 and 3.3. In addition, myriad federal programs mandated research or evaluation of programs for children; and this evaluation at least indirectly contributed to increased test use. For example, one study identified more than 1,500 test titles proposed for use in federally funded research projects (Heyneman and Mintz 1976).

The following federal education acts were the most prominent (See Haney, Madaus, and Lyons in press, for a more detailed legislative history):

1. *The National Defense Education Act (NDEA) of 1958,* which included a section entitled "Guidance, Counseling and Testing: Identification and Encouragement of Able Students." That section authorized funds for local testing programs in both public and private school

systems. Many of the NDEA's testing provisions were included in the *Elementary and Secondary Education Act of 1965*.

2. *The 1964 Civil Rights Act* made an impact on testing in important ways. For programs and activities receiving federal funding, Title VI mandated nondiscrimination in employment by reason of race; and it was widely used to challenge educational testing practices. Two of the most famous of these legal challenges were the *Larry P. v. Riles* case in California, which resulted in the prohibition on the use of IQ tests to place students in classrooms for "educable" mentally retarded students, and the landmark *Debra P. v. Turlington* case in Florida, which ruled that a minimum competency test used for high school graduation had to be a fair test of what was taught in the classrooms of the state (Madaus 1983). The 1964 Civil Rights Act also mandated the *Coleman Report*, which helped to shift the definition of equal opportunity from inputs to educational outcomes, as measured by tests.

3. *The National Assessment of Educational Progress* (NAEP), founded in 1963, marks another milestone in the growing federal influence on educational testing. NAEP, almost entirely funded by the federal government since the late '60s, is important, not because it contributed to increased volume in testing but for several other reasons. First, NAEP was the first systematic effort to gather nationally representative achievement test data. Second, NAEP contributed to the shift to focusing on outcomes when considering educational quality. Third, NAEP data were used to support calls for educational reform in the '70s, '80s, and '90s. (Over the past decade, NAEP's capability to provide accurate information to policymakers and the public stands in sharp contrast to many state and district high-stakes testing programs implemented during the late '70s and '80s in response to a growing dissatisfaction with our schools.) Fourth, NAEP has contributed to the development of curriculum frameworks and to the technology of testing in areas like scaling, matrix sampling, and the reporting of results.

In 1991, Congress authorized state-by-state comparisons that had initially been prohibited to NAEP. Thirty-five states participated in the effort. (See Glaser and Linn 1992 for an evaluation of the Trial State Assessment Project.) A recommendation by the National Assessment Governing Board (NAGB 1990) and a proposal in the *America 2000* report would extend NAEP downward to district, school, and even individual levels (Haney and Madaus 1992). These later proposals have the potential to change the character of NAEP, perhaps even destroy its usefulness as an independent, valid indicator of the nation's educational progress, and need to be watched closely (Haney and Madaus 1992).

4. *The Elementary and Secondary Education Act (ESEA) of 1965* and its subsequent amendments and reauthorizations have had an enormous impact on test use. For example, ESEA provided funds for statewide testing programs and helped upgrade the capacity of state agencies to conduct testing programs. It also provided money under Title IV for the training of personnel conducting tests and measures.

Standardized test scores became the yardstick to evaluate Title I programs for the disadvantaged and other interventions, such as Head Start [Title II of the Economic Opportunity Act (ECO) of 1964] and Follow Through (included in a 1967 amendment to the ECO). In 1975, the U.S. Department of Education developed six models for districts to use with either norm- or criterion-referenced tests when evaluating Title I (later Chapter 1 of P.L. 100-297). Section 22 of the 1978 revision included a provision for periodic testing of basic skills achievement and the publication of performance by grade level and school. Because of ESEA, all major achievement-test series were revised in the late '70s and early '80s and included a provision for interpreting results in terms of NCEs. The redesigned achievement series of the late '70s contained a higher density of easier items, making them more useful in the evaluation of programs for the educationally disadvantaged because the change permitted low-achieving students to more reliably show what they knew and could do (Rudman 1987).

5. *The Education for All Handicapped Children Act of 1975* (P.L. 94-142), together with its accompanying regulations and amendments, was another federal windfall for the testing industry. It required that tests and other evaluation materials be used to determine individual placement, assess specific areas of need, and evaluate the effectiveness of individual educational plans of students with disabilities or other special needs (Haney and Madaus 1992).

6. *The Augustus F. Hawkins-Robert T. Stafford Elementary and Secondary School Improvements Amendments of 1988 (P.L. 100-297)* contained the first-of-its-kind provisions for a federal test of individual students. It authorized the Secretary of Education

> after consultation with appropriate State and local educational agencies and public and private organizations, to approve comprehensive tests of academic excellence or to develop such a test where commercially unavailable, to be administered to identify outstanding students who are in the eleventh grade of public and private secondary schools .... The tests of academic excellence shall be tests of acquired skills and knowledge appropriate for the completion of a secondary school education (P.L. 100-297, p. 102, STAT. 247–248).

The bill also authorized the Secretary to award certificates to students who scored at a high level. Students would receive these certificates, signed by the Secretary, within 60 days of taking the test.

Bureaucratization of Education

Perhaps the greatest single change in American education over the past fifty years has been the increased bureaucratization of education (see Hall 1977; Wise 1979; and Haney, Madaus, and Lyons in press for detailed discussions of testing and bureaucratization). For instance:

• Tests provide means for categorizing people, educational institutions, and problems according to abstract, impersonal, and generalizable rules. They expedite formal and impersonal yet generalizable administrative procedures. Individual test scores can easily be "aggregated" across students to describe the performance of such units as classrooms, schools, school districts, or states.

• Test results have become a standard against which bureaucrats and policymakers can measure the performance of students and educators. Gains or declines in score patterns for aggregated units can then be used as a standard by which to judge the "success" or the "progress" of teachers, administrators, schools, districts, and states toward the realization of certain expectations.

• Tests provide society with a mechanism for the allocation of opportunities on the basis of objective qualifications or merit.

• Testing is an efficient, cheap, administratively convenient, quantifiable, outwardly objective and valid, apparently scientific instrumentality in the service of accountability. Tests provide bureaucrats and policymakers with a convenient mechanism to mete out rewards or sanctions. Affixing important rewards or sanctions to these aggregated mean scores permits bureaucrats and policymakers to put teeth into the accountability system.

• Test scores permit the quantifiable objectification of individuals and of groups. Students' scores on mandated tests easily become part of their permanent records. Students' scores also can be used to make decisions about placement, promotion, or graduation—a form of student-level accountability.

The Future of Testing

Testing will surely remain in the forefront as the policy tool of choice in efforts to reform our educational system. There will be a further push to develop a "voluntary," national, but not federal, testing system along the lines outlined in the NCEST report. Much of the focus on testing as a tool of policy will revolve around "authentic" or "innovative" performance-based assessments. These "new"—actually quite old—forms of assessment have been, and will continue to be, touted as beneficial: as providing real incentives, driving instruction and learning in positive ways, and focusing learning on "higher order or complex thinking skills" (NCEST 1992, p. 28). Such claims about the efficacy of these assessments need to be carefully evaluated. It is not the form of the tests (e.g., multiple choice, performance task, portfolio, or product to be evaluated) that is important in determining the impact of a testing program on students, teachers, and schools. Instead it is the use to which the results are put (Messick 1989).

Thus, many issues need careful study before we embark on a new type of national, high-stakes testing program. First, we need to be certain that delivery standards—the necessary inputs and processes that students need to help them meet standards—are in place for all students.

Second, we need more evidence that assessments are preferable to traditional written tests in terms of their effects on the ways teachers and students spend their time and the aspects of the curriculum to which they pay attention. We need to continuously monitor whether a national testing system is narrowing instruction and eventually corrupting the assessments themselves, as happened during the '70s and '80s. New assessment techniques may be more useful to teachers than traditional tests—but how can they be integrated into the normal routines of the classroom? And what happens when we try to use the same techniques simultaneously for making high-stakes decisions about students, teachers, or schools?

Third, the technical issues associated with these assessment techniques will not go away. Evidence is mounting that student performance often generalizes poorly across related performance tasks purporting to measure the same domain or skills. As a result, a student might be judged to fail on the basis of one limited sample of tasks when he would have passed if given equally defensible alternative tasks (Koretz, Madaus, Haertel, and Beaton 1992; Madaus and Kellaghan in press). Much more research on the validity and fairness of "new" assessment techniques is needed.

Fourth, if we move to a cluster of testing bodies or boards, we need to take seriously the need to have comparable tests across the United States. However, we know from Europe that comparability of performance on exams across diverse examining bodies is very difficult to achieve (Madaus and Kellaghan 1991). Finally, we must address the serious practical problems that occur with new assessments used for high-stakes policy purposes. Among these problems are manageability; standardization of conditions, which relates to comparability of results even within a single examining body; time constraints; and costs (Koretz, Madaus, Haertel, and Beaton 1992; Madaus 1991; Madaus and Kellaghan 1991, in press). For example, when England administered the Standard Assessment Tasks (performance tasks) to all 7-year-olds in the spring of 1991, specific issues became apparent: the need for extra support staff in schools, the need for procedures to minimize the disruption of school and classroom organization, and the difficulty (and perhaps undesirability) of imposing standardized conditions of administration that would permit comparability of results across schools. If the English experience taught us anything, it is that there is no quick and easy way of rating large numbers of performance tasks (Madaus and Kellaghan in press).

Testing/assessment, like other technologies, needs to be periodically reevaluated to determine whether it has shifted from being a means used to satisfy a need, to being an end in itself (Staudenmaier 1985). This shift in testing from a means to an end is wonderfully illustrated in the following observation from a 19th century British school inspector who observed firsthand the negative effects of a high-stakes testing program operating in England and Ireland. This program tied pupil examination results to teacher salaries:

> Whenever the outward standard of reality (examination results) has established itself at the expense of the inward, the ease with which worth (or what passes for such) can be measured is ever tending to become in itself the chief, if not sole, measure of worth. And in proportion as we tend to value the results of education for their measurableness, so we tend to undervalue and at last to ignore those results which are too intrinsically valuable to be measured (Holmes 1911, p. 128).

Sixty years later, Ralph Tyler echoed the same message when he warned that society conspires to treat scores on important certifying tests as the major end of secondary schooling, rather than as a useful but not infallible indicator of student achievement (Tyler 1963).

Over ASCD's history, tests have too often been uncritically accepted by far too many people as authoritative and appropriate, without properly evaluating their impact. This is especially true of tests mandated by state law or regulation. The mandate itself lends a legitimacy to a test that is not true of most other technologies. Because testing is so entrenched in our culture, and so taken for granted, most people fail to consider how education is transformed by the mediating role of testing (Madaus 1988). Our hope is that in the coming years, testing and assessment—call it what you may—will be evaluated not only for their contributions to bureaucratic goals of efficiency and productivity, and for their positive and negative side effects, but also for the ways in which they can objectify specific forms of power and authority (Madaus 1990, Messick 1989). Testing and assessment have important roles to play in education; what we need for the remainder of this century—and into the next—are ways to properly evaluate, prioritize, and monitor those roles.

References and Further Resources

Angoff and Dyer. (1971). *The College Board Admissions Testing Program: A Technical Report on Research and Development Activities Relating to the Scholastic Aptitude Test and Achievement Tests.* New York: College Entrance Examinations Board.

Aries, P. (1962). *Centuries of Childhood: A Social History of Family Life.* New York: Vintage Books.

Basalla, G. (1988). *The Evolution of Technology.* New York: Cambridge University Press.

Black, H. (1963). *They Shall Not Pass.* New York: Morrow.

Block, N.J., and G. Dworkin. (1976). *The IQ Controversy.* New York: Pantheon Books.

Bloom, B.S. (1968). "Learning for Mastery." *University of California Comment* 1, 2: 1–12.

Boorstin, D.J. (1978). *The Republic of Technology: Reflections on Our Future Community.* New York: Harper and Row.

Bowker Annual. (1970–1987). New York: R.R. Bowker.

Bowler, R.F. (1983). "Payment by Results: A Study in Achievement Accountability." Doctoral diss., Boston College.

Bruner, J.S. (1966). *Toward a Theory of Instruction.* Cambridge, Mass.: Belknap Press of Harvard University Press.

Buros, O.C. (1938). *Nineteen Thirty-Eight Mental Measurements Yearbook of the School of Education.* Rutgers University: Rutgers University Press.

Burton, E. (1979). "Richard Lowell Edgeworth's Education Bill of 1979: A Missing Chapter in the History of Irish Education." *Irish Journal of Education* 13, 1: 24–33.

Cannell, J.J. (1987). *Nationally Normed Elementary Achievement Testing in America's Public Schools: How All Fifty States Are Above the National Average.* Daneils, W.V.: Friends for Education.

Cannell, J.J. (1988). "Nationally Normed Elementary Achievement Testing in America's Public Schools: How all Fifty States are Above the National Average." *Educational Measurement: Issues and Practice* 7, 2: 5–9.

Carroll, J. (1963). "A Model for School Learning." *Teachers College Record* 64: 723–733.

Carroll, J.B. (1987). "The National Assessments in Reading: Are We Misreading the Findings?" *Phi Delta Kappan* 68, 6: 424–430.

Coleman, J.S., E.Q. Campbell, C.J. Hobson, J. McPartland, A.M. Mood, F.D. Weinfield, and R.L. York. (1966). *Equality of Educational Opportunity.* Washington, D.C.: Office of Education, U.S. Department of Health,

Education, and Welfare, U.S. Government Printing Office.

Conant, J.B. (1961). *Slums and Suburbs: A Commentary on Schools in Metropolitan Areas*. New York: McGraw-Hill.

Conoley, J.C., and J.J. Kramer, eds. (1989). *Tenth Mental Measurements Yearbook*. Lincoln, Nebr.: Buros Institute of Mental Measurements of the University of Nebraska-Lincoln.

Coolahan, J.M. (1975). "The Origins of the Payment-by-Results Policy in Education and the Experience of It in the National and Intermediate Schools of Ireland." Master's thesis, Trinity College, Dublin.

Crouse, J., and D. Trusheim. (1988). *The Case Against the SAT*. Chicago: University of Chicago Press.

Edmonds, R.R. (1980). "Schools Count: New York City's School Improvement Project." *Harvard Graduate School of Education Association Bulletin* 25: 33–35.

Ellul, J. (1990). *The Technological Bluff*. Grand Rapids, Mich.: Williams B. Eerdmans.

Foucault, M. (1977). *Discipline and Punish. The Birth of the Prison*. New York: Viking.

Glaser, R., and R. Linn. (1992). "Assessing Student Achievement in the States." The first report of the National Academy of Education Panel on the Evaluation of the NAEP Trial State Assessments: *1990 Trial State Assessment*. Stanford, Calif.: National Academy of Education.

Gordon, S.C. (1968). *Reports and Repercussions in West Indian Education. 1835–1933*. London: Ginn.

Gould, S.J. (1981). *The Mismeasure of Man*. New York: Norton.

Gross, M.L. (1962). *The Brain Watchers*. New York: Random House.

Haertel, E. (1989). "Student Achievement Tests as Tools of Educational Policy: Practices and Consequences." In *Test Policy and Test Performance: Education, Language and Culture*, edited by B. Gifford. Boston: Kluwer Academic Publishers.

Hall, E.T. (1976). *Beyond Culture*. Garden City, N.Y.: Anchor Press.

Haney, W., and G.F. Madaus. (1992). "Cautions on Removing the Prohibition Against the Use of NAEP Tests and Data Reporting Below the State Level." In *Studies for the Evaluation of the National Assessment of Educational Progress (NAEP) Trial State Assessment*. Stanford, Calif.: National Academy of Education.

Haney, W., G.F. Madaus, and R. Lyons. (in press). *The Fractured Market Place for Standardized Testing*. Boston: Kluwer Academic Publishers.

Hearn, W.E. (1872). *Payment by the Results in Primary Education*. Melbourne: Stellwell and Knight.

Herrnstein, R. (September 1971). "IQ." *Atlantic Monthly*, pp. 63–64.

Heyneman, S.P., and P. Mintz. (1976). *The Frequency and Quality of Measures Utilized in Federally Sponsored Research on Children*. Washington, D.C.: Social Research Group, George Washington University.

Hoffman, B. (1962). *The Tyranny of Testing*. New York: Crowell-Collier Press.

Holmes, E.G.A. (1911). *What Is and What Might Be: A Study of Education in General and Elementary in Particular*. London: Constable.

Hoskins, K. (1968). "The Examination, Disciplinary Power and Rational Schooling." *History of Education* 8: 135–146.

Houts, P. (1977). *The Myth of Measurability*. New York: Hart.

Hughes, R.N. (March 15, 1979). "Education Could Pay." *New York Times*, A23.

Hughes, T.P. (1989). *American Genesis: A Century of Invention and Technological Enthusiasm*. New York: Penguin Books.

Jensen, A. (1969). "How Much Can We Boost IQ and Scholastic Achievement?" *Harvard Educational Review* 33: 1–123.

Judd, C.H. (1918). "A Look Forward." In *The Measurement of Educational Products*, edited by G. M. Whipple. Bloomington, Ill.: Public School

Publishing Co.

Kamin, L.J. (1974). *The Science and Politics of I.Q.* Potomac, Md.: Lawrence Erlbaum Associates.

Kellaghan, T., G.F. Madaus, and P.W. Airasian. (1982). *The Effects of Standardized Testing.* Boston: Kluwer-Nijhoff.

Keppel, F. (1966). *The Necessary Revolution in American Education.* (1st ed.). New York: Harper and Row.

Koretz, D.M., G.F. Madaus, E. Haertel, and A. Beaton. (February 19, 1992). Statement before the Subcommittee on Elementary, Secondary, and Vocational Education Committee on Education and Labor, U.S. House of Representatives, Washington, D.C.

Laffer, A.B. (1982). "For Better Schools, Pay Achievers." *Education Week* 24: 25.

Lawler, J.M. (1978). *IQ, Heritability, and Racism.* New York: International Publishers.

Lazarus, M. (1981). *Goodbye to Excellence: A Critical Look at Minimum Competency Testing.* Boulder, Colo.: Westview Press.

Levine, D.M. (1971). *Performance Contracting in Education. An Appraisal: Toward a Balanced Perspective.* Englewood Cliffs, N.J.: Educational Technology Publications.

Lowrance, W.W. (1986). *Modern Science and Human Values.* New York: Oxford University Press.

Madaus, G.F. (1983 ed.). *The Courts, Validity, and Minimum Competency Testing.* Boston: Kluwer-Nijhoff.

Madaus, G.F. (1985). "Public Policy and the Testing Profession—You've Never Had It So Good? *Educational Measurement: Issues and Practices* 4, 4: 5–11.

Madaus, G.F. (1988). "The Influence of Testing on the Curriculum." In *Critical Issues in Curriculum*, edited by L. Tanner. Chicago: University of Chicago Press.

Madaus, G.F. (1990). "Testing as a Social Technology: The Inaugural Boisi Lecture in Education and Public Policy." Center for the Study of Testing, Evaluation, and Public Policy, Boston College.

Madaus, G.F. (1991). "The Effects of Important Tests on Students: Implications for a National Examination or System of Examinations." *Phi Delta Kappan* 73, 3: 226–231.

Madaus, G.F., P.W. Airasian, and T. Kellaghan. (1980). *School Effectiveness: A Reassessment of the Evidence.* New York: McGraw-Hill.

Madaus, G.F., and T. Kellaghan. (1991). *Student Examination Systems in the European Community: Lessons for the United States.* Contractor Report submitted to the Office of Technology Assessment, U.S. Congress, Washington D.C.

Madaus, G.F., and T. Kellaghan. (1992). "Curriculum Evaluation and Assessment." In *Handbook of Research on Curriculum*, edited by P.W. Jackson. New York: Macmillan.

Madaus, G.F., and T. Kellaghan. (in press). "British Experience with 'Authentic' Testing." *Phi Delta Kappan.*

Madaus, G.F., and J.T. McDonagh. (1979). "Minimum Competency Testing: Unexamined Assumptions and Unexplored Negative Outcomes." *New Directions for Testing and Measurement* 3: 1–15.

Marx, L. (1988). *The Pilot and the Passenger: Essays on Literature, Technology, and Culture in the United States.* New York: Oxford University Press.

Massachusetts Historical Society Documents. (1845–46). "Horace Mann Papers." Microfilm Collection 372, Reel 8 (August 29, 1845).

Messick, S. (1989). "Validity." In *Educational Measurement*, edited by R. Linn. 3rd ed. New York: Macmillan.

Montgomery, R.J. (1967). *Examinations: An Account of Their Evolution as Administrative Devices in England.* Pittsburgh: University of

Pittsburgh Press.

Nairn, A., and Associates. (1980). *The Reign of ETS: The Corporation That Makes Up Minds.* The Ralph Nader Report on the Educational Testing Service. Washington, D.C.: Ralph Nader.

National Commission on Excellence in Education. (1983a). *A Nation at Risk.* Washington D.C.: U.S. Government Printing Office.

National Commission on Excellence in Education. (1983b). *Meeting the Challenge: Recent Efforts to Improve Education Across the Nation.* Washington D.C.: U.S. Government Printing Office.

National Commission on Testing and Public Policy (NCTPP). (1990). *From Gatekeeper to Gateway: Transforming Testing in America.* Chestnut Hill, Mass.: NCTPP, Boston College.

National Council on Education Standards and Testing (NCEST). (1992). *Raising Standards for American Education: A Report to Congress, the Secretary of Education, the National Education Goals Panel, and the American People.* Washington, D.C.: NCEST.

Owen, D. (1985). *None of the Above: Behind the Myth of Scholastic Aptitude.* Boston: Houghton-Mifflin.

Pacey, A. (1989). *The Culture of Technology.* Cambridge: Massachusetts Institute of Technology Press.

Packard, V.O. (1964). *The Naked Society.* New York: D. McKay.

Popham, W.J. (1983). "Measurements as an Instructional Catalyst." *New Directions for Testing and Measurement* 17: 19–30.

Romberg, T.A., E.A. Zarinnia, and S.R. Williams. (1989). *The Influence of Mandated Testing on Mathematics Instruction: Grade 8 Teachers' Perceptions.* Madison: University of Wisconsin, National Center for Research in Mathematical Science Education.

Rosenthal, R., and L. Jacobson. (1968). *Pygmalion in the Classroom.* New York: Holt, Rinehart and Winston.

Rudman, H.C. (1987). "The Future of Testing Is Now." *Educational Measurement: Issues and Practice* 6: 5–11.

Samelson, F. (1987). "Was Early Mental Testing: (a) Racist Inspired, (b) Objective Science, (c) A Technology for Democracy, (d) The Origin of Multiple-choice Exams, (e) None of the Above?" In *Psychological Testing and American Society: 1890–1930,* edited by M.M. Sokal. New Brunswick, N.J.: Rutgers University Press.

Shanker, A. (October 26, 1986). "Power v. Knowledge in St. Louis: Professionalism Under Fire." *New York Times,* E7.

Simon, B. (1971). *Intelligence, Psychology, and Education: A Marxist Critique.* London: Lawrence and Wishart.

Snow, R., and E. Yalow. (1982). "Education and Intelligence." In *Handbook of Human Intelligence,* edited by R.J. Sternberg. Cambridge: Cambridge University Press.

Sokal, M.M., ed. (1987). *Psychological Testing and American Society: 1890–1930.* New Brunswick, N.J.: Rutgers University Press.

Spring, J.H. (1976). *The Sorting Machine: A National Educational Policy Since 1945.* New York: McKay.

Starch and Elliott. (1912). "Reliability of Grading High School Work in English." *School Review* 21: 442–457.

Starch and Elliot. (1913). "Reliability of Grading Work in Mathematics." *School Review* 21: 254–259.

Staudenmaier, J.M. (1985). *Technology's Storytellers: Reweaving the Human Fabric.* Cambridge: Massachusetts Institute of Technology Press.

Staudenmaier, J.M. (1989). "U.S. Technological Style and the Atrophy of Civic Commitment." In *Beyond Individualism Toward a Retrieval of Moral Discourse in America,* edited by D.L. Gilpi. South Bend, Ind.: Notre Dame Press.

Stedman, L.C., and M.S. Smith. (1983). "Recent Reform Proposals for American Education." *Contemporary Education Review* 2, 2: 85–104.

Strenio, A.J. (1981). *The Testing Trap: How It Can Make or Break Your Career and Your Children's Futures*. New York: Rawson, Wade Publishers.

Sutherland, G. (1973). *Elementary Education in the Nineteenth Century*. London: London Historical Association.

Thorndike, R.M., and D.F. Lohman. (1990). *A Century of Ability Testing*. Chicago: Riverside.

Travers, R.M.W. (1983). *How Research Has Changed American Schools: A History from 1840 to the Present*. Kalamazoo, Mich.: Mythos Press.

Tyack, D.B. (1974). *The One Best System: A History of American Urban Education*. Cambridge: Harvard University Press.

Tyack, D., and E. Hansot. (1982). *Managers of Virtue: Public School Leadership in America*. New York: Basic Books.

Tyler, R.W. (1963). "The Impact of External Testing Programs." In *The Impact and Improvement of School Testing Programs*, edited by W.G. Findley. Chicago: University of Chicago Press.

U.S. Department of Education. (1991). *America 2000: An Education Strategy: Sourcebook*. (ED/0S91–13). Washington, D.C.: U.S. Department of Education.

White, E.E. (1888). "Examinations and Promotions." *Education* 8: 519–522.

Winner, L. (1977). *Autonomous Technology: Technics-Out-of-Control as a Theme in Political Thought*. Cambridge: Massachusetts Institute of Technology Press.

Winner, L. (1986). *The Whale and the Reactor: A Search for Limits in an Age of High Technology*. Chicago: University of Chicago Press.

Wise, A.E. (1979). *Legislated Learning: The Bureaucratization of the American Classroom*. Berkeley: University of California Press.

Woody, C., and P.V. Sangren. (1933). *Administration of the Testing Program*. New York: World Book Co.

4

Curriculum Reform

William H. Schubert

I n 1943, at ASCD's birth, more than a decade of attempts to recover from the Great Depression had clearly left its mark; and World War II was the overriding concern in a world political context that few had felt as powerfully in earlier eras. An historical perspective on curriculum reform must consider the context of the past fifty years, including the cultural and social spheres (Cawelti 1985). Here, however, I maintain a more limited focus. Therefore, in examining fifty years of curriculum reform, I first consider the meaning of curriculum and reform; second, sketch the historical baggage of ideas and practices brought by earlier generations; third, examine factors that contribute to reform (society, learners, subject matter, and technology); and fourth, review key events and players that shaped curriculum reform. Finally, noting that questions are forged by our sense of history, I raise some questions that may help us consider, plan for, and create the next fifty years of curriculum reform.

Definitions of Curriculum and Reform

Reform is easier to define than curriculum. *Reform* merely means to reshape, to reconfigure, to make different. But mere change does not mean improvement. So, too, with reform; thus, the saga of *re-form* that we review here is not intended to imply an evolutionary development. Reformers themselves generally hope that their brand of reform will bring improvement; it is their inspiration to pursue their cause. Therefore, as we think about the past fifty years of curriculum reform, we need to ask whether the re-forming carried out was improvement or not.

The term *curriculum* is shrouded in definitional controversy, so much so that it would require a book-length treatment to begin to deal with it (Schubert 1986). For our discussion, curriculum means whatever is advocated for teaching and learning. This includes both school and nonschool environments; both overt and hidden curriculums; and broad as well as narrow notions of content—its development, acquisition, and consequences.

Historical Perspective

Under the surface of concern for World War II in 1943, there lingered a deeply felt concern for what human beings are and what they might become. One might argue that such a self-conscious interest is, indeed, what makes us human. In the curriculum literature from 1900 to 1980, three orientations to curriculum thought emerge with some persistence—the intellectual traditionalist, the social behaviorist, and the experientialist (Schubert and Lopez-Schubert 1980). In addition, Thomas (1991) added a category I call the "conciliator." Let us briefly consider each of these and some recent variations, noting that few educators are wholly devoted to one position.

Intellectual Traditionalists

People with this orientation adhere to the ideals of Western intellectual history, stemming back to ancient Greece and greatly influencing U.S. educators, including Hollis Caswell and other founders of ASCD. Current examples of this approach to curriculum include the "great books" advocacy of Robert Maynard Hutchins and Mortimer Adler of the Britannica "Great Books of the Western World" and, most recently, Adler's (1982) several iterations of the Paideia Proposal. The main emphasis of this approach is on great ideas derived from the classics of a Western intellectual tradition and from the attendant disciplines of knowledge. The great works are great because they cut to the essential ideas that persons of all backgrounds and from all eras need to consider: truth, beauty, goodness, liberty, equality, and justice (Adler 1981). Thus, the intellectual traditionalist curriculum not only augments knowledge and skill acquisition, but also brings the learner closer to the deepest concerns of humanity throughout the ages.

Today, E.D. Hirsch, Allan Bloom, Diane Ravitch, William Bennett, and Chester Finn are among those who advocate an intellectual traditionalist approach to curriculum reform. The argument is quite familiar: that all students deserve access to the best ideas that the human race has achieved, that pursuit of such ideas enables the best development of the human mind, and that society will be served most fully by people who are steeped in these traditions.

One finds the intellectual-traditionalist values in elite private schools, such as those discussed in *Preparing for Power* (Cookson and Presell 1985), as well as the upper tracks of public schools well known in different parts of the United States for having high numbers of National Merit Scholars and high SAT and ACT scores. Every city and its surrounding suburbs readily can give examples of such schools. In many different environments (affluent, inner city, rural, and suburban middle class), Mortimer Adler's "Paideia Schools" (Adler 1982) have made headway to broaden the constituencies who promote intellectual traditionalist perspectives.

Social Behaviorist

This orientation emerged out of a positivist notion of science. Social behaviorists were strongly influenced by the scientific psychology of E.L. Thorndike, the management science of Frederick Taylor, and the critiques by Joseph Mayer Rice of inefficient and ineffective schooling. Writers such as Franklin Bobbitt and W.W. Charters had a considerable effect on the curriculum reform ideas of 1943—and even to the present. Believing in empirical evidence, in a world where truth can be discerned by objective inquiry, Bobbitt (1918, 1924) and Charters (1923) set out to determine curriculum scientifically. They identified what successful people spend their time doing and used those activities and ideals they represent as a basis for inducting the young into society. Historically, social behaviorists (advocates of "social efficiency," according to Kliebard 1986; and *essentialists*, according to Brameld 1955) favored the use of tests as a basis for determining curriculum. Carefully controlled studies were their hallmark.

Many of today's advocates of social behaviorist perspectives call for attention to "time on task" and link behavioral aspects of teaching to standardized test scores. Similarly, they hold quantitative modes of evaluation to be the best indicators of valid and reliable results in education. The selection of curricular materials and methods for reform should be based on an analysis of convincing documentation by research studies. Such curricular reform should begin with a systematic needs analysis, followed by detailed planning of objectives and content and activities to further the objectives; organizational matters such as scope and sequence; the learning environment; and evaluation that leads to revision in subsequent course offerings. The central argument is that curriculum reform should be based on the best scientific evidence available. Schools in middle-class suburban environments, some in university communities where research is valued, and some large city school systems adopt curriculum policies and teaching strategies that are social behaviorist in orientation.

Experientialists

Experientialist curriculum thought has its origins in the work of John Dewey, who referred to his own pragmatic philosophy as "instrumentalism" (Dewey 1930). Brameld's (1955) categories of *progressivism* and *reconstruction* both apply to the experientialist orientation to curriculum, as do a hybrid of what Kliebard (1986) labels *developmentalists* and *social meliorists*. With Dewey (1902, 1916), experientialists advocate the progressive organization of curriculum by moving from what Dewey called "the psychological" to what he referred to as "the logical."

To begin with the psychological is to start with the interests and concerns that emerge from learners' experience. As learners air their interests and concerns, they begin to see that at a deeper level they are similar to the concerns and interests of others. This vividly provides insight into a realization that gives basis to participatory democracy, namely, that there are common human interests. Seeing such interests as the perennial wonderings of human beings about great existential questions, Robert Ulich (1955) referred to them as the "great mysteries and events of life: birth, death, love, tradition, society and the crowd, success and failure, salvation, and anxiety" (p. 255). Interests and concerns of the moment coalesce around such existential questions, issues that have plagued humanity in every cultural and historical setting. Teachers and learners, together, build projects to understand more deeply the problems that grow from their lived experience.

Then the Deweyan logical, the disciplines of knowledge or funded knowledge of the human race, becomes relevant to learners. Thus, the disciplines are drawn upon in eclectic and interdisciplinary fashion, combined with experiential insights, and valued for the consequences they offer to the reconstruction of meaning and sense of direction in the lives of individuals and groups alike.

Dewey and prominent progressive theorists (such as George S. Counts, Harold O. Rugg, William H. Kilpatrick, Boyd Bode, and L. Thomas Hopkins) furthered this notion of curriculum reform emerging from the philosophizing-in-action of teachers and learners. This philosophizing-in-action is at once democratic, scientific, and integrative (of both diverse groups and dualistic ideas). It relies more on the understanding of those embedded in everyday dilemmas than that of detached experts, though both are deemed helpful. Some of these dilemmas surely relate to today's increased consciousness of persons who are oppressed or silenced because of race, class, gender, health, age, place, and so forth. The central assumption is that curriculum reform is enhanced by grass roots participation of those who will be affected most directly by the reform.

The Central Park East schools, founded by Deborah Meier in New York City; the Fratney School, guided by Bob Peterson in Milwaukee; schools associated with the Institute for Democracy and Education under the leadership of George Wood at Ohio University and Eliot Wigginton's work at Foxfire Rabun Gap, Georgia, are notable varieties of experientialist experiences (see Wood 1992). So are private schools, some that remain from the free school movement of the 1960s and others that are associated with the revived emphasis on progressive education and the Progressive Education Association (see Jervis and Montag 1991). However, many private schools associated with this movement cater to wealthy student populations; thus, it could be argued that the innovations are only possible because the advantaged can learn in a counterculture way without incurring negative repercussions. Examples provided by Wood (1992), Fratney School (Milwaukee), and Central Park East (New York) are counterexamples, in that they reflect an experientialist orientation with children who are far from wealthy.

Conciliators

For decades, intellectual traditionalists, social behaviorists, and experientialists have struggled for power in curriculum reform. One early conciliating effort was the publication of the Twenty-sixth Yearbook (Vol. 2) of the National Society for the Study of Education (NSSE, Rugg 1927). The result of several years of deliberation by major figures in the field of curriculum, this report marked an early unification of the field of curriculum studies.

Another important conciliating act was the birth of synoptic curriculum texts—books designed to bring together under a single cover a holistic portrait of curriculum knowledge. Following Caswell and Campbell's (1935) text, many synoptic works—and their revisions—have appeared in subsequent decades. For instance, influential writers in the 1940s included Gwynn (1943); Alberty (1947); Stratemeyer, Forkner, and McKim (1947); and Tyler (1949). The 1950s included Smith, Stanley, and Shores (1950) and Saylor and Alexander (1954); and the 1960s, Taba (1962) and Doll (1964). It is not unusual for curriculum leaders or scholars to recall the synoptic text(s) that provided initiation to the curriculum field early in their own careers.

One text, which was perhaps too brief to genuinely be called synoptic, had an extraordinary impact on curricular theory and practice: Ralph Tyler's (1949) *Basic Principles of Curriculum and Instruction* (also called the "Tyler Rationale"). Tyler's text, initially written as a course syllabus at the University of Chicago, is the seedbed of thinking about curriculum in terms of purposes, learning experiences, organization, and evaluation—and in perceiving sources of curricular purpose in the study of learners, society, and subject matter (see the "Chronology" section, "1943 to 1953").

It is fair to say that the Twenty-sixth Yearbook of the NSSE, the synoptic texts begun by Caswell and Campbell, and the Tyler Rationale were major conciliating forces that gave intellectual justification to the emergence of ASCD. Each of these events, including the creation of ASCD, was a major effort to bring together the best of each of the evolving schools of curriculum theory and practice. The hope was that curriculum reform could best develop as an eclectic endeavor in which each of the major orientations could be tapped for insight in the leadership of educational practice. The extent to which this was (is being) accomplished, the extent to which it is possible to combine the different sets of assumptions without inoperative contradiction, is of course problematic. Too many schools are conciliatory in the negative sense of trying to integrate a range of popular "hot topics" that conflict with one another. However, inclusive approaches that are productive include the work of Theodore Sizer (1984) in the Coalition of Essential Schools and James Comer (1980) in schools for inner-city populations.

Analysis of the Four Orientations

The strengths of intellectual traditionalists lie in the transmission of the Western cultural heritage. Critics argue that other traditions are equally valid, for example, those from the Far East, Latin America, Africa, and Oceania. Proponents of the Western tradition claim that because it has spawned great divergent insights as a basis for inquiry and that any cultural tradition embodies the great ideas, we should stick with the one with which we are most familiar. Critics, however, add that insights do differ among these and other traditions, often criticizing the Western tradition as being the ideas of affluent white men. Proponents counter by asserting that the Western tradition is, in fact, multicultural, having evolved from great cosmopolitan centers, such as Athens, Alexandria, Rome, Constantinople, Madrid, Paris, and London.

The strengths of social behaviorists are evident in their reliance on findings of scientific, educational, and psychological research. Criticisms focus on their overreliance on highly generalized information. Critics of the empirical, analytical assumptions of social behaviorists say that they should investigate problems found in actual states of affairs, not conjured-up problems in researchers' minds (e.g., the best method to teach science or the best curriculum for at-risk students). Critics claim that we should avoid overgeneralizations, and that we should find situational insights that enhance decision and action rather than search for laws that produce knowledge for its own sake (which they claim is a search for the will-o'-the-wisp). Advocates, however, maintain that empirical study is the only sure route to truth, and that the failures of many past curriculums have been caused by lack of documented evidence to support them.

Experientialists' strengths reside in their recognition that much important learning is from life itself. A fundamental asset lies in the recognition that it is valuable to start with learners' actual concerns. In principle, this brings a higher chance of engagement in learning. However, critics suggest that it is impossible, impractical, and too costly to think about building a curriculum for each learner. Advocates counter this by arguing that it is a misconception to hold that the experientialist position requires a separate curriculum for each learner. Advocates hold that starting with immediate concerns and interests of learners is only the beginning. It leads to democratic communication that probes to deeper inquiry through group investigation into common interests. Critics argue that pursuit of interests does not cover the requisite realms of knowledge. Experientialists say that the pursuit of any genuine human interest in depth requires interdisciplinary study that taps many realms of knowledge.

The strengths of conciliation lie in the view that none of the three "pure" positions can be completely right. Conciliation favors an eclectic position that draws on the other approaches as situations and interpretations require. Critics claim that most conciliators merely advocate "hot topics" or whatever is in vogue due to the winds of politics and economics. Advocates, however, retort that it requires the most creative and critical thinking to function in the best eclectic traditions.

Currently, the status of the conciliatory position is greatest in school practice, probably in theory as well. The publications of ASCD, especially *Educational Leadership*, exemplify conciliation in both practice and theory. It is interesting that the experientialist position is quite dominant among curriculum theorists today, and yet its pure form is least represented in policy and practice. Though the social behaviorist position is strong and quite stable in the research community and in practice, the intellectual traditionalist position has grown in strength through the concerted efforts of political leaders such as William Bennett, Chester Finn, and Lamar Alexander, and scholars such as Diane Ravitch, Allan Bloom, and E.D. Hirsch.

Factors Contributing to Reform

Each "pure" curriculum position—intellectual traditionalist, social behaviorist, and experientialist—could have its own set of factors that contributes to reform. The conciliators, however, come to the rescue by providing something of a common language, with special emphasis on the contribution of the Tyler Rationale (Tyler 1949). Granted, when one thinks of the Tyler Rationale, the quartet of categories (purposes, learning experiences, organization, and evaluation) comes to mind immediately.

At least as great, however, is Tyler's contribution to sources for determining purposes, noted previously: studies of learners, studies of contemporary life outside school, and suggestions from subject matter specialists. These three topics can be traced back through work by Harold Rugg and other progressive theorists to Dewey (1902), who called for balanced attention to the *learner*, to *subject matter*, and to *society*. Two decades after Tyler's book was published, Joseph Schwab (1969) added the *teacher* to the curriculum universe. One can easily see the compatibility of these categories. It is impossible to consider curriculum reform in any meaningful sense without addressing the impact of these factors on curriculum development. Curriculum development, too, as a technology has been re-formed over the past fifty years. That reform must be seen in the context of (1) social forces, (2) learners, and (3) subject matter.

How have these three factors changed over the years? And how do we see society, students, and subject matter through the alternative lenses of the intellectual traditionalist, the social behaviorist, the experientialist, and the conciliator? Looking at these issues necessarily involves a fourth factor—curriculum development and the technologies that support it.

Societal Forces

The intellectual traditionalist sees societal forces, the political and economic activity of the day, as a possible impediment to realizing a curriculum through the classics and disciplines of knowledge. Nevertheless, these forces must be met with the greatest of wisdom, which is derived from the classics and the disciplines of knowledge. Therefore, to understand societal forces, one should pursue a liberal education. An intellectual traditionalist might argue, for instance, that urban social life can be understood better by reading Dickens' *Oliver Twist* and Upton Sinclair's *The Jungle* than from studying the great tomes of mediocre sociological research. The central point, however, for the intellectual traditionalist, is to clear away societal factors that might be impediments to learner access to the classics and the disciplines of knowledge.

The social behaviorist sees societal forces as factors to research—on the one hand, to have better information as a basis for behavior and, on the other, as factors to orchestrate for increased control of the environment.

The experientialist sees curriculum reform as situated in and largely created by societal forces. Looking to an interaction of culture, politics, and economics—sometimes referred to as ideology—the experientialist sees schools as frequently perpetuating inequities. Advocating greater justice, the experientialist sees democratic action as the means to enter into serious discourse about ways to contest oppressive ideological societal forces, through the opening of channels of dialogue from all realms of society, especially from those who have been silenced in the past.

Conciliators see social forces from the vantage point of each position, almost at once, or alternatively in whatever way seems expedient. The matter of holding contradictory positions at the same time, however, needs to be addressed. For instance, is it logically or pragmatically defensible to hold with the experientialist view that powerful structures of inequality in society are reproduced by schooling and, at the same time, agree with a social behaviorist that individuals should be expected to pull themselves up by the bootstraps regardless of social class background?

Learners

Another factor contributing to curriculum reform is the conception of *learner* that is held by curriculum reformers. Intellectual traditionalists essentially hold that learners are passive recipients of the wisdom of the ages; nevertheless, they expect learners to actively engage in Socratic discussions, demonstrate knowledge and skills through oral and written presentations, and exemplify the attributes of self-directed learners in search of a liberal education.

Social behaviorists usually share the idea that a learner is a subject to be altered into a more desirable state by methods and materials that are supported by research. Both social behaviorist and intellectual traditionalists think it is important to know about student interests and concerns—but not as the starting point of curriculum. Rather, both social behaviorists and traditionalists see student interests and concerns as aspects of student life to use as linkages to gain access for "delivery" of curriculum determined by adult experts for students.

In contrast, the experientialist holds that learners' interests must be the key to understanding what the curriculum should be, and educators and students should be cooperative partners in determining the purposes and experiences of learning. This, they hold, is the only defensible way to encourage genuine learning and participation in democratic living.

The conciliator might hold that learners vary greatly from one another and, moreover, that any one learner varies from situation to situation. Therefore, one needs to have a repertoire of perspectives to draw on to fit situational needs, sometimes seeing the learner as self-directive and sometimes as needing considerable direction.

Subject Matter

To the intellectual traditionalist, subject matter is contained in the disciplines of knowledge and in the great books, and it should be disseminated with the logic or chronology of organization that fits the structure given by experts in each of the several disciplines.

The social behaviorist tends in the same direction, but is much more open to delivering or engineering what the public wants. The social behaviorist's view of democratic leadership in curriculum reform is to find out what the public wants, ask questions to see if enough options are provided for people to choose from, help them anticipate the probable outcomes of what they want, and then engineer the desired results. Thus, the social behaviorist is not wedded to a highly academic curriculum; instead, a variety of social and individual needs might be met that have little directly to do with the great books or the disciplines of knowledge, such as curriculums for prevention of teen pregnancy, parenting, anti-drug use, thinking skills, computer literacy, and consumer education.

The experientialist views subject matter more as process than product, emphasizing the experience of learning more than specific, discrete bodies of knowledge and skills to be acquired. Subject matter, in this orientation, is created by learners and teachers who pursue concerns together and develop an understanding of those concerns. This is a kind of personal knowledge, to be sure, but it does not neglect public knowledge; for learning must tap what has been learned before, what is stored in the disciplines.

The conciliator, in a desire to meet situational needs, must try to bring together different types of subject matter. On the one hand is the content of the various disciplines, and on the other is the experience of many people as they share their subjective realities. The question of whether to emphasize the disciplines or experiences is not necessarily an either-or matter; yet it must be thought about carefully so that incompatible notions of subject matter are not uncritically merged.

Curriculum Development Technologies

The term *technology* refers here to systematic treatment, not the kind of hardware used in curriculum development for reform. Thus, a popular approach, such as strategic planning, is a form of technology. The intellectual traditionalist would be less supportive than the others of placing great emphasis on curriculum development, claiming that the curriculum (the classics and knowledge disciplines) are already developed. It is merely a matter of providing students with what is known.

In great contrast, the social behaviorist calls for a detailed needs analysis as a basis for forming purposes, followed by in-depth analysis as purposes are translated into manageable behavioral objectives. Behaviorists systematically delineate learning activities that serve as vehicles for the objectives; design the route (scope, sequence, environment, and instructional models) through which the objectives and activities take shape; and evaluate how well the objectives are realized. The evaluation of the process then guides revision and shapes the next curriculum reform.

For the experientialist, the steps of curriculum development appear to be much less systematic; yet, structure is there but more deeply embedded in the fabric of human interaction. Rather than a top-down orientation to curriculum development (i.e., planning by experts, to be distributed to teachers and learners), curriculum development is seen as a natural function of school and classroom life. The structure or systematic treatment (technology) of curriculum development is evolutionary—formed through communication in small groups who work on projects that evolve into other projects in a continuing sequence.

The conciliator admits that such "natural" curriculum development can sometimes occur when certain kinds of ideal teachers and students meet. On the other hand, the conciliarist tends to lean heavily on more overtly structured forms of curriculum development. The conciliator encourages input from teachers, learners, parents, and relevant others, but usually stops short of giving these groups full reign in actually creating the curriculum.

Clearly, there is a tendency among three of the four orientations discussed here to favor a top-down rather than a grass roots approach to curriculum development. The experientialist stands largely alone in the naturalistic approach to curriculum development. Nevertheless, each of the other orientations acknowledges the need for some grass roots participation, if only to make all those affected by curriculum *feel* that they had some input.

The top-down versus grass roots debate is well illustrated by a decade or more of reform in the area of assessment. Outcome-based education, for instance, can be seen as national, state, or even school district-level impingement, leading to a top-down situation in which political authorities determine curriculum by specifying outcome criteria. In contrast, strategic planning at the school level (or even within democratic classrooms or teams of teachers and learners) can become an interpretation of outcome-based learning that is grass roots in character. Cronbach (1980) and a team of evaluators and scholars formulated a productive statement about needed reforms in program evaluation that goes considerably beyond traditional models. Eisner (e.g., 1985) has called for "connoisseur-based evaluation," educational criticism that is an imaginative blend of outside expertise and grass roots participation. Lee Shulman is exploring new forms of evaluation of teachers through a broadly based configuration of portfolios, tests, demonstrations, and oral components, with considerable input from practitioners in both curriculum and the assessment.

Illustrations of Contributing Factors in Major Reforms

The major reforms of the past decades clearly reflect all four contributing factors (society, learner, subject matter, and curriculum development technology). For example, since the founding of ASCD in 1943, reforms have resulted in changes in science education, elective subjects, Chapter 1 (formerly Title I) programs, special education, and bilingual education. A careful policy analysis of these reforms is far beyond the scope of this chapter, but let's look at these reforms in terms of influences from society, learners, subject matter, and curriculum development.

The heyday of change in science education was triggered by Sputnik. It was societal and political reform at its roots. Quite simply, the society (especially its economic and political moguls) wanted the United States to be competitive with the Russians, a strikingly similar phenomenon as that with the Japanese today. To make the advances necessary to reach the aspired goal, a range of government and private agencies provided funds; however, The National Science Foundation was chief among them. Through funding, research projects that heretofore operated on shoestring budgets were able to engage in development and dissemination, as well as in more research. The curriculum projects often advocated a new conception of the learner as an active inquirer, rather than passive recipient. Although changes in science education from post-Sputnik reform crept into the experiences of students in schools, it is ironic that too many of the "reforms" in science education did not give teachers the same accord as the curriculums offered students. Instead of treating teachers as active inquirers capable of reforming curriculum in their own school settings, they were subjected to what was pejoratively called "teacher-proof curriculum." Many curriculum developers saw teachers, at best, as followers of orders.

Elective subjects have a much longer history, harkening back to Charles Eliot's call in the 1890s for electives in secondary education to parallel the history of elective subjects at Harvard, where he was president. Thus, status and academic tradition in subject matter organization was an initial boon to elective subjects. As social interest broadened to accommodate learners from a wider variety of cultural backgrounds, it was thought appropriate to have course offerings that paralleled the interests of learners.

A dominant interest that emerged was the call for curriculums to facilitate the emergence of large groups of underserved student populations. One such group was special education students. The need to understand and serve a broad range of students with special needs emerged as a grass roots movement. The result was large-scale legislation to identify, carefully analyze, and provide for students with many different kinds of disabilities and potentials. Bilingual education also grew as a grass roots social development and, simultaneously, from teacher perception of a set of needs presented by a new and growing body of Latino students.

Similarly, Chapter 1 evolved from the War on Poverty and The Elementary and Secondary Education Act of the mid-1960s. Thus, it was societal in origins and grew from a desire to overcome the cycle of poverty and its adverse educational implications. The impact on schools, teachers, subject matter, and students of programs and funding in this area is far too enormous to be dealt with fully here. Nevertheless, Chapter 1 programs are part of attempts at curriculum reform in the past fifty years.

As with the other examples of curriculum reform, the societal dimension had a great effect on students and subject matter. Moreover, any reform effort always carries an orientation to curriculum development, that is, a technology of intervention and change, with top-down or grass roots emphasis.

Reflection on Perspectives and Reforms

The four historical perspectives (intellectual traditionalist, social behaviorist, experientialist, and conciliator) and the four factors contributing to curriculum reform (societal forces, learners, subject matter, and curriculum development technology) are *analytic* categories. As such, they are devised to enhance thinking about tendencies in curriculum. They are not intended to be pure categories, compatible in a one-to-one way with real-world instances. Rather, we should keep them in mind when reviewing curriculum events of the past fifty years, or even those of today. It would be unproductive to try to classify noted figures in the curriculum field as "members" of one or another orientation, but it is helpful to perceive researchers and educators as having different degrees of emphasis toward or away from these orientations in their theory and practice. Likewise, we may find it helpful to reflect on the stance of a given curriculum scholar or on the perspectives apparent in a reform movement. Do some scholars, for example, take some factors for granted, such as societal forces, or one conception of the learner, or one interpretation of subject matter? Do others take the time to consider a wide range of different perspectives?

To note some familiar examples from early in the 20th century, Bobbitt's scientific curriculum-making took for granted the rightness of successful members of society when using them as exemplars from whom to fashion objectives, and did not seem to consider the possibility that certain dominant strands of value and belief in a society may be headed on a detrimental course. Deweyan experiential theorists may hold such a dynamic faith in the goodness of human nature that they fail to accept the need for certain benevolent kinds of external control and authority. Advocates of the classics may not want to see the possibility that powerful societal forces have designated certain works classics (perhaps due to the race, class, or gender of the authors) and omitted others from high rank, because of a wish to have a clear and decided picture of the best and wisest for subsequent generations.

No doubt, social behaviorist, experientialist, and intellectual traditionalist influences are present in today's curriculum reform proposals and practices; but conciliation is probably more widespread in practice than any of the other three. This state of affairs holds the promise of developing into a *principled eclecticism*, whereby educational decision makers carefully clarify assumptions, survey theory and research, and select a course of policy and action that fits the needs and interests of particular situations. In other words, they engage in a process that Cronbach and Suppes (1969) called "disciplined inquiry." This process involves carefully studied and defensible inquiry, reflection, decision making, and action—sometimes at the same time.

More problematic, however, and more prevalent is the conciliar tendency to uncritically choose whatever theory, research, and practical approaches seem most expedient, most intriguing, most valuable for public relations, or most in vogue at a given moment. Such decision making runs the risk of being inconsistent—subject to being dictated by the flow of economic, political, and social events of the day. It is passive, not active and creative. It operates on unclear or nonexistent assumptions and is responsible for the phenomenon known as "the educational bandwagon."

In the following chronology, consider the character of conciliation that formed the events in education during the past fifty years. Why did certain movements and decisions move in the direction of social behaviorist, experientialist, or intellectual traditionalist assumptions? Were such reform tendencies based on disciplined inquiry or were they left to the fate of events? Moreover, how did educators and other decision makers (politicians, legislators, community members, and others) respond to factors such as social forces, changes in learners, subject matter interpretations, and the technology of curriculum development and enactment?

Chronology of Key Events and Players in Curriculum Reform: 1943–1993

No era begins on an empty stage. The stage for curriculum reform of the past fifty years includes the following influential works:

• *The Eight Year Study*, a five-volume work led by Wilford Aikin (1942), presented convincing evidence that progressive approaches in high schools yielded results that at least matched and usually exceeded those of traditional schools, even when it came to success of students in traditional colleges. But the publication of results received scant attention in a world at war. Thus, societal forces effectually prevented what in another day might have been a fertile seedbed of experientialist curriculum reform.

- Publications of the Educational Policies Commission (EPC) of the National Education Association—2.5 million copies of almost 100 books and booklets—were widely distributed during the late 1930s and the early 1940s. Works included *A War Policy for American Schools* (EPC 1942), *Education and the People's Peace* (EPC 1943), and *Education for ALL American Youth* (EPC 1944).

- A strongly influential synoptic curriculum text was published by Gwynn (1943) and subsequently went into several editions. This book particularly emphasized the influence of social trends on curriculum. Meanwhile, Franklin Bobbitt, architect of detailed procedures that swept the curriculum world for two decades (e.g., Bobbitt 1924, *How to Make a Curriculum*) shocked curriculum developers when he asserted in his last major work, "Curriculum making belongs with the dodo and the great auk." He went on to argue, "Current curriculum discovery, one for each child and youth, takes its place" (Bobbitt 1941, p. 298). This is clearly a move from the social behaviorist toward the experientialist position, and if nothing else shows that curriculum reformers, not just the curriculum, can reform!

- In *Progressive Education at the Crossroads*, Boyd Bode (1938) addressed the experientialists' often divisive concerns with the either-or dualism of child versus society. And Dewey's last major book on education, *Experience and Education* (Dewey 1938), was a conciliatory attempt to undo the misinterpretations done in his name under the label of "progressivism" since the turn of the century.

- Harold Benjamin (1939) poignantly satirized the still-dominant traditionalist curriculum as equivalent to that in prehistoric times. Prehistoric curricularists, for instance, he asserted, once had necessary courses such as "Fish-grabbing with the Bare Hands" and "Saber-tooth Tiger Chasing with Fire"; these courses, however, were retained long after the glaciers had frozen the streams and pushed tigers to warmer climes, the intellectual traditionalist justification being that they trained the mind. Studies by eminent social behaviorists, such as Edward L. Thorndike, did much to dispel myths of faculty psychology and the notion that certain traditional subjects (classical languages, geometry, etc.) exercised "muscles" of the mind (the "faculties" of reason, imagination, and the like) in a way that physical exercise develops the bodily muscles. But the sentiments of faculty psychology persisted for a long time.

• Alfred North Whitehead, a conciliator of the first order, elegantly called for the removal of inert ideas (social behaviorist efficiency) from the curriculum; the study of only a few essential subjects but in great depth (intellectual traditionalist); and the acquisition of the art of using knowledge (experientialist)—all in one profound essay on curricular purposes, *The Aims of Education* (Whitehead 1929).

These works form a sizable part of the backdrop that set the stage for another conciliar move led by Hollis Caswell and others: the formation of ASCD in 1943, by curriculum specialists, supervisors, and other educational leaders from diverse intellectual persuasions and a wide range of contextual backgrounds.

Let us now turn to a decade-by-decade look at curriculum reform that evolved from the foregoing perspectives, contextual factors, and events.

1943 to 1953

The mid-'40s saw World War II grind to a halt; and as the decade moved along, people asked why the world got to the point of war and how it might be prevented in the future. To get back to basics in work as well as in education became a major concern, and basic values (moral and political) were reinstated. McCarthyism was one of the more inimical forms of control set forth to ensure adherence to basic American values. In a more constructive vein, the world was trying to pull together through such ventures as the United Nations, the Marshall Plan, the Warsaw Pact, and NATO; nevertheless, the decade ended with the Korean War. The advent of the atomic age issued at once feelings of fear and hope—fear of annihilation, as well as hope for technological achievement.

At the beginning of the 1940s, 49 percent of the seventeen-year-olds graduated from high school, a substantial increase over 29 percent in 1930; by 1950 it was 57 percent in the United States (Cawelti 1985). The G.I. Bill also contributed to a great influx of members of the military who entered college after World War II. These gains in student populations affected all levels of education by bringing a broader population to the curriculum encounter. Debate was, therefore, heightened about what knowledge and experiences were most worthwhile for this new group. It was not at all certain that classic subjects, even the modified or (more pejoratively) watered down classics and disciplines of knowledge were appropriate for all of the newcomers. Already in place were varieties of vocational education, since the Smith-Hughes Act of 1917, but it was not clear that the only option to scholarly preparation should be training in trades, service industries, home economics, and agriculture.

Charles Prosser and others argued persuasively that only about 40 percent of the students' needs were met by the extremes of classic education on one end of the continuum and vocational and distributive education on the other. Thus, these advocates called for "life adjustment education" to meet the needs of the vast 60 percent of students who they claimed had been essentially ignored. Some see life adjustment as a social behaviorist variation on tracking; others perceive it as an experientialist interest in more adequately meeting life needs. Most likely, life adjustment curriculum reform was a blend of both social behaviorist and experientialist origins; nonetheless, it was a far cry from the radical experientialist call of George S. Counts (1932) for schools to change the social order. Indeed, life adjustment was more efficiency oriented, harkening back to Joseph Mayer Rice (1913), whose school visitations in search of experientialist schools had led him to conclude that such schools were so rare and most schools were so inefficient that the only recourse was to manage them with a tight hand. So, life adjustment was a blend, a conciliar creation.

The intellectual traditionalist orientation received considerable impetus in the mid-1940s from a landmark book, *General Education in a Free Society*, by the Harvard Committee on the Objectives of Education in a Free Society (1945). Known as the *Harvard Red Book*, this volume rekindled the kind of rationale that Robert Maynard Hutchins and Mortimer J. Adler cultivated through their call for a liberal education that could keep alive the spirit of learning and a quest for the most worthwhile as the basic necessity of a free and democratic society. The impact of the experientialists had dwindled because of internal argument; yet several efforts pointed to the continuation of progressive strands after the war: L. Thomas Hopkins' (1937, 1941) emphasis on integration among subjects and between subjects and the self, and interaction as a democratic process of the organic human group; Arthur Jersild's (1946) attempt to integrate child development and curriculum development; Alice Miel's (1946) call for curriculum as a social process; Harold Alberty's (1947) delineation of several interpretations of core curriculum—ranging from combining subjects to a problem-centered study to study of self; and the work of Florence Stratemeyer and her colleagues (1947), who emphasized the need to build curriculum around "persistent life situations."

Interestingly, whether experientialist or intellectual traditionalist, the fear of loss of freedom from the war experience did much to ensure that almost any brand of curriculum reform had to be justified in terms of the contribution it could make to preserving freedom.

Ironically, however, another strand of reform, one that accompanies the educational aftershock of most wars, is a back-to-basics response, a return to the "nuts and bolts" to prevent any future loss. This is ironic, because in the intent to preserve freedoms, we often establish a control-laden education system, arguing that too much freedom of choice in early learning may lose our freedom in the long run. Experientialists, in contrast, had long argued that the only way to have genuine freedom and democracy in the adult world is to live democracy and experience freedom of choice in childhood and youth.

Perhaps the single most influential event of the 1943–1953 period was the creation of a small text on curriculum, *Basic Principles of Curriculum and Instruction*, by Ralph W. Tyler (1949), former evaluation director of the *Eight Year Study*. Tyler, having been trained originally by Charles Judd at the University of Chicago in social behaviorist methods of educational science and measurement, was at once respectful of the intellectual traditionalist value of liberal education (as he was brought back to chair the Department of Education at the University of Chicago in 1936, after having been influenced by Dewey, Bode, and others in the experientialist work of the *Eight Year Study*).

Tyler had the ideal background to draw disparate perspectives together in a new conciliar position known afterward as the Tyler Rationale. His book, now translated into more than a dozen languages, influenced curriculum development and design throughout the world by creating what now may seem to be conventional wisdom—that curriculum and instruction should have carefully determined purposes, defensibly selected learning experiences, organizational character that facilitates the purposes and the learning experiences, and evaluation that furthers understanding of consequences and provides a basis for revision. Purposes, he said, should be conceived from a balanced study of contemporary society, subject matter, and the nature of learners. Decision and action should be carefully filtered through both philosophical and psychological screens. For some years, the Tyler Rationale was used by advocates of curriculum reform from many different orientations. Its basic categories today are still evident in state and school district planning documents, guides to the use of textbooks and other instructional materials, and teacher education classes on lesson and unit planning.

1953 to 1963

The Cold War—and its later manifestation in the "space race" and post-Sputnik cries for catching the Russians—was an almost all-encompassing influence on curriculum reform of this period. This was so much the case that it even overshadowed the landmark court case *Brown v. The Board of Education of Topeka* in 1954 and the use of federal troops to integrate Central High School in Little Rock, Arkansas, in 1957. Although these events may symbolize salient struggles in a more important journey than the Cold War, the latter was the focal point for a decade of education.

Even before post-Sputnik curriculum reform, the nation had begun to question the schools, to force them back to the basics, to the essentials. Rudolf Flesch (1955) severely criticized reading instruction in *Why Johnny Can't Read*; English professor Arthur Bestor (1953) called the schools "educational wastelands" and later (1955) called for "the restoration of learning"; Albert Lynd (1953) coined the phrase "quackery in the public schools"; and Hyman Rickover (1959), in *Education and Freedom*, spelled *freedom* with *control*.

Meanwhile, progressivism was on its last legs (until its next reincarnation in the mid-to-late 1960s); and even Hollis Caswell (experientialist of the conciliar vein) called for less emphasis on process and more on substance (Cawelti 1985). While his call was similar to Dewey's (1938)—to show that the best experiential education has considerable content and to avoid the misinterpretive emphasis on process alone—those who wanted to end progressive education interpreted it as recanting from within.

When the Soviet Union put Sputnik in orbit, the criticism took a new turn, achieving enormous power. Research on teaching and learning that had gone virtually unnoticed since the late 1940s (e.g., Max Beeberman's work on mathematics education at the University of Illinois) was brought immediately to the center of attention in 1957 as a basis to regain the competitive edge in the space race. So great was the perceived need to win this race, that the National Defense Education Act of 1956 was used in the late 1950s to justify federal funds for education on the basis of defense needs. Because education was constitutionally to be handled by the states and localities, not the federal government, the funding had to be justified as fulfilling defense needs, rather than educational needs alone (Tyler 1991). To use the money well, it was deemed necessary to act quickly and to bring in psychologists and other social scientists, if not to completely replace educators, then to at least tap sources thought more credible than those who had contributed to the current state of affairs. There was, of course, no small amount of scapegoating; something seems amiss in blaming educators as major reasons for decline of power in military and space exploration. At least, many educators felt that way when large numbers of prominent psychologists, social scientists, and natural scientists were brought to the fore to reform curriculum in the late 1950s and early 1960s.

Those who lived through the era as educators or as students remember the so-called "new math," which mathematicians acknowledge as mathematics as it has always been (except in schools). They remember language teaching that involved actually speaking the language being studied and learning it from experience in cultural context, and they remember the raft of acronyms of science education projects such as BSCS, CBA, CHEM Study, and PSSC at the secondary level, and at the elementary level ESS, SAPA, MINNEMAST, and SCIS—to name but a few (many are reviewed by Goodlad, Von Stoephasius, and Klein 1966, in *The Changing School Curriculum*). Most of the projects drew in eclectic fashion from several different roots.

Probably the most influential scholar in this movement was Jerome Bruner (1960), whose book *The Process of Education* had overtones that were at once experientialist, intellectual traditionalist, and social behaviorist. He inspired other curriculum developers from each of these perspectives. Bruner's emphasis on having students learn science as scientists engage in inquiry was clearly experientialist, and he acknowledged his debt to Dewey; his emphasis on teaching students in ways commensurate with the structure of the disciplines invokes an intellectual traditionalist respect for the logical organization of knowledge.

The projects of reform, the ready-made packages delivered to schools with specified instructions for conveyance to students, however, smacked of a social behaviorist efficiency often known as "teacher proofing." While students were to learn how to learn by engaging in problem solving, those who taught them were to follow predetermined recipes. Some teachers did not understand what they were asked to do, while others understood quite fully but refused to do it because they saw the contradiction or thought they had a better way to reach students. Whatever the case, evaluations of the success of the costly curriculum reform projects were disappointing to those who devoted huge amounts of time and effort in making them. The goals of inquiry— insight into the structure of the disciplines, and enhanced problem-solving in science and other subjects—were rarely realized. What was the explanation? The projects were carefully developed and designed. What about implementation?

Much of the answer was found by Goodlad, Klein, and Associates (1970) and reported in *Behind the Classroom Door*. Behind the rhetoric of reform, they found little reformed practice; traditional practice still dominated the scene. Therefore, we cannot conclude that the post-Sputnik curriculum reform packages failed as indicated by evaluation. Rather, evaluation did not indicate much difference in outcomes because the reform packages frequently were not implemented. Indeed, *no implementation* should mean *no project* rather than the failure of an experiment. On the other hand, implementation itself must be seen as a salient feature of any experimental reform; thus, failure to implement is itself a failure in the reform design.

Much of the evaluation of post-Sputnik curriculum reform was social behaviorist in nature, despite the intellectual traditionalist and experientialist themes of reform advocacy. The demands for definitive evidence of increased achievement, not unlike those of today, pushed the balance toward a greater social behaviorist mind-set. It is not surprising that such an emphasis brought the end of progressive education. In fact, Lawrence Cremin's (1961) classic history of progressive education, *The Transformation of the School*, dates the progressive era in American education as extending from 1876 to 1957.

The dismissal of progressive or experientialist curriculum by some, however, brought voices of others who called for balance in the curriculum in quite different ways from one another. Margaret Willis (1961) tried this by doing an elaborate follow-up study of participants in the *Eight Year Study*, finding them highly adept in many aspects of life after school as well as during school. Bloom's (1956) *Taxonomy of Educational Objectives* called for balance in another way, by setting forth a cognitive domain of objectives; in the long run, this work led his colleague and former student, David Krathwohl (1964) to issue a similar handbook on the affective domain of objectives. Later, others wrote psychomotor and social handbooks. The images of cognitive, affective, psychomotor, and social domains influenced a great many curriculum reform designs for at least two decades.

Balance was highlighted in several other sources as well. In the realm of practices of school organization, it is difficult to find a greater influence on yet another version of balance than James B. Conant. In *The American High School Today*, Conant (1959) argued for the comprehensive high school, one large enough to provide for many different kinds of learning on one campus. Through substantial grants from Carnegie, Conant was able to distribute his book to most school boards, again illustrating the power of funding, which added substantially to the sweeping consolidations of small schools into large ones in the 1960s. ASCD also tried to make sense of the issue of balance in the 1961 Yearbook, *Balance in the Curriculum* (Halverson 1961).

Finally, a steadily growing intellectual thrust in curriculum, one emphasizing theory, resulted from the publication of papers from a 1947 curriculum theory conference organized by Virgil Herrick and Ralph Tyler (1950). Theory, it was argued, could become a sound rationale for the careful justification of balance in the curriculum. This early work on curriculum theory held closely to positivistic notions, and it admittedly inspired the contributions of George Beauchamp to curriculum theory from 1961 into the 1980s. But commentaries on curriculum reform assembled by Eisner (1971) illustrated a wider range of theoretic contribution on the horizon.

1963 to 1973

The middle '60s and early '70s were times of questioning authority; of grass roots political action; of steadfast consumer activism; of debate over what was worth fighting for; and of how to achieve greater equity, justice, and human well-being. These concerns were national, they were worldwide, and they were curricular. Books about curriculum, which did not look like curriculum books of previous decades, actually appeared on the popular book market. These were usually first-person accounts of teaching and thoughtful reflections about how counterculture activist teachers made a difference in the lives of children and youth by thinking deeply about what is worthwhile to know and learn, how that contributes to better human beings and to a more just society. Exemplary authors included Myles Horton, A.S. Neill, John Holt, Sylvia Ashton-Warner, Jonathan Kozol, James Herndon, and Paulo Freire (e.g., Neill 1960; Holt 1964; Freire 1970; Kohl 1968; Kozol 1967).

The wide circulation of such books did much to fuel curriculum reforms that some contend were revivals of the experientialist position, such as individualized education, open education, open-space schooling, and personalized education, schools without walls, schools within schools—to note just a few of the labels. The alternative school movement, with its free schools, freedom schools, and folk schools, by the early 1970s made alternatives a much greater presence in the public and traditional private schools. Attention to the hidden curriculum, advocacy of humanistic curriculum, confluent learning, ecstasy in education, affective instruction, classroom meetings, nongraded school organization, and values clarification are but a few of the ideas now etched in the minds of those who taught in this era.

But this era was not all experientialist, to be sure. Funding wars for education had reached a fever pitch. In fact, "Great Society" funding (the National Defense Education Act and the Elementary Secondary Education Act, the "titles" and later "chapters," the opportunities of Head Start, Follow Through, Upward Bound, and the like) put the old Educational Policies Commission out of business by 1968. Some claim the EPC was replaced by the funding initiatives of the federal government and private foundations as the real policy determiners in education generally and especially in curriculum. It was possible to see funding origins as the dictators of curriculum reform.

Funding, however, had its price. Those who received funding faced heavy demands to be accountable. It was not enough to claim successful use of funds; strong measures of accountability needed to be provided. Educators turned for help to business, where funding had always been "the bottom line," and the result was behavioral objectives—presented to educators by a successful instructor from the business world, Robert Mager (1962), and shortly after by James Popham and Eva Baker (Popham and Baker 1970, Baker and Popham 1973).

With this "golden age" of funding, then, came a similar emphasis on evaluation models. The growth of curriculum evaluation through the work of Ralph Tyler, Michael Scriven, Lee J. Cronbach, Malcolm Provus, Robert Stake, Daniel Stufflebeam, Elliot Eisner, George Willis, and others brought great debate about the best ways to get a handle on assessment of education. The National Assessment of Educational Progress (NAEP) began its periodic testing of four age groups (9, 13, 17, and 26) in 1969, adding to questions about how to deal with large data sets in ways that could contribute to curriculum reform.

Similarly, this period saw the inflow of initial results of the International Education Assessment (IEA) Studies, international comparisons that began in 1959 to examine achievement in science, mathematics, reading comprehension, foreign languages, literature, and civic education in some 250,000 students, 50,000 teachers, and twenty-two nations. Again, the question was how to use the results to sensibly form policy for reform. Was it enough to see where one nation lagged behind another and to compel it to catch the other? Surely not, but that characterizes some of the criticisms, that is, a lack of serious study of the complexity of achievement and its multiple causes, meanings, and consequences.

ASCD yearbooks often captured the spirit of the times, the interplay of and tension between the humanistic and the accountability emphases. The following yearbooks captured central moments of this volatile period: *Perceiving, Behaving, and Becoming* (Combs 1962), one of ASCD's best sellers; *New Insights and the Curriculum* (Frazier 1963); *Individualizing Instruction* (Doll 1964b); and *Life Skills in School and Society* (Rubin 1969).

It was quite clear that a bona fide area of curriculum studies was emerging. This was represented in several ways. The field was becoming more conscious of itself; it was beginning to forge a history (Seguel 1966, on the field itself; and Elson 1964, on the impact of early textbooks). Scholarly journals, too, were emerging; *Curriculum Inquiry* (originally as *Curriculum Theory Network*) in 1968, and the *Journal of Curriculum Studies* (1968), and they remain influential in scholarly circles today. Collections of journal articles in book form became popular during the 1963–1973 decade; witness books of readings led by Glen Hass (1986), Short and Marconnit (1968), and Van Til (1974). A conceptual unity amid this diversity of writing provided by synoptic texts continued through persistent use of books by Smith and colleagues (1950, 1957), Saylor and Alexander (1954, 1966, 1974, 1981), and Tyler (1949, 1969 reprint), Taba (1962, 1971 reprint), and Doll (1964)—a newcomer in the 1960s whose book, *Curriculum Improvement*, went through eight editions.

This unity, however, was more of a bringing together, while diversity of curricular orientations continued to expand. The notion of "hidden curriculum" or the lessons embedded in institutional life in schools expanded the notion of curriculum itself (e.g., Jackson 1968; Snyder 1970). In the same year that the structure of the disciplines was heavily debated through books by Elam (1964) and Ford and Pugno (1964), Philip Phenix (1964) brilliantly interpreted a range of ways of knowing and deriving meaning. Similarly, writing to curriculum developers and teachers as well as fellow scholars, Louise Berman (1968) went beyond the usual subject areas to explore new priorities, such as perceiving, communicating, loving, knowing, decision making, patterning, creating, and valuing; and Raths, Harmin, and Simon (1966) translated valuing thoroughly into the level of concrete classroom approaches through the promotion of values clarification strategies. Meanwhile, Norman Overly (1970) argued that curriculum as it occurs in the lives of students is virtually unstudied, calling for broader attention to the hidden curriculum; and Philo Pritzkau (1970) called for existential awareness in curriculum. Of perhaps greatest impact on scholars, and indirectly on practitioners, was Joseph Schwab's (1970) call for broadening curriculum inquiry from an almost exclusive reliance on the "theoretic," which looks for problems in generalized categories, uses methods geared to seek law-like statements about education, and finds its ends in knowledge production or publication. His recommendation was that curriculum inquiry move to the "practical, quasi-practical, and eclectic"; that is, curriculum inquiry should seek insights about how to better decide and act in concrete educational situations.

1973 to 1983

The emergent pluralism of the previous decade was accentuated in curriculum theory of the 1973–1983 period, as evidenced by the continuation of the journals *Curriculum Inquiry* and *Journal of Curriculum Studies*, noted above, and the establishment of *The Journal of Curriculum Theorizing* in 1979 (now *JCT: An Interdisciplinary Journal of Curriculum Studies*) and *Journal of Curriculum and Supervision* by ASCD in 1985. Though there was an air of the back-to-basics sentiment that follow wars and other times of crisis, it was longer in coming during this time period after the Vietnam War. Reform reports of the 1970s were more experientialist with some overtones in the intellectual traditionalist vein. Those that emphasized high school revitalization of different types were reviewed and critiqued by Cawelti (1974).

By the end of the 1970s, a back-to-basics movement had quite fully come into its own; however, during the first half of the 1970s, reform emphases were on the left side of the political spectrum. This was true of the turn in curriculum scholarship throughout the decade and well into the next. Considerable attention was generated in the early 1970s, for instance, by the critical work of Latin American scholar-practitioners, Ivan Illich (1972) on de-schooling society and Paulo Freire (1970) on how to respond to the needs of oppressed peoples. In England, critical sociologists (such as Michael F.D. Young 1971) raised questions about how knowledge is reproduced by schools to serve interests of dominant social classes, and Lawrence Stenhouse (1975) and colleagues from the University of East Anglia explored ways in which teachers and scholars could augment the efforts of one another by joining their expertise to create curriculum reform.

In the United States, new intellectual traditions were tapped in curriculum inquiry. These include critical theory, radical psychoanalysis, literary and art criticism, existentialism, phenomenology, feminist theory, and more. William Pinar (1975) convened a group of eminent curriculum scholars in the form of a book; Pinar argued that this new brand of scholar was "reconceptualizing" curriculum as an area of study, partly because of an emphasis on "theorizing" (verb form) rather than the more static image of "theory" (as a noun, or finished product). Surrounding and flowing from this work (which reconceptualized curriculum in many different ways), we find such prominent examples as Maxine Greene's *Teacher as Stranger* (1973) and *Landscapes of Learning* (1978); *Reschooling Society*, an ASCD publication, by James B. Macdonald, Bernice Wolfson, and Esther Zaret (1973); Michael Apple's *Ideology and Curriculum* (1979) and *Education and Power* (1982); Elliot Eisner's (1979) *The Educational Imagination*; Henry Giroux's (1983) *Theory and Resistance in Education*; and *Toward a Poor Curriculum* by William Pinar and Madeleine Grumet (1976).

It should be made clear that these and related scholars are not part of a "card carrying club"; in fact, they disagree fundamentally on certain matters. Moreover, while Pinar signaled a change in the field of curriculum studies, he should not be considered the leader of a movement or of the aforementioned scholars, many of whom developed their ideas before he began to make his own contributions. The variety of emergent curriculum thought in the 1973–1983 period can be gleaned from some of the collections of essays that were developed, for example, *Curriculum Theory* (an ASCD book by Molnar and Zahorik 1977), *Conflicting Conceptions of Curriculum* (Eisner and Vallance 1974), and *Qualitative Evaluation: Concepts and Cases in Curriculum Criticism* (G. Willis 1978).

Major synoptic texts during the period tried to keep pace with the field, but often found it hard going to bring past and present developments, and the variety of intellectual sources, under a single cover. Firth and Kimpston (1973), Tanner and Tanner (1975, rev. ed. 1980), and Zais (1976) attempted this formidable task by relying heavily on philosophy, history, and other educational foundations as a stable basis for dealing with the multiplicity of ideas and approaches beginning to appear in the literature. The extent to which these books and the widely read aesthetic perspective of Eisner (1979) actually affected curriculum reform is debatable, but the influence must have been at least provided by the fact that curriculum reformers were influenced by the synoptic texts. In fact, one might argue that because of the great expansion of curriculum literature, curriculum reformers were educated by summaries, that is, the synoptic texts. Conversely, one might also say that curriculum reform can no longer be informed adequately by a one-book summary and analysis of extant literature. Instead, one might be advised to turn to historical treatments (bibliographies, interpretations, categorizations), such as Bantock's (1980) *Dilemmas of the Curriculum*, Connell's (1980) *A History of Education in the Twentieth Century World*, and Schubert and Lopez-Schubert's (1980) *Curriculum Books: The First Eighty Years* as a starting point for reform efforts.

1983 to 1993

Because analysis requires time and distance, it is especially difficult to discuss the curricular developments in the past decade, particularly since this chapter was written a year before the 1993 publication date. Let us begin by identifying several prominent topics in curriculum theory and practice and briefly looking at the precedent for understanding them that the past fifty years can provide (see Schubert 1986).

Historical Awareness. It seems fitting to begin with historical awareness itself, since the whole thrust of this chapter is along this line. Ironically, there is little precedent for curriculum history in the curriculum field. There are many self-criticisms that note the condition of "ahistoricism." In the 1980s, however, the field had access to Kliebard (1986), Goodson (1984), Franklin (1986), Van Til (1986), Cuban (1984), Schubert and Lopez-Schubert (1980), Kridel (1989), and in the next decade Tanner and Tanner (1990). Increased awareness of lack of awareness of curriculum history inspired work to create curriculum history. Through associations such as ASCD, the American Educational Research Association, and the Society for the Study of Curriculum History, this subfield is likely to grow and to influence curriculum reform.

Paradigm Discourse. A great deal of study and debate has centered on the kinds of inquiry that best provide understanding about what is most worthwhile to know and experience. Scholars in this area include Short (1991), van Manen (1990), Carr and Kemmis (1986), Sears and Marshall (1990), Pinar (1988), Connelly and Clandinin (1990), Eisner (1991), and G.H. Willis and Schubert (1991). The study of assumptions behind inquiry helps us understand the lenses through which we perceive the world and evaluate different aspects of it. Major curriculum writers of earlier decades have much to contribute to this kind of understanding: Dewey, Bode, Rugg, Counts, and Whitehead in earlier years of the curriculum field, and more recently Maxine Greene, Dwayne Huebner, James B. Macdonald, Arthur W. Foshay, Philip Phenix, and Harry S. Broudy, among others. As long as curriculum is taken seriously, the question of paradigms will be significant.

Collaboration. This is a term used widely today to refer to partnership ventures by scholars and practitioners who share expertise to resolve problems encountered in educational settings. Today, Ann Lieberman (e.g., 1988), well known for collaborative school improvement efforts, has brought together an array of contemporary exemplars. Precedent for this kind of work can be found in Deweyan theory, to be sure. Hollis Caswell, L. Thomas Hopkins, and others from the progressive era consulted in a collaborative spirit. More than most, Alice Miel (1946) saw curriculum reform as a dynamic social process, and her colleague at Teachers College, S.M. Corey (1953), wrote what was regarded by many as the central guide on action research. In England, as noted earlier, Stenhouse did a great deal to further teacher and university faculty cooperation.

Too many who do collaborative action research are virtually unaware of the heritage of similar work at their disposal. If collaborative researchers of today immersed themselves in similar work of the progressive education era, they might well determine more ways to involve not only teachers, administrators, and scholar-researchers, but students and parents as well. The work of several reformers of today clearly moves in this direction—for example, George Wood at the Institute for Democracy in Education (Ohio University), Theodore Sizer and the Coalition of Essential Schools out of Brown University, James Comer of Harvard and his work with schools in oppressed urban areas, and William Ayers and Chicago School Reform through Local School Councils. The progressive literature would help collaborators see their work as an effort to ask how all affected by reform can play a key role in its development and enactment.

Popular Curricular Approaches. Too many to cover here, popular curriculum ideas as we move into the 1990s include whole language, literacy, cooperative learning, individual education plans (IEPs), and basics. This is a motley assortment of efforts that are well known to the inservice education crowd. Each of these "hot topics," as they are sometimes called, could become more fully developed by careful attention to precedent.

Beginning with basics, it is of benefit to realize that a return to basics has occurred in 20th century American education with great regularity after wars and other crises. Therefore the current basics thrust that stems from *A Nation at Risk* (National Commission on Excellence in Education 1983) and its fear of an economic crisis that gives lower status to the United States in the world market is not dissimilar to post-Sputnik reform and a fear of loss in the space race and Cold War. It is similar to the worry of unpreparedness that accompanied the ends of World War I and World War II.

The IEP that has been part of special education literature for almost a decade, especially connected with the emphasis on mainstreaming, also has roots that run deep historically. Many remember the behavioral objectives movement that added the semblance of precision to statements of purpose in the late 1960s and provided the appearance of efficiency in response to accountability pressures of the 1970s. Behavioral objectives, however, had origins in the advocacy of scientific curriculum building by Franklin Bobbitt and W.W. Charters in the 1920s, and was strongly related to E.L. Thorndike's earlier work in behavioristic psychology and to Joseph Mayer Rice's calls for efficiency of management near the turn of the century.

Cooperative learning, as promoted by Roger Johnson and David Johnson and studied extensively by Robert Slavin (see, e.g., the ASCD 1990 videotapes, *Cooperative Learning Series*) has had great appeal. Yet, precedent for it in the experimental schools of the *Eight Year Study* and in progressive schools generally has not been explored systematically. Were it explored, new dimensions would likely be unearthed, ways to more fully develop the content of cooperation out of the life experience of the students. Of equal import, it would lead to tough questions about the connections and discontinuities between a cooperative ambience in classroom life and an ethos of competitiveness in the world outside. John Nicholls (1989) has addressed competitiveness relative to democratic education, and Donald Hellison and Thomas Templin (1991) have emphasized cooperation in physical education under the rubric of "social responsibility."

The current emphasis on literacy and whole language is largely a return to experientialist roots in several ways (see Goodman 1992). The stress on wholeness bespeaks an integrated frame of reference that counterculture and open educators of the 1960s and early 1970s pushed, and earlier it was spoken to by progressive educators who perceived the dynamic relational character of language in human development. Another dimension of the literacy emphasis today is surely its relevance to the poor and oppressed, minority, and limited-English or non-English proficiency populations. In this regard, it has important connections to the international work in developing countries by Paulo Freire over the past thirty years. Some of this is tapped, but to tap it fully we must address the political and ideological context in which it is embedded and that gives it meaning. Thus, we must address head-on the potentially powerful social dimensions of whole language and other attempts to enhance literacy. When we accomplish real wholeness and relevance, George Counts' (1932) great question of whether the schools dare change the social order will emerge as central to literacy education.

Curriculum Questions

To centralize or decentralize? This is perhaps the major question of curriculum reform today and tomorrow. It deals with the fundamental nature of democracy in education; and the precedent for this issue is found in the works of John Dewey and debates on his perspectives. Today's calls for national standards in America 2000 (see U.S. Department of Education 1991), a national curriculum, national testing, and the already established centralization of accountability standards in state departments of education provide ample evidence of the move toward centralization.

Ironically, many nations of the world, some that proponents of centralization wish to emulate in America, have long had a centralized curriculum and are moving away from it precisely because of the reasons to oppose tracking that Oakes (1985) presents. Nevertheless, some kinds of increased centralization are likely to emerge more fully in the years ahead. A careful comparative look at curriculums in different cultures and the implications for global awareness in curriculum policymaking (such as provided by Tye in the 1991 ASCD Yearbook) is essential. Just as essential, however, is the question of who decides. The following related questions require great reflection:

• Who decides what is worthwhile to know and experience, in order that human beings might reach greater potential and develop a more just social order?

• Do national standards, formulated necessarily by authorities who live outside of the specific context for which they are making curricular policy, fit the needs and interests of people who live in those contexts?

• Fundamentally, how can genuine grass roots curriculum development (in an era when many educators value site-based management) become a reality under the auspices of centralized standards?

• How can the interplay of centralized and grass roots reform yield excellence, equity, and genuine human growth (see Klein 1991; Beyer and Apple 1988)?

• Finally, what should children know and experience to become democratic participants?

These are haunting questions; at the same time, they are the most hopeful questions we can ask. If these questions lie at the heart of curriculum reform during the next fifty years, we must be prepared to experience forms of education that go far beyond schooling as we now know it. We must be prepared to facilitate the curriculum implicit in new coalitions of teachers, curriculum developers, administrators, teacher educators, researchers and scholars, publishers, parents, and especially, learners themselves.

References

Adler, M.J. (1981). *Six Great Ideas*. New York: Macmillan.

Adler, M.J. (1982). *The Paideia Proposal: An Educational Manifesto*. New York: Macmillan.

Aikin, W. (1942). *The Story of the Eight Year Study*. New York: Harper and Brothers.

Alberty, H.B. (1947). *Reorganizing the High School Curriculum*. New York: Macmillan.

Apple, M.W. (1979). *Ideology and Curriculum*. London: Routledge and Kegan Paul.

Apple, M.W. (1982). *Education and Power*. Boston: Routledge and Kegan Paul.

Association for Supervision and Curriculum Development. (1990). *Cooperative Learning Series* (videotapes). Alexandria, Va.: ASCD.

Baker, E., and W.J. Popham. (1973). *Expanding Dimensions of Instructional Objectives*. Englewood Cliffs, N.J.: Prentice-Hall.

Bantock, G.A. (1980). *Dilemmas of the Curriculum*. Oxford: Martin Robertson.

Beauchamp, G.A. (1981). *Curriculum Theory*. Itasca, Ill.: F.E. Peacock. (Previous editions: 1975, 1968, 1961 by Kagg Press, Wilmette, Ill.)

Benjamin, H. (1939). *The Saber-Tooth Curriculum*. New York: McGraw Hill. (Author pseudonym, J.A. Peddiwell.)

Berman, L. (1968). *New Priorities in the Curriculum*. Columbus, Ohio: Merrill.

Bestor, A. (1953). *Educational Wastelands*. Urbana, Ill.: University of Illinois Press.

Beyer, L.E., and M.W. Apple, eds. (1988). *The Curriculum: Problems, Politics and Possibilities*. Albany: State University of New York Press.

Bloom, B.S., ed. (1956). *Taxonomy of Educational Objectives: Cognitive Domain*. New York: David McKay.

Bobbitt, F. (1918). *The Curriculum*. Boston: Houghton Mifflin.

Bobbitt, F. (1924). *How to Make a Curriculum*. Boston: Houghton Mifflin.

Bobbitt, F. (1941). *The Curriculum of Modern Education*. New York: McGraw-Hill.

Bode, B.H. (1938). *Progressive Education at the Crossroads*. New York: Newson.

Brameld, T. (1955). *Philosophies of Education in Cultural Perspective*. New York: Dryden.

Bruner, J.S. (1960). *The Process of Education*. New York: Vintage.

Carr, W., and S. Kemmis, S. (1986). *Becoming Critical*. London: Falmer.

Caswell, H.L., and D.S. Campbell. (1935). *Curriculum Development*. New York: American Book Company. (Reprinted by R. West 1978).

Cawelti, G. (1974). *Vitalizing the High School: A Critique of Major Reform Proposals*. Washington, D.C.: ASCD.

Cawelti, G. (1985). *Great Events of the Twentieth Century* (a wall chart). Alexandria, Va.: Author.

Charters, W.W. (1923). *Curriculum Construction*. New York: Macmillan.

Combs, A.W., ed. (1962). *Perceiving, Behaving, Becoming: A New Focus for Education*. 1962 ASCD Yearbook. Washington, D.C.: ASCD.

Comer, J.P. (1980). *School Power*. New York: Free Press of Macmillan.

Conant, J.B. (1959). *The American High School Today*. New York: McGraw-Hill.

Connell, W.F. (1980). *A History of Education in the Twentieth Century World*. New York: Teachers College and the Curriculum Development Centre of Australia.

Connelly, F.M., and D.J. Clandinin. (1990). "Stories of Experience and Narrative Inquiry." *Educational Researcher* 19, 5: 2–14.

Cookson, P.W., and C.H. Persell. (1985). *Preparing for Power*. New York: Basic Books.

Corey, S.M. (1953). *Action Research to Improve School Practices*. New York: Bureau of Publications, Teachers College, Columbia University.

Counts, G.S. (1932). *Dare the School Build a New Social Order?* New York: John Day.

Cremin, L.A. (1961). *The Transformation of the School*. New York: Knopf.

Cronbach, L.J., and Associates. (1980). *Toward the Reform of Program Evaluation*. San Francisco: Jossey-Bass.

Cronbach, L.J., and P. Suppes, eds. (1969). *Research for Tomorrow's Schools*. London: Macmillan.

Cuban, L. (1984). *How Teachers Taught: Constancy and Change in American Classrooms, 1890–1980*. New York: Longman.

Dewey, J. (1902). *The Child and the Curriculum*. Chicago: University of Chicago Press.

Dewey, J. (1916). *Democracy and Education*. New York: Macmillan.

Dewey, J. (1930). "From Absolutism to Experimentalism." In *Contemporary American Philosophy* (pp. 13–27), edited by G.P. Adams and W.P. Montague. New York: Macmillan.

Dewey, J. (1938). *Experience and Education*. New York: Macmillan.

Doll, R.C. (1964a). *Curriculum Improvement: Decision Making and Process*. Boston: Allyn and Bacon. (Other editions: 1970, 1974, 1978, 1982, 1986, 1989, and 1992).

Doll, R.C. (1964b). *Individualizing Instruction*. 1964 ASCD Yearbook. Washington, D.C.: ASCD.

Educational Policies Commission. (1942). *A War Policy for American Schools*. Washington, D.C.: National Education Association.

Educational Policies Commission. (1943). *Education and the People's Peace*. Washington, D.C.: National Education Association.

Educational Policies Commission. (1944). *Education for ALL American Youth*. Washington, D.C.: National Education Association.

Eisner, E.W., ed. (1971). *Confronting Curriculum Reform*. Boston: Little, Brown.

Eisner, E.W. (1979). *The Educational Imagination: On the Design and Evaluation of School Programs*. New York: Macmillan.

Eisner, E.W. (1985). *The Educational Imagination*. 2nd ed. New York: Macmillan.

Eisner, E.W. (1991). *The Enlightened Eye: Qualitative Inquiry and the Enhancement of Educational Practice*. New York: Macmillan.

Eisner, E.W., and E. Vallance, eds. (1974). *Conflicting Conceptions of Curriculum*. Berkeley, Calif.: McCutchan.

Elam, S., ed. (1964). *Education and the Structure of Knowledge*. Chicago: Rand McNally.

Elson, R.M. (1964). *Guardians of Tradition: American Schoolbooks of the Nineteenth Century*. Lincoln: University of Nebraska Press.

Firth, G.R., and R.D. Kimpston. (1973). *The Curricular Continuum in Perspective*. Itasca, Ill.: F.E. Peacock.

Flesch, R. (1955). *Why Johnny Can't Read: And What You Can Do About It*. New York: Harper.

Ford, G.W., and L. Pugno, eds. (1964). *The Structure of Knowledge and the Curriculum*. Chicago: Rand McNally.

Franklin, B.M. (1986). *Building the American Community and the Search for Social Control*. London: Falmer.

Frazier, A., ed. (1963). *New Insights and the Curriculum*. 1963 ASCD Yearbook. Washington, D.C.: ASCD.

Freire, P. (1970). *Pedagogy of the Oppressed*, trans. by M.B. Ramos. New York: Seabury.

Giroux, H.A. (1983). *Theory and Resistance in Education: A Pedagogy for the Opposition*. South Hadley, Mass.: Bergin and Garvey.

Goodlad, J.I., M.R. Klein, and Associates (1970). *Behind the Classroom Door*. Worthington, Ohio: Charles A. Jones.

Goodlad, J.I., R. Von Stoephasius, and M.F. Klein. (1966). *The Changing School Curriculum*. New York: Fund for the Advancement of Education.

Goodman, Y.M. (April 23, 1992). "Roots of Whole Language in John Dewey and Women Progressive Educators of the Early Twentieth Century." Paper presented at the Annual Meeting of the American Educational Research Association, San Francisco.

Goodson, I., ed. (1984). *Social Histories of the Secondary Curriculum: Subjects for Study*. London: Falmer.

Greene, M. (1973). *Teacher as Stranger*. New York: Wadsworth.

Greene, M. (1978). *Landscapes of Learning*. New York: Teachers College Press.

Gwynn, J.M. (1943). *Curriculum Principles and Social Trends*. New York: Macmillan.

Halverson, P.M., ed. (1961). *Balance in the Curriculum*. 1961 ASCD Yearbook. Washington, D.C.: ASCD.

Harvard Committee on Objectives of Education in a Free Society. (1945). *General Education in a Free Society*. Cambridge, Mass.: Harvard University Press.

Hass, G., ed. (1986). *Curriculum Planning: A New Approach*. Boston: Allyn and Bacon.

Hellison, D.R., and T.J. Templin. (1991). *A Reflective Approach to Teaching Physical Education*. Champaign, Ill.: Human Kinetics.

Herrick, V.E., and R.W. Tyler, eds. (1950). *Toward Improved Curriculum Theory*. Chicago: University of Chicago Press.

Holt, J. (1964). *How Children Fail*. New York: Delta.

Hopkins, L.T. (1937). *Integration, Its Meaning and Application*. New York: D. Appleton Century.

Hopkins, L.T. (1941). *Interaction: The Democratic Process*. New York: D.C. Heath.

Illich, I. (1972). *De-schooling Society*. New York: Harper and Row.

Jackson, P.W. (1968). *Life in Classrooms*. New York: Holt, Rinehart and Winston.

Jersild, A.T. (1946). *Child Development and the Curriculum*. New York: Teachers College, Columbia University.

Jervis, K., and C. Montag. (1991). *Progressive Education for the 1990s*. New York: Teachers College Press.

Klein, M.F., ed. (1991). *The Politics of Curriculum Decision-Making*. Albany: State University of New York Press.

Kliebard, H.M. (1986). *The Struggle for the American Curriculum: 1893–1958*. Boston: Routledge and Kegan Paul.

Kohl, H.R. (1968). *36 Children*. New York: Signet.

Kozol, J. (1967). *Death at an Early Age*. Boston: Houghton Mifflin.

Krathwohl, D. R., ed. (1964). *Taxonomy of Educational Objectives: Affective Domain*. New York: David McKay.

Kridel, C., ed. (1989). *Curriculum History*. Lanham, Md.: University Press of America and The Society for the Study of Curriculum History.

Lieberman, A., ed. (1988). *Building a Professional Culture in Schools*. New York: Teachers College Press.

Lynd, A. (1953). *Quackery in the Public Schools*. Boston: Little, Brown.

Macdonald, J.B., B. Wolfson, and E. Zaret. (1973). *Reschooling Society: A Conceptual Model*. Washington, D.C.: ASCD.

Mager, R.F. (1962). *Preparing Instructional Objectives*. Palo Alto, Calif.: Fearon.

Miel, A. (1946). *Changing the Curriculum: A Social Process*. New York: Appleton-Century.

Molnar, A., and J.A. Zahorik, eds. (1977). *Curriculum Theory*. Washington, D.C.: ASCD.

National Commission on Excellence in Education. (1983). *A Nation at Risk: The Imperative for Educational Reform*. Washington, D.C.: U.S. Government Printing Office.

Neill, A.S. (1960). *Summerhill: A Radical Approach to Child Rearing*. New York: Hart.

Nicholls, J.G. (1989). *The Competitive Ethos and Democratic Education*. Cambridge, Mass.: Harvard University Press.

Oakes, J. (1985). *Keeping Track: How Schools Structure Inequality*. New Haven: Yale University Press.

Overly, N.V., ed. (1970). *The Unstudied Curriculum: Its Impact on Children*. Washington, D.C.: ASCD.

Phenix, P.H. (1964). *Realms of Meaning: A Philosophy of the Curriculum for General Education*. New York: McGraw-Hill.

Pinar, W.F., ed. (1975). *Curriculum Theorizing: The Reconceptualists*. Berkeley, Calif.: McCutchan.

Pinar, W.F., ed. (1988). *Contemporary Curriculum Discourses*. Scottsdale, Ariz.: Gorsuch Scarisbrick.

Pinar, W.F., and M.R. Grumet. (1976). *Toward a Poor Curriculum*. Dubuque, Iowa: Kendall/Hunt.

Popham, W.J., and E. Baker. (1970). *Establishing Instructional Goals*. Englewood Cliffs, N.J.: Prentice-Hall.

Pritzkau, P.T. (1970). *On Education for the Authentic*. Scranton, Pa.: International Textbook Company.

Raths, L., M. Harmin, and S. Simon. (1966). *Values and Teaching*. Columbus, Ohio: Merrill. (Revised edition: 1978).

Rice, J.M. (1913). *Scientific Management in Education*. New York: Nobel and Eldridge.

Rickover, H. (1959). *Education and Freedom*. New York: Dutton.

Rubin, L.J., ed. (1969). *Life Skills in School and Society*. 1969 ASCD Yearbook. Washington, D.C.: ASCD.

Rugg, H.O., ed. (1927). *The Foundations of Curriculum Making*. Twenty-sixth Yearbook of the National Society for the Study of Education (Part II). Bloomington, Ill.: Public School Publishing Co.

Saylor, J.G., and W.M. Alexander. (1954). *Curriculum Planning for Better Teaching and Learning*. New York: Holt, Rinehart and Winston. (Revised 1966, 1974, 1981, with Lewis).

Schubert, W.H. (1986). *Curriculum: Perspective, Paradigm, and Possibility*. New York: Macmillan.

Schubert, W.H. (1991). "Historical Perspective on Centralizing Curriculum." In *The Politics of Curriculum Decision-making* (pp. 98–118), edited by F.M. Klein. Albany: State University of New York Press.

Schubert, W.H., and A.L. Lopez-Schubert. (1980). *Curriculum Books: The First Eighty Years*. Lanham, Md.: University Press of America.

Schwab, J.J. (1969). "The Practical: A Language for Curriculum." *School Review* 78: 1–23.

Schwab, J.J. (1970). *The Practical: A Language for Curriculum*. Washington, D.C.: National Education Association. (Revised and expanded version of Schwab 1969).

Sears, J., and D. Marshall, eds. (1990). *Teaching and Thinking About Curriculum: Critical Inquiries*. New York: Teachers College Press.

Seguel, M.L. (1966). *The Curriculum Field: Its Formative Years*. New York: Teachers College Press, Columbia University.

Short, E.C., ed. (1991). *Forms of Curriculum Inquiry*. Albany: State University of New York Press.

Short, E.C., and G.D. Marconnit, eds. (1968). *Contemporary Thought in Public School Curriculum*. Dubuque, Iowa: William C. Brown.

Sizer, T. (1984). *Horace's Compromise*. Boston: Houghton Mifflin.

Smith, B.O., W.O. Stanley, and J.H. Shores. (1950). *Fundamentals of Curriculum Development*. New York: World Book, Yonkers-on-the Hudson. (Revised edition, New York: Harcourt Brace and World 1957).

Synder, B.R. (1970). *The Hidden Curriculum*. New York: Knopf.

Stenhouse, L. (1975). *An Introduction to Curriculum Research and Development*. London: Heinemann.

Stratemeyer, F.B., H.L. Forkner, and M.G. McKim. (1947). *Developing a Curriculum for Modern Living*. New York: Bureau of Publications, Teachers College, Columbia University. (Revised edition: 1957, with A.H. Passow).

Taba, H. (1962). *Curriculum Development: Theory and Practice*. New York: Harcourt Brace and World.

Tanner, D., and L.N. Tanner. (1975). *Curriculum Development: Theory Into Practice*. New York: Macmillan. (Revised edition: 1980).

Tanner, D., and L.N. Tanner. (1990). *History of the School Curriculum*. New York: Macmillan.

Thomas, T.P. (1991). "Proposals for Moral Education Through the American Public School Curriculum: 1897–1966." Doctoral diss., University of Illinois at Chicago.

Tye, K.A., ed. (1991). *Global Education: From Thought to Action*. 1991 ASCD Yearbook. Alexandria, Va.: ASCD.

Tyler, R.W. (1949). *Basic Principles of Curriculum and Instruction*. Chicago: University of Chicago Press.

Tyler, R.W. (April 6, 1991). "Shared Leadership, Empowered Teachers, and the Politicization of Curriculum." Presentation at the annual meeting of the American Educational Research Association, Chicago.

Ulich, R. (1955). "Comments on Ralph Harper's Essay". In *Modern Philosophies of Education*, edited by N.B. Henry. Fifty-fourth Yearbook (Part I) of the National Society for the Study of Education (pp. 254–257). Chicago: University of Chicago Press.

U.S. Department of Education (1991). *America 2000: An Education Strategy*. Washington, D.C.: U.S. Department of Education.

van Manen, M. (1990). *Researching Lived Experience*. London, Ontario: Althouse Press, and Albany, N.Y.: State University of New York Press.

Van Til, W., ed. (1974). *Curriculum: Quest for Relevance*. Boston: Houghton Mifflin. (Previous edition 1972).

Van Til, W., ed. (1986). *ASCD in Retrospect*. Alexandria, Va.: ASCD.

Whitehead, A.N. (1929). *The Aims of Education and Other Essays*. New York: Macmillan.

Willis, G., ed. (1978). *Qualitative Evaluation: Concepts and Cases in Curriculum Criticism*. Berkeley, Calif.: McCutchan.

Willis, G.H., and W.H. Schubert, eds. (1991). *Reflections From the Heart of Educational Inquiry*. New York: State University of New York Press.

Willis, M. (1961). *The Guinea Pigs After Twenty Years*. Columbus: Ohio State University.

Wood, G. (1992). *Schools That Work: America's Most Innovative Public Education Programs*. New York: Dutton.

Young, M.F.D., ed. (1971). *Knowledge and Control: New Directions for the Sociology of Education*. London: Collier-Macmillan.

Zais, R.S. (1976). *Curriculum: Principles and Foundations*. New York: Thomas Y. Crowell.

5

Innovation, Reform, and Restructuring Strategies

Michael Fullan

The history of the large-scale focus on educational innovation and reform is remarkably short. Although ideas about progressive education and the need for improvement in schools in the United States have been debated and tried since the turn of the century, only in the post-Sputnik era has the push for reform taken on national proportions. Thus, the intensive study of change has essentially occurred only in the last half of the 20th century. Those of us working in this period are privileged to have literally grown up with the field.

Our wisdom about change processes has become increasingly sophisticated; our focus for reform has become more comprehensive and deeper. Simultaneously, the problems appear more formidable and intractable. In this chapter, I trace this evolution of sophistication in change—concentrating on how far we have come, what lessons we have learned, and what we are facing for the future.

Evolution of the Study and Practice of Change

The terms *innovation*, *reform*, and *restructuring* are used loosely and inconsistently in the literature. Of the three, innovation is less sweeping, usually confined to specific single changes, such as a new curriculum, an instructional strategy, a new technology, or a particular organizational change like flexible scheduling or team teaching. Innovations are discrete, usually affecting only a particular aspect of schooling.

Reform and restructuring refer to more fundamental and potentially sweeping changes. Both terms are vague until linked to particular initiatives (and even then tend to be less than clear). Thus, governments engage in major "reforms," such as the Kentucky Education Reform Act of 1990 or Great Britain's Education Reform Act of 1989. But the term is also used more generally, for example, to refer to the need to reform teacher education. Restructuring has taken on a particular focus (but still vague) in recent years. It takes many forms, but usually involves school-based management; enhanced roles for teachers in instruction and decision making; restructured programs and timetables, collaborative work cultures, and new designs for teaching-learning; new roles such as mentors, coaches, and other teacher leadership arrangements (see Murphy 1992). People also talk about "restructuring" entire systems at all levels.

In this chapter, I consider four distinct themes of change over the past four decades, each of which implies a different focus and is associated with different assumptions and strategies. The four themes can be seen approximately in terms of each decade since 1960, although the exact transition points often overlap and are somewhat blurred:

1960s—Adoption of Reforms
1970s—Implementation Problems
1980s—Multiple Innovations
1990s—Systemic Reform

The first three themes set the stage for what we know and face for the future. The fourth theme, Systemic Reform, reflects the complexity and comprehensiveness of changes we face in the last decade of the 20th century. In the next sections, I describe each theme briefly, noting its contributions and its limitations.

Adoption of Reforms

The adoption era of the 1960s was generated by a national concern that U.S. education was falling behind scientific accomplishments in Russia. National (federal) leadership and resources were needed to "kick start" a rolling curriculum reform across the country. Federal coffers were opened for major curriculum reforms (PSSC Physics, Chem Study, Chemistry, New Math), technology innovations (television instruction, teaching machines), and organizational innovations (open schools, flexible scheduling, and team teaching).

At the same time, the civil rights movement in the 1960s pinpointed scores of inequities. These simultaneous concerns—academic excellence and equity for the socially and ethnically disadvantaged—drove federal strategies for improving education. A dramatic presence and influx of federal funds was signaled by the passage of the Elementary and Secondary Education Act of 1965, which channeled resources to the disadvantaged, to desegregation, and to the development and dissemination of exemplary innovations.

These were heady days. Cawelti (1967) reflects the spirit of the time in the opening sentence of a review of "innovative practices in high schools": "Innovation is one of the *magic words* influencing school planning in 1967" (p. 1, my emphasis). And it was. The contributions of this adoption era included putting innovation and change into the national consciousness and mobilizing the development of new ideas, resources, and efforts of innovators at all levels of the educational system.

Some fundamental flaws, however, became apparent. The first was the assumption that developing major innovations on a national scale and making them available would lead to widespread adoption. In Cawelti's (1967) survey of more than 7,000 high schools, an average of six out of twenty-seven identified innovations were reported to have been adopted. But this was a start and not by itself a fatal limitation. A second and more telling problem was that schools that reported "adoption" were in fact using the innovation hardly at all, let alone effectively. Cawelti reports a "high abandonment" rate for many of the innovations. In considering how to evaluate the impact of innovations in the 1960s, Charters and Jones (1973) worried about "the risk of appraising non-events." A third, unquestioned assumption of the day was that innovation was "good." To be innovating was to be on the cutting edge; to question or show disinterest was to be a laggard. Change for the sake of change had the upper hand because innovation was the name of the game. A fourth defect was the strategy assumption that you could accomplish change on the ground from afar. Federal initiative would find its way into local practice.

Implementation Problems

The second phase occurred abruptly. Around 1970, almost overnight, innovation got a bad name. The term *implementation*—what was happening (or not happening) in practice—came into use. Goodlad and his colleagues' (1973) *Behind the Classroom Door*, Sarason's (1971) *The Culture of the School and the Problem of Change*, Gross and associates' (1971) *Implementing Organizational Innovations*, and Smith and Keith's (1971) *Anatomy of Educational Innovation* exposed the problem. People were adopting innovations without asking why, and they were giving no forethought to follow through. Most of the 1970s was a decade of acknowledged failure. The economy was stagnant; there was a surplus of teachers; and from an innovation perspective, the focus was on "failed implementation." Although the initial implementation studies told us what *not* to do, after 1975 we gradually began to look for factors related to successful implementation. Alan Pomfret and I conducted a major review of implementation, and we identified fourteen "determinants of implementation" under four categories:

A. Characteristics of the Innovation
    1. Explicitness (what, who, when, how)
    2. Complexity

B. Strategies
    1. In-service training
    2. Resource support (time and materials)
    3. Feedback mechanisms
    4. Participation

C. Characteristics of the Adopting Unit
    1. Adoption process
    2. Organizational climate
    3. Environmental support
    4. Demographic factors

D. Characteristics of Macro Sociopolitical Units
    1. Design questions
    2. Incentive system
    3. Evaluation
    4. Political complexity (Fullan and Pomfret 1977,
       pp. 367–368)

Our confidence in the validity of these factors was buoyed by the fact that the evidence was coming from a variety of research and practice traditions that were compatible but were arrived at seemingly independently. Implementation research and practice, school improvement, effective schools, staff development (e.g., coaching), and leadership (e.g., the role of the principal) all more or less independently documented success stories and provided lists of key factors and processes associated with these accomplishments.

Clearly we were getting somewhere. We were now in a position to identify key factors for putting chosen innovations into practice. Armed with this knowledge, we could do a better job of planning for successful implementation. Moreover, local schools and school districts were paying more attention to developing the instructional leadership of principals, using effective schools research, and providing staff development. The federal role was still evident. Maybe federal and local initiatives could become connected (the role of states was still relatively dormant). Berman and McLaughlin (1977) provided the most comprehensive study of the implementation of federally sponsored programs. In addition to confirming many examples of failed implementation, Berman and McLaughlin emphasized local orientation and capacity: districts and schools fared better when they had a "problem solving" versus an "opportunistic" approach to new initiatives; received active support from principals and other administrators; engaged in ongoing inservice and support focused on the innovation; and, above all, engaged in a process of "mutual adaptation." Instead of attempting to implement innovations "faithfully" (the fidelity perspective) according to their initial design, local users had to interact with the innovation, reworking and redeveloping it according to local needs and contexts (mutual adaptation).

We were making progress, but we still had nagging doubts and problems. First, we still did not know enough about the dynamics of change. It was one thing to have a list of factors, and another to know how these factors interact and unfold. We did not have enough insights about the "microprocesses" of successful change projects. Second, and more fundamentally, we gained a growing realization that knowing how to implement single innovations, one at a time, was not the full story. Schools were not in the business of implementing innovations one after the other. They were in the business of implementing *multiple innovations simultaneously*.

Multiple Innovations

The futility of attempting to implement one innovation at a time, even substantial innovations, was attacked forcefully by the National Commission on Excellence in Education with the publication of *A Nation at Risk* in 1983. The book's subtitle contained the new call to arms: "The Imperative for Educational Reform." The Carnegie Forum's (1986) *A Nation Prepared: Teachers for the 21st Century* and the National Governors' Association's (1986) *A Time for Results* were two among several high-powered, nationwide mandates for action that followed, not to mention the many omnibus reform bills passed at the state level across the United States. Everyone seemed to agree that comprehensive reform was urgently needed.

During the 1980s, educators attempted more basic reform through two strategies, frequently but not always incompatible. These developments involved, respectively, a greater state role and site-based restructuring. In the last half of the 1980s, states led more reform activity than in the previous twenty-five years. The federal share of expenditures for elementary and secondary education declined from 8.7 percent in 1981 to 6.2 percent in 1989. By contrast, state funds rose dramatically. Between 1982–83 and 1986–87, state funding climbed over 21 percent, adjusted for inflation, although it has since leveled off (Firestone, Fuhrman, and Kirst 1989). The share of state funding of local school revenues has risen to a high of 50.7 percent (compared with 40 percent in 1970), with local districts at 42.5 percent and the federal government at 6.8 percent (p. 43). Part and parcel of greater funding was increased legislation and policy requirements.

At the same time, many states and school districts pursued "restructuring" strategies that sought to empower schools to work on shared governance and schoolwide improvement. The federally funded Center for Policy Research and Education (CPRE) has been tracking these state and reform initiatives. Firestone and colleagues (1989) report that every state joined in the movement to address the concerns raised in *A Nation at Risk*. We can examine these developments more closely through CPRE's study of six states: Arizona, California, Florida, Georgia, Minnesota, and Pennsylvania. In 1986, CPRE began a five-year tracer study of the implementation and effects of the reforms in these six states, which were chosen for their diverse approaches to reform. The states were selected to differ on scope of reform (comprehensive vs. small pieces), strategies used (mandates vs. other approaches like building local capacity), and geographical location (representative of regions). Firestone and associates report that:

> California, Florida and Georgia undertook comprehensive reform, symbolized by one major piece of legislation . . . . Reform in the other states was more incremental . . . . Florida, Georgia and Pennsylvania counted on state mandates to change local behavior. California used inducements and Minnesota favored strategies that build local capacity and broadened the state system of service providers. Arizona's plan balanced mandates and inducements (p. 1).

Among the main interim findings, after three years of study, are the following:

• All six states passed special legislation focusing on student standards (and curriculum), teacher policies, and corresponding finances.

• Strategies and policy instruments varied according to tradition and state political culture. For example, California used comprehensive reform and incentives; Georgia mandated reform.

• Most state reform packages lacked coherence. It was not that specific provisions conflicted, but that they were unrelated. The exception was California, where the state superintendent orchestrated the integration of existing and new provisions and coordinated implementation requirements.

• First-order changes involving graduation requirements, curriculum specifications, and the like, were more likely to occur and be retained than second-order changes involving career ladders, new decision-making structures, and so forth.

• District responses were crucial and varied greatly.

The state-level strategies have had differential success. Those that pursued a high-stakes testing strategy fared less well. Corbett and Wilson (1990) identified several unintended consequences, including the diversion of attention and energy from more basic reforms in the structure and practice of schools and reduced teacher motivation, morale, and collegial interaction necessary to bring about reform. They conclude: "When the modal response to statewide testing by professional educators is typified by practices that even the educators acknowledge are counterproductive to improving learning over the long term, then the issue is a 'policymaking problem'" (p. 321).

On the other hand, aggressive state leadership that coupled comprehensive focus with local district and school development did have an impact (Odden and Marsh 1988). Nonetheless, the key variable seemed to be local district capacity. State-level strategies can go only so far in affecting the district.

Site-based restructuring, however, has its own problems. It may have altered governance procedures, but does not necessarily affect the teacher-learning core of schools. Taylor and Teddlie (1992) found this to be true in their study of the extent of classroom change in "a district widely acclaimed as a model of restructuring" (p. 4). They examined classrooms in thirty-three schools [sixteen from pilot schools that had established school-based management (SBM) programs and seventeen from nonpilot schools in the same district]. Taylor and Teddlie found that teachers in the pilot schools reported higher levels of participation in decision making, but they found *no* differences in teaching strategies used. In both sets of schools, instruction continued to be teacher directed, with low student involvement. Further, there was little evidence of teacher collaboration. Extensive collaboration was reported in only two of the thirty-three schools—and both were from nonpilot schools. Taylor and Teddlie observe:

> Teachers in this study did not alter their practice . . . . Increasing their participation in decision-making did not overcome norms of autonomy so that teachers would feel empowered to collaborate with their colleagues (p. 10).

Other evidence from classroom observations failed to indicate changes in classroom environments and student learning activities. Despite considerable rhetoric and what Taylor and Teddlie saw as "a genuine desire to professionalize teaching," "the core mission of the school seemed ancillary to the SBM project" (p. 19). Substantive changes in pedagogy (teaching strategies and assessment) and in the way teachers worked together on instructional matters proved to be elusive. These findings would not be as noteworthy, claim the authors, except for the fact that "the study occurred in a district recognized nationally as a leader in implementing restructuring reforms" (p. 16). Similarly, Hallinger, Murphy, and Hausman (1991) found that teachers and principals in their sample were highly in favor of restructuring, but did not make connections "between new governance structures and the teaching-learning process" (p. 11).

Virtually identical findings arise in Weiss' (1992) investigation of shared decision making (SDM) in twelve high schools in eleven states in the United States (half were selected because they had implemented SDM; the other half were managed in a traditional, principal-led manner). Weiss found that teachers in SDM schools were more likely to mention decisions *about* the decision-making process (i.e., composition of committees, procedures, etc.) but that "schools with SDM did not pay more attention to issues of curriculum than traditionally managed schools, and pedagogical issues and student concerns were low on the list for both sets of schools" (p. 2).

Similar findings were obtained in the implementation of the Chicago Reform Act of 1989. In essence, this legislation shifted responsibility from the Central Board of Education to Local School Councils (LSCs) for each of the city's 540 public schools and mandated that each school develop School Improvement Plans (SIPs). The LSCs by law consist of eleven or twelve members (six parents, two teachers, two community representatives, the school principal—and in the case of high schools, a student). Easton (1991) reports that the majority of elementary teachers said that "their instructional practices had not changed as a result of school reform and will not change as a result of SIP" (p. 41).

In summary, the 1990s represent a new potential watershed. We have learned that neither centralization (federal or state or district) nor decentralization (school) by itself works. We also see that reform strategies struggle between *overcontrol* and *chaos* (Pascale 1990). The realization that initiating multiple innovations is the problem has shifted our attention to more comprehensive perspectives, but has failed to provide a solution. Evidently, change is more complex than we realized.

Systemic Reform

The response to the need to map and carry out comprehensive reform has been to advocate "systemic" strategies (Smith and O'Day 1990). Assessment, curriculum and instruction, staff development, personnel selection and promotion, and state/district/school action—hitherto uncoordinated—are to be systemically linked. The National Board for Professional Teaching Standards (NBTS 1992), focusing on "what teachers should know and be able to do," represents one component. The New Generation of American Schools "winning designs" program represents another as they attempt to integrate curriculum, school and community, structure and governance, and technology and assessment ("Winning Designs" 1992). The limitations of the systemic strategy are twofold. First, people vastly underestimate the dynamic complexity of how systems operate. Second, even if we coordinate the systemic components in one situation, we cannot necessarily extend the process to new situations. For example, producing good systemic ideas either through NTBS or through the New Generation of American Schools is not the same as seeing them spread to new situations. For the latter, we need a different paradigm.

What We Have Learned

We have come a long way in our short history of fifty years. We are now at the early stage of a much more complex phase of unpredictable and dynamic complexity. The next phase—essentially the beginning of the next century—will either build on or ignore the key lessons of the past half-century of experience with educational innovation and reform. I see eight main lessons,* each of which represents dilemmas, with corresponding lines of action. I believe these lessons represent a new mindset about educational change, one that is more in tune with systemic reality and dynamic complexity (see Fullan in press a).

---

* My thanks to Matt Miles, who has identified several of these lessons (Fullan and Miles 1992).

Senge (1990) makes the distinction between "detailed complexity" and "dynamic complexity." The former involves identifying all the variables that could influence a problem. Even this would be enormously difficult for one person or a group to orchestrate. But detailed complexity is not reality. Dynamic complexity is the real territory of change—"when 'cause and effect' are not close in time and space and obvious interventions do not produce expected outcomes" (Senge, p. 365) because other "unplanned" factors dynamically interfere. And we keep discovering, as Dorothy in Oz did, that "this is not Kansas anymore." Complexity, dynamism, and unpredictability, in other words, are not merely things that get in the way. They are *normal*. Such a mindset allows us to uncover a number of basic lessons about the process of educational change.

Eight Lessons of Change

Lesson 1. You Can't Mandate What Matters.

Mandates are important. Policymakers have an obligation to set policies, establish standards, and monitor performance. But to accomplish certain kinds of purposes—in this case, important educational goals—you cannot mandate what matters, because what really matters for complex goals of change are skills, creative thinking, and committed action (McLaughlin 1990). Mandates are not sufficient; and the more you try to specify them, the more narrow the goals and means become. Teachers are not technicians.

To elaborate, you can effectively mandate things that (1) do not require thinking or skill to implement them and (2) can be monitored through close and constant surveillance. You can, for example, mandate the cessation of the use of the strap, or mandate a sales tax on liquor or gasoline. These kinds of changes do not require skill on the part of implementers to comply; and provided that they are closely monitored, they can be enforced effectively.

Even in the relatively simple case—detailed, not dynamic complexity—almost all educational changes of value require new (1) skills, (2) behavior, and (3) beliefs or understanding (Fullan 1991). For example, think of computers across the curriculum, teachers' thinking and problem-solving skills, developing citizenship and teamwork, integration of special education in regular classrooms, dealing with multiculturalism and racism, working with social agencies to provide integrated services, responding to *all* students in the classroom, cooperative learning, and monitoring the performance of students. All of these changes, to be productive, require skills, capacity, commitment, motivation, beliefs, and insights—and discretionary judgment on the spot. If there is one cardinal rule of change in the human condition, it is that you cannot *make* people change. You cannot force them to think differently or compel them to develop new skills.

Lesson 2. Change Is a Journey, Not a Blueprint.

Another reason that you can't mandate what matters, is that you don't know what is going to matter until you are into the journey. If change involved implementing single, well-developed, proven innovations one at a time, perhaps it could be blueprinted. But school districts and schools are in the business of implementing a bewildering array of multiple innovations and policies simultaneously. Moreover, restructuring reforms are so multifaceted and complex that solutions for particular settings cannot be known in advance. If you try to match the complexity of the situation with complex implementation plans, the process becomes unwieldy, cumbersome, and usually wrong.

Lesson 3. Problems Are Our Friends.

It seems perverse to say that problems are our friends, but we cannot develop effective responses to complex situations unless we actively seek and confront the real problems—which are in fact difficult to solve. Problems are our friends because it is only through immersing ourselves in problems that we can come up with creative solutions. Problems are the route to deeper change and deeper satisfaction. In this sense, effective organizations embrace problems rather than avoid them.

Louis and Miles (1990) found that the least successful schools they studied engaged in "shallow coping"—doing nothing, procrastinating, doing it the usual way, easing off, or increasing pressure—whereas the successful schools went deeper to probe underlying reasons and to make more substantial interventions, such as comprehensive restaffing, continuous training, and redesigning programs. Successful schools did not have fewer problems than other schools; they just coped with them better. Moreover, the absence of problems usually indicates that not much is being attempted. Smoothness in the early stages of a change effort is a sure sign that superficial or trivial change is being substituted for substantial change attempts.

Lesson 4. Vision and Strategic Planning Come Later.

Visions are necessary for success, but few concepts are as misunderstood and misapplied in the change process. Visions come later for three reasons. First, under conditions of dynamic complexity, people need a good deal of *reflective experience* before they can form a plausible vision. Vision emerges from, more than it precedes, action. Even then it is always provisional. Second, *shared* vision, which is essential for success, must evolve through the dynamic interaction of organizational members and leaders. This takes time and will not succeed unless the vision-building process is somewhat open ended. Third, skill development is essential because without skill, vision remains superficial. In other words, vision building takes work; but the delay in formation means that people pursue the vision more authentically while avoiding premature formalization.

Visions come later because the process of merging personal and shared vision takes time. The critical question is not whether visions are important, but *how* they can be shaped and reshaped, given the complexity of change. Deep ownership comes through the learning that arises from engagement in solving problems. In this sense, ownership is stronger in the middle of a successful change process than at the beginning, and stronger still at the end than at the middle or beginning. Ownership is a process as well as a state. Saying that ownership is crucial begs the question, unless you know how it is achieved.

Lesson 5. Individualism and Collectivism Must Have Equal Power.

Productive educational change is a process of overcoming isolation while not succumbing to groupthink. There are few more endemic paradoxes in humankind than the creative tension between individual and group development.

Teaching has long been called "a lonely profession," always in pejorative terms. The professional isolation of teachers limits access to new ideas and better solutions; fails to recognize and praise success; and permits incompetence to exist and persist to the detriment of students, colleagues, and the teachers themselves. Isolation allows, even if it does not always produce, conservatism and resistance to innovation in teaching (Lortie 1975).

Isolation also imposes a ceiling effect on inquiry and learning. Solutions are limited to the experiences of the individual. Complex change depends on the efforts of many people working insightfully on the solution and committing themselves to concentrated action together.

Educational problems are complex; collaborative "learning enriched" schools do better than those lingering with the isolationist traditions of teaching (Rosenholtz 1989, Fullan and Hargreaves 1991). Site-based management, peer coaching, and mentoring become valued strategies.

There is nothing automatically good, however, about collaboration. Pushed to extremes, it becomes groupthink—uncritical conformity, unthinking acceptance of the latest solution, and suppression of individual dissent. Groups are more vulnerable to faddism than are individuals. Having a healthy respect for individuals and for personal visions is a source of renewal when the future is unknown and the environment is changing in unpredictable ways. The most productive schools value individualism *and* collectivism simultaneously (Nias, Southworth, and Campbell 1992).

Lesson 6. Neither Centralization nor Decentralization Works.

Centralization errs on the side of overcontrol, decentralization errs toward chaos. We have known for decades that top-down change doesn't work (Lesson 1: You can't mandate what matters). Leaders keep trying because they don't see any alternative, and they are impatient for results (either for political or moral reasons). Decentralized solutions like site-based management also fail because groups get preoccupied with governance and frequently flounder when left on their own.

To put it most clearly, individual schools can become highly collaborative despite the school system they are in, but they cannot *stay* highly collaborative despite their systems. Key people leave, people get transferred, and so on. Two-way, top-down/bottom-up solutions are needed in which schools and districts influence each other through a continually negotiated process and agenda (Fullan in press).

This process works in our Learning Consortium (Fullan in press b). For example, the Halton School Districts use the following strategies to integrate school- and district-level development:

• A broad-based mission statement and strategic directions (instruction, school planning, and staff development) provide a core focus while enabling flexibility.

• A school-growth planning process helps achieve continued growth geared to each community's context.

• Performance appraisals for teachers, vice-principals, and principals are integrated with the three strategic directions.

- A selection and promotion process for all staff stresses collaborative skills, staff development participation and leadership, implementation planning, and knowledge of the change process.
- Schools and districts make a systematic commitment to continuous development through allocating staff development funds to each school and conducting systemwide institutes.
- A reorganization of the system is designed to bring instructional support closer to the school, including in-school resource teachers and area support staff.
- A districtwide assessment and evaluation system provides periodic feedback into all processes.

Lesson 7. Connection with the Wider Environment Is Critical for Success.

Many schools work hard at internal development but fail to keep a proactive learning stance toward the environment. To prosper, schools must be actively plugged into their environments; schools must respond to the issues of the day—and contribute to them. Schools must engage state policies (not necessarily implement them literally), if they are to protect themselves from wrongheaded imposition.

Rosenholtz's (1989) "moving" schools were not disrupted by the latest state policies. Because these schools were proactive, they actively endorsed and enlarged certain state policies. These schools could also blunt or openly challenge other policies that they perceived as wrong or undeveloped.

In the same vein, in England, Nias and her colleagues (1992) found that collaborative schools committed to teacher learning reacted differently from other schools to the National Curriculum. Collaborative schools neither wholeheartedly rejected nor embraced the reform, but considered the whole school curriculum in a way that was open to the external stimulus. Nias and her colleagues conclude:

> The staff of these schools used an external initiative which they might have seen as a constraint to serve their own educational purposes. In the process they came to feel both that it was part of their own curricular thinking and that they were in control of it. That is, by the time that our fieldwork ended, the staff in these schools felt that they "owned" the relevant parts of the National Curriculum (p. 195).

"Learning" schools know that there are far more ideas "out there" than "in here." Successful schools tap into these ideas and contribute to the demands of change that are constantly churning around in the environment.

Thus teachers in Rosenholtz's (1989) "moving" schools believed that good teachers never stopped learning. They were more likely to value the sharing of expertise, and they sought advice and help both inside and outside (see also Fullan in press a).

Lesson 8. Every Person Is a Change Agent.

For two reasons, *every person* working in an enterprise committed to making continuous improvements must be effective at managing change. First, because no one person can possibly understand the complexities of change in postmodern society, we cannot leave the responsibility to others. Second, and more fundamental, the conditions for the new paradigm of change to thrive cannot be established by formal leaders working by themselves. Each teacher has the responsibility to help create an organization capable of individual and collective inquiry and continuous renewal, or it will not happen. Only when individuals take action to alter their own environments is there any chance for deep change. As more people take such action, they have greater chances of intersecting and of forming the critical mass necessary for system change.

What Lies Ahead?

There is no question that the focus has shifted from an innovation concern to a reform and restructuring agenda. Three major strategic issues face the educational system. The first is whether the public system itself will survive given the combination of fewer economic resources, public dissatisfaction, deteriorating social and economic conditions in large cities, growing teacher stress, and the push for a free-market choice system. A lot will depend on how the remaining two strategies fare.

The second strategic area relates to how much substantial progress will be made on "systemic" reform. We need concrete, knowledge- and skill-based examples of systemic reform in action in which actual connections are made through implementing new designs. We should see some development along these lines in the New Generation of American Schools, because the "winning designs" are attempts to achieve synergy of curriculum, technology, teacher development, assessment, structure and governance, and school-external agencies. The development of these new models per se is not a strategy for widespread change, because the latter always requires local development, not just borrowing good ideas. We may also see progress at the state level, because many states are seeking systemic integration among curriculum, assessment, staff development, and school development. The key will be to restructure so that bottom-up and top-down initiatives can feed on each other. This process requires not only greater *systemic* emphasis, but also a much stronger knowledge and skill base about teacher learning. In other words, both systemic connections and good ideas will be necessary. You have to have something worthwhile to connect; and even if it is worthwhile it must be evident in the day-to-day skilled practice of teachers.

The third area that requires much attention is the relationship between *restructuring* and *"reculturing"*—establishing a culture conducive to change.*Change cultures* encompass the values, beliefs, norms, and habits of collaboration and continuous improvement as, for example, contained in the eight lessons. Restructuring, such as site-based management, as many have found out, does not by itself result in reculturing. In most restructuring reforms, the structure attempts to push cultural change, and mostly fails (Fullan in press b). Clearly there must be a reciprocal relationship between the two; but restructuring might be more effective if the attempted conceptual and normative changes were to accumulate to drive structural changes conducive to new ways of working. When teachers and administrators begin working in new ways and, in the process, discover that school structures must be altered, reform and restructuring are much more powerful and meaningful than when the reverse happens. Rapidly implemented new structures create confusion, ambiguity, and conflict, ultimately leading to retrenchment. Therefore, we need to work directly on revamping and upgrading the profession of teaching and teacher education, from preservice throughout the career. At the same time, new school cultures must evolve in which continuous teacher development and continuous school development go hand in hand. Many examples of this are now happening in the works of Comer, Levin, Sizer, and others; but these are only small pockets of activity compared with what will be needed.

* * *

The past fifty years have been the formative ones in establishing the field of educational change. Our knowledge of the change process, and insights into the dynamics of what makes for unsuccessful and successful change have become considerably sophisticated. At the same time, the problems and society have become more complex, which means that the change process has become more complex and intractable. We have learned that understanding even complex change processes is only half the battle. Doing something about it is far more of a challenge, which should occupy us for years to come.

References

Berman, P., and M. McLaughlin. (1977). *Federal Programs Supporting Educational Change*. Vol. 7. Factors Affecting Implementation and Continuation. Santa Monica, Calif.: Rand Corporation.

Carnegie Forum on Education and the Economy. (1986). *A Nation Prepared: Teachers for the 21st Century*. (Report of the Task Force on Teaching as a Profession). New York: Carnegie Corporation.

Cawelti, G. (1967). "Innovative Practices in High Schools: Who Does What and Why and How." In *The Nation's Schools*, edited by G. Cawelti. New York: McGraw-Hill.

Charters, W., and J. Jones. (1973). *On the Neglect of the Independent Variable in Program Evaluation*. (Occasional paper). Eugene: University of Oregon.

Corbett, H.D., and B. Wilson. (1990). *Testing, Reform and Rebellion*. Norwood, N.Y.: Ablex.

Easton, J. (1991). *Decision Making and School Improvement*. Chicago: Chicago Panel on Public School Policy and Finance.

"Winning Designs for a New Generation of American Schools." (1992). *Education Week*.

Firestone, W., S. Fuhrman, and M. Kirst. (1989a). *The Progress of Reform: An Appraisal of State Education Initiatives*. New Brunswick, N.J.: Rutgers University Center for Policy Research in Education.

Fullan, M. (in press a). *Change Forces: Probing the Depths of Educational Reform*. London: Falmer Press.

Fullan, M. (in press b). "Coordinating School and District Development in Restructuring." In *Restructuring Education: Learning from Ongoing Efforts*, edited by J. Murphy and P. Hallinger. Calif.: Corwin Publishers.

Fullan, M., with S. Stiegelbauer. (1991). *The New Meaning of Educational Change*. New York: Teachers College Press.

Fullan, M., and A. Hargreaves. (1991). *What's Worth Fighting For? Working Together for Your School*. Toronto, Ontario, Canada: Ontario Public School Teachers' Federation; Andover, Mass.: The Network.

Fullan, M., and M. Miles. (1992). "Getting Reform Right: What Works and What Doesn't." *Phi Delta Kappan* 73, 10: 744-52.

Fullan, M., and A. Pomfret. (1977). "Research on Curriculum and Instruction Implementation." *Review of Educational Research* 47, 1: 335-37.

Goodlad, J.I., M. Klein, and associates. (1970). *Behind the Classroom Door*. Worthington, Ohio: Charles A. Jones.

Gross, N., J. Giacquinta, and M. Bernstein. (1971). *Implementing Organizational Innovations: A Sociological Analysis of Planned Educational Change*. New York: Basic Books.

Hallinger, P., J. Murphy, and Housmann. (1991). "Conceptualizing School Restructuring: Principals' and Teachers' Perceptions." Paper presented at the Annual Meeting of the American Research Education Association.

Lortie, D. (1975). *School Teacher: A Sociological Study*. Chicago: University of Chicago Press.

Louis, K., and M. Miles. (1990). *Improving the Urban High School: What Works and Why*. New York: Teachers College Press.

McLaughlin, M. (1990). "The Rand Change Agent Study Revisited." *Educational Researcher* 19: 11-16.

Murphy, J. (1992). *Restructuring Schools: Capturing the Phenomenon*. New York: Teachers College Press.

National Commission on Excellence in Education. (1983). *A Nation at Risk*. Washington, D.C.: National Commission on Excellence in Education.

National Governors' Association. (1986). *A Time for Results*. Washington, D.C.: National Governors' Association.

Nias, J., G. Southworth, and P. Campbell. (1992). *Whole School Curriculum Development in the Primary School*. Philadelphia: Falmer Press.

Odden, A., and D. Marsh. (1988). "How Comprehensive Reform Legislation Can Improve Secondary Schools." *Phi Delta Kappan* 68, 8: 593-598.

Pascale, R. (1990). *Meaning on the Edge*. New York: Simon and Schuster.

Rosenholtz, S. (1989). *Teachers' Workplace: The Sound Organization of Schools*. New York: Longman.

Sarason, S. (1971). *The Culture of the School and the Problem of Change*. Boston: Allyn and Bacon.

Sarason, S. (1990). *The Predictable Failure of Educational Reform*. San Francisco: Jossey Bass.

Senge, P. (1990). *The Fifth Discipline*. New York: Doubleday.

Smith, L. and P. Keith. (1971). *Anatomy of Educational Innovation: An Organizational Analysis of an Elementary School*. New York: Wiley.

Smith M.., and J. O'Day. (1990). "Systemic School Reform." In *The Politics of Curriculum and Testing* (pp. 233-267), edited by S. Furham and B. Malen. Philadelphia: Falmer Press.

Taylor, D., and C. Teddlie. (1992). "Restructuring and the Classroom: A View from a Reform District." Paper presented at the Annual Meeting of the American Educational Research Association, San Francisco.

Weiss, C. (1992). "Shared Decision Making About What?" Paper presented at the Annual Meeting of the American Educational Research Association, San Francisco.

6

Inventing and Reinventing Ideas: Constructivist Teaching and Learning in Mathematics

Penelope L. Peterson and Nancy F. Knapp

When the parent organization of ASCD, the National Conference on Educational Methods, published its first yearbook in 1928, the dominant view of learning expressed by education researchers was that people learn by forming connections between environmental stimuli and useful responses. This view had developed from the work of associationists like E.B. Thorndike (1922), who recommended that in mathematics, for example, students do lots of drill and practice on correct procedures and facts to strengthen correct mental bonds and habits. At the same time, associationists said, curriculums should be structured to keep related concepts well separated, so that students did not form incorrect bonds. Thorndike argued for a science of education built on experimental methods, and he suggested the need to design objective measures of students' learning in the form of valid and reliable test items.

By 1943, the behaviorists were asserting that a real science of education could only be built on direct observation. Absent from the

Authors' Note: Our work on this chapter was supported in part by the Center for the Learning and Teaching of Elementary Subjects funded by the Office of Educational Research and Improvement (OERI) (Cooperative Agreement No. G0087C0226). Peterson's research on Annie Keith's class, reported here, was supported in part by a grant from the National Science Foundation (MDR-8954679). The opinions expressed in this chapter do not necessarily reflect the position, policy, or endorsement of OERI or the National Science Foundation.

We thank Deborah Ball and Annie Keith for their willingness to share these examples of their teaching and for their insightful commentaries on their practice. We are also grateful to them and to Elizabeth Fennema for their careful reading and helpful comments on an earlier draft of this chapter.

research and discourse of behaviorists were "meaning," "thinking," or other such unobservable and possibly nonexistent phenomena. Though behaviorists, led by B.F. Skinner, denied the theory of "mental bonds" that associationists had put forth, their prescriptions for mathematics teaching were similar: plenty of drill and practice, with reinforcement by reward for desirable behavior (i.e., correct answers) and extinguishing or punishment for undesired behavior.

Programmed learning curriculums developed by the behaviorists, combined with the new standardized testing techniques developed by psychometricians from achievement and aptitude measures used to evaluate draftees for the U.S. Army during World War II, offered hope for a true "science" of education. Educational research promised to discover curricular materials and teaching methods that could be used by trained teachers to produce learning in students in much the way that newly developed machines were being used in factories to produce ever-increasing numbers and types of manufactured goods, and accompanying tests that could measure the exact degree of learning produced. Extending the behavioral view of learning to the study of teaching, "process-product" researchers searched for the types of teaching behavior that led to greater student achievement, under the assumption that with such a list, they could construct a prescription for effective teaching (Gage 1963, Dunkin and Biddle 1974).

Yet there existed other views of knowledge and learning during these same years, acknowledged alternatives in the scholarly community, although not dominant in the policies and practices of public schooling (Lagemann 1989, Darling-Hammond and Snyder 1992). As early as 1895, John Dewey wrote with James McLellan: "Number is not a property of objects which can be realized through the mere use of the senses or impressed upon the mind . . . . Objects (and measured things) aid the mind in its work of constructing numerical ideas" (McLellan and Dewey 1895, p. 24). In 1935, William Brownell wrote about a theory of instruction that "makes meaning, the fact that children shall see sense in what they learn, the central issue in arithmetic instruction" (p. 19). Later, based on detailed interviews with hundreds of children, Piaget and his coworkers proposed that children "make sense" in ways very different from adults, and that they learn through the process of trying to make things happen, trying to manipulate their environment (Piaget 1970).

Today, theories like these, which hold that "people are not recorders of information, but builders of knowledge structures" (Resnick and

Klopfer 1989, p. 4), have come to be grouped under the heading of "constructivism."[1]

Reemergence of Constructivism Within the Context of Reform

Over the past two decades, disappointment with public schools has been mounting; calls for reform are increasingly heard. The goal of "producing" learning in all children seems to be ever receding. Arguments have multiplied about the validity of "scientific" measures of learning, especially as applied to various nonmainstream groups, such as minorities and disadvantaged students. Schools are called on to help students learn in increasingly complex ways, because in their lives and work and thought, people do not need simply to be able to recall facts or preset procedures in response to specific stimuli. They need to be able to plan courses of action, weigh alternatives, think about problems and issues in new ways, converse with others about what they know and why, and transform and create new knowledge for themselves; they need, in short, to be able "to make sense" and "to learn."

At the same time, dissatisfaction has been growing within scholarly communities with behaviorist models of learning and objectivist views of knowledge or truth (Kuhn 1970, Lakatos 1970; Toulmin 1985). Psychologists are focusing less on the simple conditioned responses that humans share with many animals and more on *the uniquely human aspects of learning in language, art, science, mathematics, cultural groups, and societal institutions* (e.g., Resnick and Klopfer 1989). In addition, scholars are rethinking their views of knowledge, moving away from the idea that we can know something "objectively," and toward the idea that *knowledge is necessarily subjective, interpretive, and contextualized*. For these reasons, education scholars have been increasingly interested in the ideas about learning that were advanced by people like Dewey, Brownell, and Piaget, thinkers who put forth constructivist ideas. In addition, scholars are interested in more recent, "social" aspects of constructivism that portray inquiry and the growth of knowledge as occurring within communities through the processes of conversation, argumentation, justification, and "proof" (Lakatos 1976; Vygotsky 1978).

[1]The views expressed in ASCD yearbooks have, as a whole, tended to favor these alternative views. We would refer those interested to the yearbooks of 1949, 1954, 1959, 1963, and 1967, particularly.

Why "Unpack" Constructivism?

Currently, most educational scholars espouse the idea that knowledge is constructed, and much current reform rhetoric in the United States is couched in terms of "constructed knowledge" (e.g., National Research Council 1989, Rutherford and Ahlgren 1990). Although "the initial statement 'I am a constructivist' has become a kind of academic lip service" (Bauersfeld 1991, p. 3), the terms *constructivist* and *constructivism* can have many meanings. Not only do different scholars who use these terms hold differing assumptions about knowledge and how one comes to know, but these assumptions and the ways in which they might influence school teaching and learning are often not made explicit.

Those within a community of scholars are usually aware of the views and assumptions that underlie the statements and work of their colleagues within the community, as well as the views and assumptions of scholars in other communities. But those outside the scholarly community typically remain unaware. For example, educators such as principals, teachers, and curriculum designers are often presented with surface-level suggestions about how they might change toward more "constructivist" practices in their schools, without being made privy to the assumptions or theoretical frames of the various authors of these reforms, who may include researchers, policy reformers, textbook writers, or expert practitioners.

Some may protest that practicing educators are more interested in practical features than in theories; but evidence exists that, for example, teachers' enactments of suggested reforms are profoundly influenced by the theories and beliefs that they currently hold (Ball 1990, Cohen 1990, Wiemers 1990, Wilson 1990). This body of research on teachers' "reading" of reforms suggests, as does research on the reading of texts, that readers interpret texts (or reform recommendations) in light of their existing assumptions and frames. If not privy to the underlying assumptions and understandings of the author, readers may attempt to incorporate the "new information" without reexamining their existing understanding. Educators who are expected to "implement" surface features of constructivist reforms without being given time and access to consider and interpret for themselves the assumptions and ideas about learning that underlie these reforms may miss the main meaning of the reform, while adhering to the letter of the suggested procedures. Teachers, particularly, may be caught in a net of conflicting expectations, as the remnants of older reforms based on more behaviorist views remain in place at the same time constructivist-based instructional activities are urged on them (Darling-Hammond 1990, Peterson 1990). Thus teachers may come to see themselves as responsible both for students' getting the "right answers" on standardized exams and simultaneously encouraging students to explore "multiple ways of knowing" in class.

Finally, constructivist theories, like all theories of teaching and learning, pose their own dilemmas for educators (Lampert 1985, Ball in press). These dilemmas arise in specific contexts, as teachers try to help particular students learn particular things in particular classrooms and schools; thus, the dilemmas cannot be resolved in advance by the "designers" of any reform. They must be resolved again and again by practicing educators as they deal with their own particular situations. The success of all these reforms ultimately depends on the wisdom of practicing educators—their understanding of and ability to flexibly interpret constructivist ideas.

Why Explore Cases of Constructivist Mathematics Teaching?

In this chapter, we consider two examples of constructivist mathematics teaching and learning that have been created by two elementary schoolteachers working within their own communities of discourse and learning.

We have chosen examples from mathematics primarily because this is the subject area with which we are most familiar; yet we see similar questions and issues emerging in constructivist teaching in other subject areas, including literacy and science.

We have chosen to look at examples of teaching for two reasons. First, it is in the classroom interactions among teacher and students that school learning finally does or does not occur. All the planning and resources of schools, all the vital activities of administrators, curriculum specialists, supervisors, counselors, and other practicing educators in our school systems lead up to and make possible the learning that we hope will occur in the classroom through the direct mediation of the teacher. Yet, and this is our second reason, teachers are often the most excluded from the scholarly discourse around issues of teaching and learning (Carter 1992).

This absence of teachers' voices seems to reflect a dominant view of knowledge over the past fifty years—knowledge was thought to be constructed by experts (researchers) and transmitted to practitioners (teachers), just as knowledge was thought to be constructed by experts (teachers and adults) and transmitted to novices (students). Just as some educators are challenging this transmission view of knowledge for students in our nation's classrooms, educators are also challenging it for teachers in our nation's schools (Lieberman 1992). Just as students need to think for themselves, so do teachers; and just as students need to be lifelong learners of new knowledge, so do teachers (Carnegie Forum on Education and the Economy 1986, Holmes Group 1990). Much dialogue and debate in scholarly and professional communities in education is now concerned with questions of whether and how teachers will be included in the ongoing discourse that is constructing a knowledge base for teaching and who will assume the roles of authorities for knowledge in the fields of teaching and learning (e.g., Carter 1992).[2]

In the cases in this chapter, both the perspectives and the voices of these two teachers are present and visible. We explore the assumptions about mathematics learning that these teachers bring to their mathematics teaching, as well as the assumptions of the researchers with whom they have worked. Although these two teachers had never met and were unacquainted with each others' practices, they independently created instructional practices that have both striking similarities and interesting differences.

One way of thinking about these cases is to consider some common themes, similar to the "common threads" identified by Davis, Maher, and Noddings (1990), including

> the emphasis on mathematical activity in a mathematical community. It is assumed that learners have to construct their own knowledge— individually and collectively. Each learner has a tool kit of conceptions and skills with which he or she must construct knowledge to solve problems presented by the environment. The role of the community— other learners and teacher—is to provide the setting, pose the challenges, and offer the support that will encourage mathematical construction. Any form of activity that takes place in a genuine community is likely to be complex. Initiates have to learn the language, customs, characteristic problems, and tools of the community, and there is a continual need to negotiate and renegotiate meaning. Because student communities necessarily lack the experience and authority of expert communities, teachers bear a great responsibility for guiding student activity, modeling mathematical behavior, and providing the examples and counterexamples that will turn student talk into useful communication about mathematics (p. 3).

---

[2]In line with recent concern for teachers' voices, both the 1990 and 1991 ASCD yearbooks include chapters authored by classroom teachers.

Another aspect of these cases is the dilemmas or tensions that emerge as these teachers work to embody constructivist theories in their practices. These cases can serve as sites for exploration for teachers who want to move toward constructivist teaching and learning in their own classrooms. They can also be used by supervisors, administrators, curriculum developers, and teacher educators to consider what kinds of resources might support teachers' attempts to teach in this way. In our ongoing research on policy and practice in more than fifty teachers' classrooms in California and Michigan, we see similar themes and dilemmas emerging as other elementary schoolteachers move toward more constructivist teaching in literacy and mathematics. However, we want readers to see these cases as "instances" of constructivist teaching, rather than "models" to be imitated. A constructivist view of knowledge implies that knowledge is continuously created and reconstructed so that there can be no template for constructivist teaching. Just as teachers' knowledge is developing and changing as teachers learn from their learners and their teaching, so too would teachers continuously recreate and transform their own teaching within their own contexts.

A third way of thinking about these cases is as texts, situated within social, cultural, and historical contexts, that may be interpreted in multiple ways by readers who also exist within such contexts. If we would practice what we preach, we cannot claim here to present *the* definitive interpretation of these excerpts, but rather simply to share some of the ideas we have about them. We expect, and indeed hope, that these cases will elicit other ideas and interpretations from other readers and thereby facilitate discourse among practitioners, policymakers, and researchers aimed at developing shared understandings and new ways to think about reform, research, teaching, and learning.

Examples of Constructivist Teaching and Learning

Deborah Ball and Annie Keith are both elementary schoolteachers who are involved in multiple communities of inquiry and discourse that include teachers, teacher educators, and researchers, as well as the students in their own classrooms. We chose these teachers because they have three important things in common. First, both teachers take social constructivist perspectives on learners' mathematical knowledge, although they have come to these views from different directions. Second, both teachers are striving to create teaching practices that are in line with the visions of teaching in the *Standards* recently published by the National Council of Teachers of Mathematics (NCTM 1991). Third, both teachers are learners themselves, and as such they are striving continuously to renew and reform their own classroom practices.

We begin each case with a short introduction to each teacher and some of her goals in teaching, followed by excerpts from a lesson, including italicized commentary, and end with an investigation of some of the issues in constructivist teaching that seem to arise out of each excerpt.

Understanding "Sean Numbers" in Deborah Ball's Class

Deborah Ball has seventeen years of experience as an elementary schoolteacher. After teaching for eight years, she returned to school and earned a Ph.D. degree in 1988. She is currently a professor of teacher education and researcher at Michigan State University, while she continues to teach mathematics daily to a class of 3rd graders. Throughout her years of teaching, Ball has worked to improve mathematics teaching. She is one of the authors of the *NCTM Professional Standards for Teaching Mathematics* (1991). With Magdalene Lampert, Ball has had a grant from the National Science Foundation (NSF) to study her own mathematics teaching and to develop videodisc materials for teacher education.

Ball has written extensively about her experiences in trying to create and revise her teaching practice. Like Magdalene Lampert (1990), she attempts to develop a "practice that respects both the integrity of mathematics as a discipline *and* of children as mathematical thinkers" (Ball 1990, p. 3). She strives to create a classroom environment in which the norms of discourse are informed by patterns of discourse in the mathematics community as well as by the culture of the classroom. Further, she strives to shift authority for mathematical knowledge from the teacher and the "text" to the community of knowers and learners of mathematics in her classroom. She also assumes that students are "sense makers" and that, as their teacher, she needs to understand their understandings.

Ball teaches 3rd grade mathematics at Spartan Village Elementary School in East Lansing, Michigan. The school has an ethnically and linguistically diverse student body; children in the school speak twenty different languages, and many attend English-as-a-Second-Language (ESL) classes. Most of the children's parents are undergraduate or graduate students who are attending Michigan State University and live in University-subsidized student housing. The following is excerpted from a whole-class discussion of odd and even numbers (Ball 1991, in press). Ball's own comments are in italics; the names of the students are pseudonyms.[3]

> *We had been working with patterns with odd and even numbers. One day as we began class, Sean announced:*
>
> Sean:[4] I was just thinking about 6, that it's a . . . I 'm just thinking it can be an odd number, too, 'cause there could be 2, 4, 6, and two, three 2s, that'd make 6.
>
> Ball: Uh-huh . . .
>
> Sean: And two 3s, that it could be an odd and an even number. Both! Three things to make it and there could be two things to make it . . . .
>
> Ball: Other people's comments?
>
> Cassandra: I disagree with Sean when he says that 6 can be an odd number. I think 6 can't be an odd number because, look . . . [she goes to the board and points to the number line there, starting with zero] even, odd, even, odd, even, odd, even. How can it be an odd number because . . . zero's not an odd number [appealing to an implicit definition of even numbers as 'every other number'] . . . .
>
> Ball: What's the definition—Sean?—what's our working . . . definition of an even number? . . .
>
> *At this point I thought that Sean was just confused about the definition for even numbers. I thought that if we just reviewed the definition, he would see that 6 fit the definition and was therefore even . . . .* (There are several minutes spent recalling and discussing the working definition. Agreement is reached).
>
> Jeannie: If you have a number that you can split up evenly without having to split one in half, then it's an even number.
>
> Ball: Can you do that with 6, Sean? Can you split 6 in half without having to use halves?
>
> Sean: Yeah.
>
> Ball: So then it would fit our working definition, then it would be even. Okay?
>
> Sean: [pause] <u>And</u> it could be odd. Three 2s could make it . . . . It fits the definition for odd, too.
>
> Ball: What is the definition for odd? Maybe we need to talk about that?

---

[3]This selection is excerpted from two sources in which Ball discusses this lesson (Ball 1991; Ball in press).

[4]Although in this chapter we have used Deborah Ball's and Annie Keith's real names, according to their wishes, all student names are pseudonyms.

We discussed a definition for odd numbers [and] we agreed that odd numbers were numbers that you could not split up fairly into two groups. But this still did not satisfy Sean . . . .

Sean: You could split 6 fairly, *and* you can split 6 not fairly . . . . Like, say there's 2 of you, and you had 6 cookies, and you didn't want to split them in <u>half</u> . . . you wanted to split them by 2s. Each person would get 2 and there would be 2 left . . . .

Ball: So, are you saying <u>all</u> numbers are odd, then?

Sean: No, I'm not saying all numbers are odd, but . . .

Ball: Which numbers are *not* odd then?

Sean: Um . . . 2, 4, 6, . . . 6 can be odd or even . . . 8 . . .

Students: <u>No!</u>

Temba: Prove it to us that it can be odd. <u>Prove</u> it to us.

Sean: Okay. [He goes to the board.] Well, see, there's two [he draws] number 2 over here, put that there. Put this here. There's 2, 2, and 2, and that would make 6.

OO I OO I OO

Temba: I know, which is even!

Mei: I think I know what he's saying . . . . I think what he's saying is that you have 3 groups of 2. And 3 is an odd number, so 6 can be an odd number <u>and</u> an even number.

Ball: Do other people agree with that? <u>Is</u> that what you're saying, Sean?

Sean: Yeah.

Ball: Okay, do other people agree with him? [pause] Mei, you <u>disagree</u> with that?

Mei: Yeah, I·disagree with that because it's not according to like . . . how many groups it is. Let's say I have [pauses] Let's see. If you call 6 an odd number, why don't [pause] let's see [pause] let's see—10. One, two . . . [draws circles on the board] and here are 10 circles. And then you would split them, let's say I wanted to split them by 2s . . . . 1, 2, 3, 4, 5 [she draws].

OO I OO I OO I OO I OO

Then why do you not call 10 an odd number and an even number, or why don't you call <u>other</u> numbers an odd number and an even number?

Sean: I didn't think of it that way. Thank you for bringing it up, so—I say it's—10 can be an odd and an even.

Mei: [with some agitation] What about other numbers? Like, if you keep on going on like that and you say that other numbers are odd and even maybe we'll end it up with <u>all</u> numbers are odd and even. Then it won't make sense that all numbers should be odd and even, because if all numbers were odd <u>and</u> even, we wouldn't be even having this discussion!

In this excerpt, Deborah Ball deals with two of the dilemmas, or issues, common to constructivist teaching. First, what is the teacher's role in constructivist learning? Second, how can the teacher honor both student-constructed knowledge and traditionally accepted knowledge?

What is the teacher's role in constructivist learning?

Constructivist theory holds that learning involves students' constructing their own knowledge. Yet students cannot be expected to construct centuries' worth of knowledge all on their own. One of the "common threads" in constructivism identified by Davis and colleagues (1990) concerns this redefinition of the teacher's role, away from *directing* all classroom discourse and *telling* students correct procedures and right answers, toward "*guiding* student activity, *modeling* mathematical behavior, and *providing* the examples and counterexamples that will turn student talk into useful communication about mathematics" (p. 3, emphasis added).

This episode from Deborah Ball's teaching reveals one way of handling this new role. The teacher was quite active in the class discussion: she clarified students' remarks, posed challenging questions, and thought hard about where she wanted the discussion to go. At the same time, the discussion was in large part shaped by the students' concerns. Sean made the original conjecture that "some numbers can be odd or even." Other students argued with Sean's conjecture, expanded it, demanded proof of it, and discussed its significance for definitions of odd and even numbers in mathematics. Although Ball was a major participant and, at times, moderator of the discussion, she maintained her posture that authority for mathematical knowledge should reside with the community of learners in her classroom. The entire classroom community, through mathematical argument, justification, and sense-making, wrestled with just how and whether Sean's conjecture would be accepted. Ball's rationale was that

> in traditional classrooms, answers are right most often because the teacher says so . . . . I am searching for ways to construct classroom discourse such that the students learn to rely on themselves and on mathematical argument for resolving mathematical sense.

How can the teacher honor both student-constructed knowledge and traditionally accepted knowledge?

Constructivist ideas about teaching emphasize the importance of listening to and valuing students' perceptions, even when their understanding differs from conventional knowledge. Listening and valuing are part of the vital "support" that Davis and colleagues suggest is necessary to encourage students to construct their knowledge, to engage in the hard and risky task of openly wondering, conjecturing, testing, and arguing about mathematics or any other subject. Such listening and valuing also reflect the constructivist, epistemological stance that knowledge, even "official" knowledge, is not fixed and static, but ever changing and growing. Yet students also need to understand the conventional knowledge that is currently accepted in their society, and teachers are responsible for helping them gain this understanding.

Sean's suggestion that "some numbers can be odd and even" because they contain an odd number of groups of two caused Deborah Ball to struggle hard with the dilemma of how to respect Sean's understanding, yet avoid confusing him and his classmates. She wrote:

> On the one hand, Sean was wrong. Even and odd are defined to be non-overlapping. . . . He was . . . paying attention to something that was irrelevant to the conventional definition for even and odd numbers . . . . On the other hand . . . Sean noticed that some even numbers have an odd number of groups of two. Hence, they were, to him, special. . . . I wrote in my journal: "I'm wondering if I should introduce to the class the idea that Sean has identified (discovered) a new category of numbers—those that have the property he has noted. We could name them after him. Or maybe this is silly—will just confuse them since it's nonstandard knowledge. . . . "

> In the end, I decided not to label his claim wrong, and, instead, to legitimize Sean's idea of a number that can be "both even and odd." I pointed out that Sean had invented another kind of number that we hadn't known before and suggested that we call them "Sean numbers." . . . And, over the course of the next few days, some children explored patterns with Sean numbers, just as others were investigating patterns with even and odd numbers.

Ball's decision to trust her students' ability to understand and discriminate worked out well. She comments:

> When I gave a quiz on even and odd numbers . . . the results were reassuring. Everyone was able to give a sound definition of odd numbers, and to correctly identify and justify even and odd numbers. And, interestingly, in a problem that involved placing some numbers into a string picture (Venn diagram), no one placed 90 (a Sean number) into the intersection between even and odd numbers. If they were confused about these classifications of number, the quizzes did not reveal it.

Ball also learned from this episode as she participated in the classroom discussion and came to understand Sean's idea. She learned a lot about how Sean and his classmates were thinking about odd and even numbers, and she also learned something about mathematics from Sean. Although Ball had never heard of "Sean numbers"—numbers composed of an odd number of groups of two—when Sean "discovered" them in class, she subsequently found out that Greek mathematicians had discovered this kind of number and worked with it centuries ago. Janine Remillard, a graduate student and colleague of Ball's, called this to her attention. Remillard found in D.E. Smith's *History of Mathematics*, Vol. II, the following:

> Euclid [studied] "even-times-even numbers," "even-times-odd numbers," and "odd-times-odd numbers." His definitions of the first two differ from those given by Nicomachus (*c.* 100) and other writers. . . . How far back these ideas go in Greek arithmetic is unknown, for they were doubtless transmitted orally long before they were committed to writing (p. 18).

Harvey Davis, of the mathematics department at Michigan State University, called to our attention that both Plato and the neo-Pythagoreans had also worked with "Sean-type" numbers—those produced by multiplying two by an odd number, resulting in "an odd number of groups of two."

Working Together on Problems in Annie Keith's Class

The second teacher, Annie Keith, had just completed her first year of teaching when she began participating six years ago in the development of Cognitively Guided Instruction (CGI)—a research-based approach to elementary mathematics learning. Keith began by participating in a month-long workshop in 1986 and became more involved in the project with each passing year. For the past two years, she has served as a mentor teacher on the CGI Project, working with researchers to "extend the principles of CGI to the primary mathematics curriculum" (Carpenter, Fennema, and Franke 1992). The full story of Annie Keith's learning and how she came to create her current mathematics practice are explored elsewhere (Peterson 1992).

The major thesis of CGI is that children enter school with a great deal of informal, intuitive knowledge of mathematics that can serve as the basis for developing much of the formal mathematics of the primary school curriculum. Although each teacher creates her own unique practice, CGI classrooms are typically characterized by a focus on problem solving, particularly the solving of word problems; students' sharing of their diverse strategies for solving the problems; and teachers' and students' listening hard to students' solutions and ideas for solving problems.[5]

Drawing on her experience in language arts with creating a classroom "community of readers and writers," Annie Keith attempts in her mathematics teaching to help her students see themselves as a community of mathematicians. At the beginning of the year, the class jointly defined the following qualities of mathematicians:

> Mathematicians listen to each other. Mathematicians never say "can't." They will always do their best and try their hardest. Mathematicians help each other. Mathematicians can solve a problem in many ways. Mathematicians use different kinds of math tools.

These qualities were not derived from any knowledge of specific or actual communities of mathematicians. Rather, they represent Keith's and her students' ideal of how *they* want to function as a community investigating mathematical ideas.

Keith encourages her students, as mathematicians, to choose and create problems and mathematical tasks that interest and challenge them and to justify their mathematical thinking to themselves and within their community. Like Deborah Ball, Annie Keith wants authority for knowing and learning to rest with the students and the community of learners rather than with her as the teacher.

Keith teaches 1st grade at Muir School in Madison, Wisconsin. For the past twenty years or so, Muir School has served a neighborhood population of white, middle-class families, as well as an additional population of students from a nearby low-rent housing area. Over the years, the latter population has changed to include a substantial number of Indo-Chinese immigrants, as well as Hispanics and African Americans. Currently, minority students make up about 30 percent of the school population, and an approximately equal number of children receive free or reduced-price lunch.

Each day, mathematics class starts with students sitting on the rug for a meeting or whole-class conversation. Then students go to math centers to work in small groups on different mathematics tasks. Students choose the center they want to work in for the day. The following selection is excerpted from field notes of a session near the end of the school year in the "Discussion" Center. Annie Keith was meeting with a group of four students involved in solving word problems that had

---

[5]For further details on this NSF-sponsored teacher enhancement and research project, see Carpenter, Fennema, Peterson, Chiang, and Loef 1989; Peterson, Fennema, and Carpenter, 1991.

been written by members of the class. Keith's comments from a follow-up interview are in italics.[6]

> Annie Keith read the first problem, written by Susan: "I found 16 icicles. I found 80 more. How many do I have now?" and then asked the students to write a number sentence that showed what they're thinking about.
>
> *[I am] linking story problems and number sentences, [so that] when my kids see number sentences they're not thrown by them. . . . If we have a story problem, the kids can put it in number sentences, and they're very comfortable with the symbols.*
>
> T.J. wrote: **80 + 10 → 90 + 6 = 96**[7]
>
> Keith looked at his solution and then asked T.J., "How can you challenge yourself?" T.J. decided to make the first number in the problem larger, changing it to: "I found 1,000,293 icicles. I found 80 more. How many do I have now?" then proceeded to work on this new, more challenging problem.
>
> Jafari made 16 tally marks. Keith led him to count by tens to 80 and then count on, using his 16 tally marks. Jafari got 96 and then wrote: **16 + 80 = 96**
>
> Heather had only written **16 + 80 = 96** on her paper. Keith said that she had heard Heather do some counting, and suggested that she find some way to show "where you started counting."
>
> *I'm really pushing them to write down on their papers how they've solved it—whether it's in words or whether it's with a number sentence that shows they're counting on or if they are putting numbers together.*
>
> Keith asked Peter how he had done the problem, and he indicated that he had first "known" that 80 + 10 = 90, and then figured 90 + 6 would be 96, "since 90 didn't have any other number on it."
>
> Keith then called on Jafari to tell the kids how he did the problem. He had written on his paper:
>
> **16 + 80 = 96**
>
> **10 + 10 + 10 + 10 + 10 + 10 + 10 + 10 + 16 = 90**
>
> He counted out loud: "10-20-30-40-50-60-70-80-90-91-92-93-94-95-96."

---

[6]These data were collected by Peterson as part of her work as an external evaluator for a current NSF-funded project, "A Longitudinal Analysis of Cognitively Guided Instruction and the Primary School," E. Fennema and T. Carpenter, principal investigators.

[7]The arrow notation was invented by elementary students in a constructivist mathematics classroom in South Africa (Oliver, Murray, and Human 1991) and shared with Elizbeth Fennema and Tom Carpenter, who shared the idea with Annie Keith, who shared it with her students.

Keith chose a problem she had written herself for the next problem: "Steve had 14 snowballs. How many more snowballs will he need to make so he has 26 snowballs altogether?"

At this point, Jafari appeared not to be listening or participating. Keith turned to him and said, "May I go on? Then I need to see you're ready; can you sit down please? Jafari, mathematicians work together, okay?" She reread the problem.

Jafari went to get an abacus and brought it back to the table, sat down, and began to use it to solve the problem. He counted out 80 and then seemed to lose interest again. Keith suggested he might draw a picture to help with the problem.

Meanwhile, T.J. had written on his paper: $14 + 10 \rightarrow 24 + 2 = 12$

Jafari seemed not to be interested in this task. He got up from the table and wandered around the room. Keith got up and went over to talk privately with Jafari. Jafari returned to the table with her, and he sat down to work again.

Sometimes Jafari will come to things hesitantly, where he thinks he can't do it, and he got really upset with this one. [I was] just saying, "I know you can do this stuff. You just need to decide. . . . Do you want to give it your best shot and work with us in this group, or do you want to join a group at another Center?"

The other three students were finished and started to share their solution strategies at Keith's urging. Meanwhile, still working on the word problem, Jafari had made 14 tally marks on his paper and put a number by each one in order from 1 to 14. Keith suggested that Jafari listen to Heather's explanation, that he might hear "the missing piece" to his solution; but Jafari did not seem to heed her suggestion, and he continued to work on his own solution.

Watching Jafari, Peter noted suddenly, "I think it clicked." Keith asked Jafari, "Are you ready to talk to us yet, or do you want us to come back?" and Jafari said, concentrating, "Come back." Jafari now had 15 tallies on his paper.

T.J. began explaining his solution strategy. As he began to explain, he erased, saying he "forgot something." He had written: $14 + 10 = 24 + 2 = 12$

He erased this and wrote, $14 + 10 \rightarrow 24 + 2 \rightarrow 26$

$2 + 10 = 12$

T.J. continued, "Fourteen plus ten is twenty-four plus two is twenty-six. Two plus ten equals twelve." Heather and Peter listened as T.J. recounted his solution strategy.

Meanwhile Jafari now had 22 tally marks. Keith asked, "How high do you need to go up to here?" Peter replied, "26." Jafari added more tally marks. Heather suggested that Jafari needed four more tally marks. Keith said to Jafari, "Keep going. You're almost there."

When Jafari had finished, Keith asked him, "How many more [snow-balls] does he need to make?" Jafari replied, "Twelve." She asked him, "How do you know? How would you prove it to us?" Jafari separated off the original 14 tallies, and counted the remaining tallies needed to make 26, "one, two, three, four, five, six, seven, eight, nine, ten, eleven, twelve." Keith replied, "Very nice job. You did not give up . . . . Good for you. It was a very hard job, and yet you guys had it. Let's see if we can do one more, okay?"

Showing great eagerness and excitement, Jafari called out, "Do mine!" (meaning do the word problem he had written). Readily agreeing, Keith read Jafari's problem aloud: "I had one hundred snowballs. My mom gave me eight. How many do I have?"

Jafari immediately answered, "108." Keith responded that he should show how he got that. Jafari wrote in his notebook: **100 + 8 = 108**.

After the other kids had a chance to work out the problem, Keith said, "Okay, Jafari, start it off . . . " Jafari said, "One hundred plus eight equals one hundred and eight." He had written ten zeroes in his notebook, each representing a ten, and then the numbers from one to ten as follows:

0 0 0 0 0 0 0 0 0 0 1 2 3 4 5 6 7 8

Jafari counted aloud the zeroes by ten: "Ten, twenty, thirty, forty, fifty, sixty, seventy, eighty, ninety, one hundred." Then he continued count-ing aloud the ones from 100 to 108: "one hundred one, one hundred two, one hundred three, one hundred four, one hundred five, one hundred six, one hundred seven, one hundred eight."

How can teachers involve diverse students in community problem solving?

In this episode, Annie Keith faced an issue common to all types of teaching: student diversity. Davis and colleagues (1990) note that "each learner has a tool kit of conceptions and skills," but each learner comes to school with different tools, depending on their personalities, cultures, and prior experiences. Annie Keith, like many constructivist teachers, placed great emphasis on children talking with and learning from each other:

Talking is a real priority in this room—getting kids to talk back and forth to each other [and] really think about what people are saying.

So Annie Keith needed to find ways to involve all four students in problem solving and enable them to confidently share their solutions, despite a wide diversity in their mathematical abilities and interests. At one extreme was T.J., who quickly solved the first problem symbolically by writing a number sentence, and at the other was Jafari, who worked more slowly, directly representing each of the quantities in the word problem with tally marks.

Giving students options is an important way in which Annie Keith involves students in mathematical problem solving in this episode. When T.J. finished quickly, she suggested he "challenge himself" by making the problem more difficult. T.J. did so by making the numbers bigger. Meanwhile the other three students had time to complete their problems, free to use whatever strategy and math tools they wanted as long as they could articulate their thinking and justify their answers.

But letting students make choices also brings its own dilemmas, for in the middle of the problem-solving session, Jafari, a student who had transferred into the class just a few weeks earlier, chose to leave the table and involve himself in something other than mathematical problem solving. Keith faced a dilemma: Should she tell Jafari to return to the table and complete the problem-solving session or should she attempt to work within the norms that had been established for the mathematical community within her classroom?

Keith chose to work within the norms of her classroom community and to make use of her ongoing, intimate knowledge of Jafari's personal background and experiences and his developing mathematical understanding. She gave Jafari the choice of whether to return to the group, where he would be expected to participate and do his best thinking, or to choose to join another mathematics group, and she gave him this choice privately.

> *What I know about Jafari is that he's the kind of kid that if I confront him in a group, he might have to . . . come off macho. . . . One on one, it's very different, because he can walk back to the class without having lost face with anybody.*

A short time after he returned to the group, Jafari asked if the group could work the word problem that he had written. When Keith and the group readily agreed, Jafari beamed and proceeded to solve the problem using his mathematical tools.

A second short excerpt points up a different issue that arises when students share ideas that may be challenged by others in the class.[8]

> The next day, during whole-class discussion, Peter began to tell his classmates about "touchpoints" on numbers, a method of calculating

---

[8]This excerpt comes from Peterson's transcription and analysis of a videotape of Annie Keith's classroom taken by Susan Baker, a CGI project staff person, on the day following the "Jafari" excerpt. Keith's remarks in italics are, as before, from the follow-up interview with Peterson. The videotape constitutes data collected by CGI researchers for their current NSF-funded project. Our analysis here is in no way intended to substitute for or supplant their own analyses of these data.

the sum of written digits by counting imaginary dots or "points" on the digits, which Peter had learned from his sister.

At one point in the discussion, Peter's interested and curious 1st grade peers began peppering him with questions.

He felt a little pushed into a corner, I think. . . And then he just turned around and he just started crying.

Keith responded by putting her arm around Peter and reminding him that students in this class "ask hard questions" because "they really want to know things."

I just wanted him to realize that they weren't attacking him. They're just really curious and trying to figure out this whole thing. And Peter tends to be one who's very, very sensitive about things.

Then she gave him the chance to leave the discussion, get a drink of water in the hall, and return to the discussion when he felt comfortable.

Peter left the room, got a drink, and returned within thirty seconds. He rejoined the discussion and returned to the board, where two other students had taken over leading the discussion on touchpoints. At the end of class, Peter volunteered to find out more information about touchpoints and bring the information back to the class. Having been supported in the risk of sharing his ideas, Peter had voluntarily rejoined the community of mathematicians in the classroom.

How can teachers help students handle the risks of publicly sharing and debating ideas?

As Davis and colleagues (1990) suggest, constructivist teaching and learning involves students and teachers in "complex" discourse, communal attempts to "negotiate and renegotiate meaning" through public discussion and debate of their conjectures, ideas, methods, solutions, and questions. Like most constructivist teachers, Annie Keith strives to find ways to help students feel safe in presenting and discussing their ideas; yet she also strives to have students think and work like mathematicians—who ask hard questions, publicly wrestle with ideas, and are called on to justify their thinking.

In the preceding excerpt, Keith had to deal with the tensions produced by these goals, which might be seen as opposing. She modeled for the class her attitude that although students may have different ideas and come from diverse backgrounds, these differences are valued, and everybody can learn from each other. She showed respect for Peter's idea, even though the "touchpoint" method of addition depends much more on rote learning than the methods she personally might espouse. Yet she also helped Peter understand that part of learning is questioning and clarifying one's own ideas and those of others—that asking "Why?"

and "How do you know?" and "What do you mean by that?" are important parts of the classroom discourse. Finally, Keith offered Peter the dignity of recovering from his upset in private and trusted him with the decision of when to rejoin the group.

> I think that's something that's really important, that they should know where their frustration point is. When [the students] feel that frustration point, [they] need to back off and come back at it again. . . . Kids will walk out of here and get a drink and come back and work. . . . I think that's really good to learn that as a kid, so as an adult you know where your point is.

Keith's concern for Peter's feelings, respect for his dignity, and trust in his judgment seemed a part of what helped Peter maintain his self-confidence and enthusiasm in the face of his critical-sounding peers and gave him the courage to return to the fray.

Inventing the Knowledge Needed for Teaching

We have used these two cases to investigate several issues faced by many teachers who are trying to teach in more constructivist ways. Deborah Ball and Annie Keith show some commonalities that may illuminate some general characteristics of successful constructivist teaching:

• Both teachers see themselves as learners—learning from their students, their colleagues, and their own investigations of mathematics. They both assert that they have changed and learned throughout the course of their teaching experiences, continuously creating and reinventing their practices as teachers.

• Both believe it is essential to listen to and respect students' ideas, yet also value students' coming to understand the mathematical constructions of the wider disciplinary community.

• Both want students to develop their own strategies for "sense-making," rather than depending on the authority of the teacher or text to determine what is the "right" answer.

• Both strive to involve students in a classroom community where they will learn to share, debate, construct, modify, and develop important mathematical ideas and ways of problem-solving.

Yet the unique flavor of these teachers also comes through clearly in these excerpts. Each teacher is an individual, not a carbon copy of some ideal model of a "constructivist teacher"; and each solves the specific dilemmas she encounters in her ongoing practice in her own ways. Indeed, a generalized model or prescription for constructivist education would be an oxymoron. A prescription implies a generalized, decontextualized list that would be good for all times and all situations, a set of procedures or solutions that some outside person could construct and then transmit or transfer to practicing educators. But just as students are continuously constructing new knowledge that is contextualized within a community of learners and within specific personal situations, so are teachers. Both Keith and Ball serve as examples of growth and change in their own knowledge, understanding, and teaching within their own learning and teaching contexts.

But these two cases raise a new puzzle and tension for practicing educators, researchers, and reformers to address, for they suggest new ways of thinking about the construction of a knowledge base for practice. In decades past, researchers, policymakers, and practitioners have worked within a model of knowledge in which researchers and policymakers construct knowledge and then "disseminate" or transmit this knowledge to administrators and teachers who are supposed to "implement" it in their schools and classrooms. Within a constructivist model, teachers, students, administrators, policymakers, and other educators would all be involved in "learning" and would participate with researchers in the ongoing construction of a knowledge base for practice (e.g., Cohen and Barnes in press). How might this be brought about?

Again, consider the cases of the two teachers we have discussed. Both Ball and Keith participate as active members of several learning or discourse communities (see Keith 1992). Ball has been an elementary schoolteacher for many years and is a major participant in the National Council of Teachers of Mathematics. Keith belongs to professional associations in reading and mathematics; she also participates in the community defined by the teachers in her school and, more specifically, by the 1st grade teachers on her primary team with whom she has weekly meetings to plan and construct curriculum.

Both teachers are also members of a community of educational scholars and researchers. In her research and communication with colleagues at Michigan State University, Ball participates in a rich discourse about the teaching and learning of mathematics. Keith also participates in a community of researchers and university professors centered around CGI. She often spends her days off at the CGI offices at the university, talking about her teaching with the researchers and graduate students involved with CGI. She also helps shape this project through her participation as a mentor teacher. Through these personal contacts, both teachers have access to the current thinking, knowledge, and understandings of scholars to which most teachers would not have access, except through reading research articles or hearing a scholar give an invited address at a national conference. The benefits of these interactions are certainly not one sided, since through conversations with Ball or Keith, other scholars also have access to the knowledge, thinking, and understanding of an elementary schoolteacher, fresh from the challenges of learning and teaching a new mathematics in new ways to a diverse group of wriggling, laughing, boisterous young learners.

A third important learning community for both Ball and Keith is that of their students. We have already mentioned how Ball sees herself as constantly learning from her students, for example, from Sean about the unique characteristics of "Sean numbers." Keith describes herself as having hated mathematics to the point of being "math phobic" throughout her own schooling. In her preservice teacher education at the University of Wisconsin-Madison, she took two courses on mathematics for elementary schoolteachers; but when she began teaching seven years ago, she still did not feel comfortable with mathematics. The turning point was when she became involved in the CGI project after her first year of teaching. Keith credits her 1st grade students for much of her growth in understanding, confidence, and interest in mathematics over the past six years:

> What have I learned? I've learned how much fun math really is, and how exciting it is. I think I probably learned even this whole idea of place value with understanding through watching these kids. You know, really getting at their thinking and understanding. . . . I just find them so incredible.

The experiences of these teachers suggest that one way practicing educators can construct a knowledge base for constructivist learning and teaching is through personally participating in diverse communities of researchers, teachers, and learners. But we do not suggest such participation is the only way. Indeed, to prescribe this as *the way* would be antithetical to constructivist views. The challenge is for scholars, administrators, teachers, and learners to work together to invent and reinvent ways in which they can construct the knowledge base needed for learning and teaching in the next fifty years.

References

Ball, D.L. (1990). "Reflections and Deflections of Policy: The Case of Carol Turner." *Educational Evaluation and Policy Analysis* 12, 3: 247–260.

Ball, D.L. (May 1991). Materials from presentation at the annual meeting of the National Council of Teachers of Mathematics, New Orleans.

Ball, D.L. (in press). "With an Eye on the Mathematical Horizon: Dilemmas of Teaching Elementary School Mathematics." *Elementary School Journal*.

Bauersfeld, H. (1991). "The Structuring of the Structures: Development and Function of Mathematizing as a Social Practice." In *Constructivism and Education*, edited by L.P. Steffe. Hillsdale, N.J.: Lawrence Erlbaum.

Brownell, W.A. (1935). "Psychological Considerations in the Learning and Teaching of Arithmetic." In *The Teaching and Learning of Arithmetic: The Tenth Yearbook of the National Council of Teachers of Mathematics* (pp. 1–31), edited by W.E. Reeve. New York: Teachers College Press.

Carnegie Forum on Education and the Economy. (1986). *A Nation Prepared: Teachers for the 21st Century*. New York: Carnegie Corporation.

Carpenter, T.P., E. Fennema, and M.L. Franke. (1992, April). "Cognitively-Guided Instruction: Building the Primary Mathematics Curriculum on Children's Informal Mathematical Knowledge." Paper presented at the annual meeting of the American Educational Research Association, San Francisco.

Carpenter, T.P., E. Fennema, P.L. Peterson, C. Chiang, and M. Loef. (1989). "Using Children's Mathematics Thinking in Classroom Teaching: An Experimental Study." *American Educational Research Journal* 26: 499–531.

Carter, K. (April 1992). "The Place of Story in Research on Teaching." Paper presented at the annual meeting of the American Educational Research Association, San Francisco.

Cohen, D.K. (1990). "A Revolution in One Classroom: The Case of Mrs. Oublier." *Educational Evalluation and Policy Analysis* 12, 3: 311–329.

Cohen, D.K., and C.A. Barnes. (in press). "A New Pedagogy for Policy." In *Teaching for Understanding: Challenges for Practice, Research, and Policy*, edited by D.K. Cohen, M.W. McLaughlin, and J.E. Talbert. San Francisco: Jossey-Bass.

Darling-Hammond, L. (1990). "Instructional Policy into Practice: 'The Power of the Bottom over the Top.'" *Educational Policy and Practice Analysis* 12, 3: 339–349.

Darling-Hammond, L., and J. Snyder. (1992). "Curriculum Studies and the Traditions of Inquiry: The Scientific Tradition." In *Handbook of Research on Curriculum* (pp. 41–78), edited by P.W. Jackson. New York: Macmillan.

Davis, R.B., C.A. Maher, and N. Noddings. (1990). *Constructivist Views on the Teaching and Learning of Mathematics*. Reston, Va.: National Council of Teachers of Mathematics.

Dunkin, M., and B. Biddle. (1974). *The Study of Teaching*. New York: Holt, Rinehart, and Winston.

Gage, N.L. (1963). "Paradigms for Research on Teaching." In *Handbook for Research on Teaching*, edited by N.L. Gage. Chicago: Rand McNally.

The Holmes Group. (1990). *Tomorrow's Schools: Principles for the Design of Professional Development Schools*. East Lansing, Mich.: The Holmes Group.

Keith, J.A. (April 1992). "Teachers' Beliefs, Thinking, and Practice in a Research-Based Mathematics Approach: A Participating Teacher's Perspective." Discussant remarks presented at the annual meeting of the American Educational Research Association, San Francisco.

Kuhn, T. (1970). *The Structure of Scientific Revolutions*. Chicago: University of Chicago Press.

Lagemann, E.C. (1989). "The Plural Worlds of Educational Research." *History of Education Quarterly* 29, 2: 185–214.

Lakatos, I. (1970). "Falsification and Methodology of Scientific Research Programmes." In *Criticism and the Growth of Knowledge* (pp. 91–196), edited by I. Lakatos and A. Musgrave. Cambridge, England: Cambridge University Press.

Lakatos, I. (1976). *Proofs and Refutations*. Cambridge, England: Cambridge University Press.

Lampert, M. (1985). "How Do Teachers Manage to Teach? Perspectives on Problems in Practice." *Harvard Educational Review* 55: 178–194.

Lampert, M. (1990). "Connecting Inventions and Conventions." In *Transforming Children's Mathematics Education: International Perspectives* (pp. 253–265), edited by L.P. Steffe and T. Wood. Hillsdale, N.J.: Lawrence Erlbaum.

Lieberman, A. (1992). "The Meaning of Scholarly Activity and the Building of Community." *Educational Researcher* 21, 6: 5–12.

McLellan, J.A., and J. Dewey. (1895). *The Psychology of Number*. New York: D. Appleton and Co.

National Council of Teachers of Mathematics. (1991). *Professional Standards for Teaching Mathematics*. Reston, Va.: National Council of Teachers of Mathematics.

National Research Council. (1989). *Everybody Counts: A Report to the Nation on the Future of Mathematics Education*. Washington, D.C.: National Academy Press.

Oliver, A., H. Murray, and P. Human. (1991). "Children's Solution Strategies for Division Problems." *Proceedings of the Thirteenth Annual Meeting of Psychology of Mathematics Education-North American Chapter*, Blacksburg, Va.

Peterson, P.L. (1990). "Doing More in the Same Amount of Time: Cathy Swift." *Educational Evaluation and Policy Analysis* 12, 3: 261–280

Peterson, P.L. (April 1992). "Using Teachers' and Learners' Knowledge to Transform Teaching." Paper presented at the annual meeting of the American Educational Research Association, San Francisco.

Peterson, P.L., E. Fennema, and T. Carpenter. (1991). "Using Children's Mathematical Knowledge." In *Teaching Advanced Skills to At-Risk Children* (pp. 68–111), edited by B. Means, C. Chelemer, and M.S. Knapp. San Francisco: Jossey-Bass.

Piaget, J. (1970). "Piaget's Theory." In *Carmichael's Manual of Child Psychology: Vol. 1*, pp. 703–732, edited by P. Mussen. New York: John Wiley.

Resnick, L.B., and L.E. Klopfer. (1989). *Toward the Thinking Curriculum: Current Cognitive Research*. Alexandria, Va.: ASCD.

Rutherford, F.J., and A. Ahlgren. (1990). *Science for All Americans*. New York: Oxford University Press.

Thorndike, E.L. (1922). *The Psychology of Arithmetic*. New York: MacMillan.

Toulmin, S. (1985). "Pluralism and Responsibility in Post-Modern Science." *Science, Technology, Human Values* 10, 1: 28–38.

Vygotsky, L.S. (1978). *Mind in Society*. Cambridge, Mass.: Harvard University Press.

Wiemers, N.J. (1990). "Transformation and Accomodation: A Case Study of Joe Scott." *Educational Evaluation and Policiy Analysis* 12, 3: 281–292.

Wilson, S.M. (1990). "A Conflict of Interests: The Case of Mark Black." *Educational Evaluation and Policy Analysis* 12, 3: 293–310.

7

Change and Continuity in Supervision and Leadership

Edward Pajak

Fifty years ago, the entire world was caught up in violent conflict between democracy and fascism. In 1946, the year after two atomic bombs abruptly ended World War II, the first computer quietly became operational; and the information age began. For many years after World War II, the planet teetered on the brink of destruction, as democracy squared off against an imposing totalitarian version of communism. The orbiting of the Soviet satellite Sputnik in 1957 triggered unprecedented national interest in education in the United States, first as a means of regaining technological superiority and later as an instrument of social policy. Just as machine and industrial technology reshaped economic, social, and political structures during the 18th and 19th centuries, information and telecommunication technology is transforming those institutions today.

A direct result of advances in information processing and telecommunications is that the challenge of a technologically sophisticated global economy has replaced the specter of totalitarianism as a rallying point for education reform. The business management theorist Peter Drucker, for example, argues that each nation's economic competitiveness depends on its schools' ability to prepare knowledgeable, self-disciplined individuals who recognize responsibility for lifelong learning, and who possess strong analytical, interpersonal, and communication skills (Drucker 1989).

In contrast to Drucker, curriculum theorist Henry Giroux (1989, 1991) is highly critical of the current education reform movement because he sees it as driven by selfish, instrumental, marketplace values while ignoring virtues like social justice and public responsibility. At a time when much of the world at last seems safe for democracy, while people around the globe risk their lives for liberty, many citizens in the traditional western democracies, especially the United States, are resolutely apathetic about political and ethical issues. Citizens demand individual rights while assiduously avoiding social obligations. Immediate advantage takes precedence over long-term interests. But above all, Giroux fears, "American youth are both unconcerned and largely ill-prepared to struggle for and keep democracy alive in the twenty-first century" (1991, p. 46).

Although major differences exist in the positions expressed by Drucker and Giroux that cannot be dismissed and should not be diminished, these authors agree on several crucial points concerning education. First, schools are critically important to the future of individuals and society because knowledge and the ability to use it increasingly represent power. For Drucker the power of knowledge is economic, whereas for Giroux that power is political. Second, both agree that schools should educate students to take responsibility for their own lives, to acquire and produce knowledge independently, to think critically and creatively, and to be capable of solving important problems. Finally, both agree that democratic society cannot well tolerate the growing disparity between the advantaged who possess knowledge and the disadvantaged who do not.

In sum, the technology of information and telecommunication is drastically reshaping political, economic, and social realities around the world. The very nature of knowledge itself, as well as its production, control, and dissemination, may be changing (Lyotard 1984). Educators are being called on today to rethink and restructure how schools operate and how teachers relate to students, to each other, to families, and to communities—as well as how schools relate to business and government. We sorely need new ways of thinking about educational supervision and leadership as we confront the technological, social, political, and moral issues of today.

An Overview

Throughout the 20th century, writers on the topic of supervision have kept the concept of educational leadership vibrant. The Association for Supervision and Curriculum Development (ASCD) has published some of the most significant literature in the field. The origin of ASCD can be traced to 1943, the year in which the National Education Association (NEA) Department of Supervisors and Directors of Instruction (DSDI) merged with the Society for Curriculum Study to form the Department of Supervision and Curriculum Development. In accordance with this momentous event, the publication committee of the 1943 Yearbook, *Leadership at Work*, set for itself an appropriately challenging task, namely:

> To track down *instructional leadership* to its lair, and once having it firmly in hand to nail its hide to the side of the house so that all good educational pilgrims who came that way in search of this golden fleece could recognize it and benefit therefrom (DSDI 1943, p. 1).

The committee eventually determined that "traces of instructional leadership were abundant," but that "no pure species" could be located. In fact, it was argued that "instructional leadership cannot be nailed down" nor even confined to "tight fences" (DSDI 1943, pp. 14–16). The title of a recent ASCD book, *Leadership: Examining the Elusive* (Sheive and Schoenheit 1987), suggests that despite occasional sightings, the golden fleece continues to evade its pursuers.

Quests for this golden fleece, however, have had some success. The supervision literature of the past fifty years reveals a remarkable consistency, in fact, in the leadership practices that have been advocated. The 1943 Yearbook, *Leadership at Work*, for example, offered advice that has an astonishingly contemporary ring:

> 1. Worry less about *having* ideas and more about *finding* them. Lots of people have ideas. . . .
> 2. Start with *real problems* that make sense to everybody and let technics come along as they're needed. The technics don't work unless they're used to help do things people want to get done. . . .
> 3. Give cooperative planning a *real* chance. . . . When people *work together* things happen that don't happen if you work alone (DSDI 1943, p. 14).

Figure 7.1 summarizes four different conceptions of educational leadership that are described in this chapter. First, an image of the supervisor as a "democratic educator" emerged early in the 20th century. This view, derived largely from the philosophy of John Dewey, coalesced around the time that ASCD was formed and dominated supervisory thought during the 1940s and 1950s. Many educators considered leadership to be a group function guided by the scientific method; and they described it as *educational* in the sense that leaders helped prepare others—students, teachers, and community members—for the responsibilities of life in a democracy. Many educators viewed schools, in turn, as microcosms and incubators of democratic citizenship.

Figure 7.1

Shifting Conceptions of Educational Leadership

Characteristic	1940s–1950s	1960s–1970s	1980s	1990s
Image of the Educational Leader	Democratic Educator	Organizational Change Agent	Corporate Visionary	Teacher
Mission	Maintain and extend democracy	Social change and curriculum implementation	Economic competition	Social, political, and economic revitalization
Method	Problem-centered cooperative action	Collaborative implementation	Legislated bureaucratic policy	Decentralized, team-focused action
Guiding Principles	Democracy and scientific method	Social systems, innovation, and organizational goals	Vision, culture, reflection, and transformation	Communication, learning organization

The image of the supervisor as "organizational change agent" developed during the 1960s and 1970s. During this time, many educators came to view schools as instruments of national policy, and educational leaders increasingly took on the tasks of implementing and facilitating changes initiated by policymakers and experts at the national level. Leaders used collaborative planning to ensure that teachers, students, and community members accepted innovations and the goals of the school organization. Educational supervision began to draw on social systems theory and business management literature for insights into the nature of leadership.

The image of the educational leader as "corporate visionary" took hold during the 1980s as the federal government championed business interests while drastically reducing funding for educational programs. The report *A Nation at Risk* blamed schools for failing to develop the human resources needed by American industry to compete successfully in the international marketplace. Heavily influenced by the literature of business management and legislation at the state level, many educators began to view educational leadership in terms of types of behavior, usually displayed by principals, who shaped school culture by manipulating symbols and rituals that conformed to personal visions of what schools might become. For example, Deal (1987) emphasized the importance of articulating values, celebrating heroes, and dignifying graduation ceremonies.

Finally, the technological and social realities of the 1990s seem to require that the educational leader be a "teacher," both in the sense that leaders are responsible for teaching those they lead and in the sense of genuine involvement by teams of teachers in creating learning-focused schools. This emerging conception resembles the "democratic leadership" advocated during the 1940s and 1950s in that it unites administrators with teachers, and schools with local communities, in cooperative, problem-solving efforts. But it also incorporates contemporary conceptions of leadership that address the learning needs of information-based organizations.

Each conception of educational leadership described here has influenced the eras that followed its emergence. Although I have suggested discrete labels, supervisory practice is actually "historically embedded" within a legacy of the past. This chapter examines how supervision and leadership have evolved as concepts in the supervision literature and speculates on where they might go next. Rather than try to capture the golden fleece and nail it to the wall, however, I have attempted a more environmentally sensitive approach. At the risk of being accused of "wool gathering," I have accumulated gleanings from bits of fleece found by others along the way; and I have woven them into a fabric that perhaps may serve "good educational pilgrims" almost as well as the fleece itself.

The Origins of Educational Supervision and Leadership

A volume entitled *Chapters on School Supervision*, by William Payne (1875), a Michigan school superintendent, is a seminal source for both supervision and administration as areas of study and practice in education (Glanz 1977, Culbertson 1988). Though supervision and administration have influenced one another subsequently, their development has not been identical.

Authors of many early supervision texts emphasized an inspectorial function and described methods for improving the efficiency and objectivity of tasks that supervisors were expected to perform, such as monitoring and overseeing the curriculum and instruction and evaluating teacher performance and student achievement (Bolin 1987). When writers mentioned leadership at all, they often associated it with personality. Stoops (1918), for example, suggested that "the personality of a supervisor contributes largely to his success." He went on to say that a male supervisor "must be a man among men," whereas "a woman supervisor should be identified with the agressive [sic] women's organizations" (p. 623).

Early in the 20th century, however, a very different theme emerged in the supervision literature that was closely related to "the democratic motive of American education" (Elliott 1914, p. 2). Edward C. Elliott distinguished "administrative efficiency," which demanded "centralization of administrative power," from "supervisory efficiency," which required "*decentralized, cooperative, expert*, supervision" (p. 78, emphasis in the original). Administrators stifled the individuality of teachers and children, Elliott argued, when they misapplied administrative control to the work of teachers and the accomplishments of students. During the 1920s, other authors began arguing that democracy should be a guiding principle of supervisory practice in education (e.g., Hosic 1920, Barr and Burton 1926, Burton 1927, Ayer and Barr 1928, Stone 1929).

The impact of Frederick Taylor's industrial logic on educational administration in the early 20th century has been well chronicled

(Callahan 1962, Tyack 1974). It would be inaccurate to suggest that Taylor's work had no effect on educational supervision, but its impact is often vastly overestimated (e.g., Lucio 1967, Gitlin and Smyth 1989). As early as 1926, Barr and Burton noted in *The Supervision of Instruction*, that Franklin Bobbitt's (1913) adaptation of Taylor's principles of scientific management "has never been especially popular and seems to have had little influence" (1926, p. 75). According to Callahan and Button (1964), the reason that scientific management failed to influence educational supervision was that "the problems of supervision and of teaching method were not readily amenable to investigation in the management frame of reference nor with the techniques available" (1964, p. 90). The field of supervision distinguished itself from administration during the 1930s, Callahan and Button (1964) note, by aligning itself instead with the process of curriculum development and "a new organization, the Association for Supervision and Curriculum Development" (p. 90).

John Dewey's combination of democracy and scientific thinking had a much greater impact on the evolution of supervision and educational leadership than is generally recognized. Dewey's definition of scientific problem solving, however, differed greatly from that of Bobbitt and other advocates of measurement and should not be confused with scientific management (McNeil 1982, McKernan 1987). When Dewey called for the application of the scientific method to the solving of educational problems, he was referring to *reflective inquiry* as a guide to practice (1929). Dewey's notion of consciously reasoned cooperative problem solving, rather than the rules generated by science, became a major guiding principle of supervisory leadership. In the early 1930s, publications by DSDI (as mentioned earlier, one of ASCD's forebears in the NEA) emphasized the need for greater involvement by teachers in decisions related to instruction, as well as group deliberation and experimentation in solving problems (DSDI 1932, 1933, 1934). Drawing heavily on this body of writing, Barr, Burton, and Brueckner announced in the preface to their 1938 textbook, *Supervision*, that they were deliberately setting out to replace the old concept of the supervisor as an inspector with a cooperative, democratic approach to supervision (1938, p. v). Democratic supervision was intended to replace traditional authority with responsible leadership and would rely on scientific reason and experimentation for direction (1938, pp. 45–74, 283–285).

The Democratic Educational Leader

At the time of ASCD's founding, supervision in education witnessed an unprecedented convergence of educational theory, national policy, and social science research. This alignment culminated in a consensus that democratic educational leadership comprised the essence of supervisory practice. From 1943 to the early 1960s, writers on supervision clarified and elaborated on the concept of democratic educational leadership.

Writing during World War II, the authors of the 1943 Yearbook, *Leadership at Work*, emphasized that leadership in a democracy is not a characteristic possessed by a few, but a responsibility of the many. The yearbook distinguished and contrasted educational leadership with totalitarianism and "old authoritarian" conceptions of supervision, as well as with leadership in military, business, and industrial settings (DSDI 1943, pp. 22–30). Educational leaders, according to this view, do not treat people as means to accomplish an end. An educational leader, whether an administrator or a teacher, "tries to educate the person he is leading," the authors maintained, to the point that "leading comes to be educating." "Leadership from an educational viewpoint" was "synonymous with stimulating people to participate in planning, executing, and evaluating the experiences" through which they learn and work together (DSDI 1943, p. 24). The 1943 Yearbook thus portrayed educational leadership as an *educative force* that expanded the horizons of the group by encouraging members to think beyond the level of existing opinion and practice. Such leadership relied on reason and built within others the ability to analyze problems and improve methods of working and living.

Published one year after the end of World War II, the 1946 ASCD Yearbook, *Leadership Through Supervision*, began with the following ominous sentence: "With earth-shattering impact, an atomic bomb dropped on Hiroshima." This terrifying historical fact marked the end of the struggle against fascism—and the beginning of the struggle to master technology. Suddenly, the "major function" of education became "to help young people understand and practice the democratic way of life in a technological age" and to help society "achieve control over its technology" (Van Til 1946, p. 2).

The authors of *Leadership Through Supervision* argued that democracy should not only guide the governance of schools, but also provide direction to curriculum and classroom experiences and serve as an arbiter of value and morality. Supervisors were encouraged to take the lead in translating democratic philosophy into educational action. The work, training, and personality of the ideal supervisor, the authors stated, should extend beyond the local and immediate problems of students and teachers to include the problems of society as well. If democracy is to survive the technological age, the 1946 Yearbook cautioned, its citizens must openly address issues of war and peace, international cooperation and understanding, class conflict, poverty amidst plenty, urban isolation and anonymity, concentration of wealth among relatively few, centralization of government, and the quality of food, health, and shelter available to young people (Van Til 1946, p. 3).

A third ASCD publication of the 1940s that helped to shape thinking in the field of supervision was *Group Processes in Supervision* (1948). This short book, which drew heavily on the research and writings of Kurt Lewin and his associates, portrayed educational leadership in the terms and concepts of social science. The purpose of educational leadership, according to this publication, was to "promote the demo-cratic way of life," among students as well as faculty. The authors emphasized that every child should serve as a leader and a follower at different times; should share and receive ideas, materials, and criticism; and should cooperate in solving group problems at each grade level.

Supervision literature during the 1950s continued to echo and refine the theme of democratic educational leadership. Two publica-tions glorified small and rural schools for exemplifying a democratic ideal. An ASCD publication, *Instructional Leadership in Small Schools* (1951), praised administrators in smaller schools for letting teachers take initiative in solving school problems. Formal leaders were encour-aged to release the talents of group members and work with them "toward common goals in order to perpetuate democracy." Another work, *Supervision in Rural Schools* (Franseth 1955), depicted supervi-sion as a "leadership service" that applied action research to problems of concern to teachers. The author considered supervision most effec-tive when it provided an atmosphere of acceptance, support, and understanding; when a scientific approach was used in the study of problems; and when teachers helped determine what supervisors should do.

The 1960 ASCD Yearbook, *Leadership for Improving Instruction*, reflected the concern then held by many that the Soviet Union might prove too powerful a competitor for the western democracies. The authors referred to a "basic and pervading fear" in the United States "that an outside force may become so strong that it will prevent this nation from continuing to practice democratic values." Despite such outpourings of national anxiety, the 1960 ASCD Yearbook represents one of the clearest statements of democratic educational leadership in the supervision literature. The application of democratic theory to schools, the authors declared, "rests upon the premise that democracy is ever in the state of becoming what people make it" (ASCD 1960, p. 26). The book placed great emphasis on leadership that emerges from within the group to meet the challenges of the situation at hand. It emphasized that all individuals and groups in the school and community have leadership potential that should be exercised.

The Organizational Change Agent

Three events forced a drastic redefinition of supervisory leadership in education during the 1960s and 1970s—a greater federal role in public education, the institution of collective bargaining in many states, and an increase in the size and complexity of schools and districts. In the mid-1960s, federal policies, such as the War on Poverty and efforts to racially integrate schools, substantially affected public education. From 1963 to 1967, federal funds appropriated for education and related activities increased from $5.4 billion to over $12 billion. Federal funds subsidized Operation Head Start for preschoolers, the Vocational Education Act, the Elementary and Secondary Education Act, and other education programs. Many educational innovations also were introduced during the 1960s, including the "new" mathematics, wider use of team teaching, audiovisual aids, bilingual education, open classrooms, and textbooks that promoted more positive images of ethnic and racial minorities (Morris, 1976). The notion of the supervisor as "change agent" emerged during this period as schools became instruments of national policy.

As early as 1961, the proposal was made that school leaders should be less concerned about whether their behavior was democratic and more concerned with whether it was effective in bringing about change and convincing others "that a new course of action is a better one" (McCoy 1961). In 1963, Cunningham suggested that supervisors needed to reexamine their roles in terms of social systems theory and begin thinking of themselves as "change agents."

The idea that educational leaders should be agents of change had been suggested years earlier by Kenneth D. Benne (1949), as a means of contributing to a more democratic society (Karier 1982). Cunningham's (1963) recommendations, however, expressed a social engineering perspective that shifted the impetus for change from teachers to supervisors. Supervisors as change agents, according to Cunningham, made their positions clear and shared their objectives with faculties and staff only *after* identifying problems; establishing priorities; discerning importance; and deciding to whom, where, and how an intervention would be introduced.

By the mid-1960s, the supervision literature touted the change-agent role as a means of empowering supervisors who felt "alienated from the educational scene" (Klohr 1965) and as a solution to the "state of confusion in many schools" (Babcock 1965) that resulted from "accelerating change" in American culture (Holmes and Seawell 1965). The call for supervisors to become change agents continued well into the 1970s (Bagby 1972, Harris 1975), resulting in the observation that the expressions "change" and "innovation" had acquired the exalted status of "God words" among educators (Hughes and Achilles 1971).

Responding to "the needs of our rapidly changing society" seemed to replace a concern for the needs of students and the problems of teachers and administrators among some authors in supervision (e.g., Sommerville 1971, Ogletree 1972). In fact, much of the supervision literature during the 1960s and 1970s became heavily concerned with gaining teacher compliance in accepting innovations. Action research became a means to "shatter the complacency which results from long experience" (Heffernan and Bishop 1965), rather than a way that supervisors, teachers, and others could solve problems together. Instead of helping teachers change the situations in which they worked, supervisors as change agents were more concerned with changing teachers and their behavior (e.g., Drummond 1964, MacDonald 1966). In the 1960s and 1970s, authors in supervision no longer considered teachers to be the source of creative ideas and solutions to problems, but a problem of "resistance" that had to be overcome (Mosher and Purpel 1972, Toepfer 1973). Authors urged broad involvement in the change process because of its "functional" value in overcoming resistance to change and ensuring that "changes are carried out" (Harris 1966, 1969). Supervisors were to keep teachers informed so that they understood the rationale for the innovation and how implementation should occur (Toepfer 1973).

The social programs and educational innovations of the 1960s and 1970s, though undeniably admirable in their intentions and necessary, effectively removed the initiative for change from educators in local schools and dislodged the tradition of leadership that had been based on democratic principles derived from educational philosophy. Increased militancy among teachers' unions during the 1960s added to the turmoil in education and made supervisors' traditional appeals to a single profession seem irrelevant. In 1968 alone, approximately 100 strikes were called over salary and working-condition issues in school districts across the United States. The NEA and the American Federation of Teachers (AFT) soon began to compete in a struggle to organize teachers nationwide (Morris 1976).

Supervisors had been in the forefront of efforts to give teachers more power and to involve them in decisions during the 1940s and 1950s. But collective bargaining effectively usurped the supervisor's tools of cooperative planning and problem solving, and reinterpreted decisions affecting instruction and curriculum as conditions of employment (Kinsella, Klopf, Shafer, and Young 1969). A specially appointed ASCD Commission on Problems of Supervisors and Curriculum Workers struggled with the fact that unionization and collective bargaining in education suddenly placed supervisors and curriculum directors in an untenable no-man's land between management and labor (Kinsella et al. 1969, Young 1969).

Thus, changing values and redistributions of power in society and education during the 1960s dramatically altered the role of the supervisor as a facilitator of change (Goldhammer, K., Suttle, Aldridge, and Becker 1967), necessitating a redefinition of the meaning of supervisory leadership. This redefinition affected the entire field, but was most obviously evident in the writings of William H. Lucio, a prominent figure in supervision at the time.

The most commonly repeated version of the development of thought in educational supervision during the 20th century is generally attributed to Lucio (Sergiovanni 1975, Anderson 1986). In a 1967 ASCD publication, *Supervision: Perspectives and Propositions*, Lucio claimed that supervision theory early in this century was heavily influenced by Frederick Taylor's book, *The Principles of Scientific Management* (1911). Partly in reaction to the severely technical nature of Taylor's prescriptions, according to Lucio's account, supervision next fell under the spell of the "human relations" school of management during the 1930s. The "human relations" perspective, based on the research of Elton Mayo and his associates, emphasized the importance of satisfying workers' psychological and social needs. School supervision followed industry, Lucio contended, in the mistaken notion that high morale would result in high productivity. Lucio next described how dissatisfaction with the results of emphasizing the interests of individuals over those of the organization led management theorists like Chris Argyris and Douglas M. McGregor to try to reconcile the scientific management and human relations viewpoints. The research and theory of Argyris and McGregor, Lucio proposed, held promising applications for school supervision (1967).

This perspective apparently represented a major intellectual departure for Lucio, who only five years earlier (Lucio and McNeil 1962) had described the history of supervisory thought with *no mention* of Frederick Taylor or Elton Mayo. Instead of praising the work of Argyris and MacGregor, he had advocated that supervision be directed by "reason and practical intelligence," a position he referenced liberally with the work of John Dewey (1910, 1927) and George S. Counts (1954).

Although other authors had already introduced concepts from business management into the supervision literature (e.g., Foster 1964), Lucio was the first to link supervision to management theory within an historical context. A careful reading of the supervision literature before the mid-1960s, however, reveals that *Lucio's 1967 version of the evolution of supervision in education is highly questionable*. On the positive side, Lucio opened the field of supervision to new perspectives on the organization of schools, motivation of teachers, and leadership (e.g., Sergiovanni 1975). A most unfortunate outcome, however, is that the wealth of supervision literature written in the tradition of progressive educational philosophy and its unique conception of educational leadership as a democratic and educative force was soon abandoned by most authors in the field.

Only one year after Lucio's 1967 publication, a report sponsored by the U.S. Department of Health, Education, and Welfare seemed to deliver the *coup de grace* to democratic leadership. The author concluded that educational supervisors should rely more on formal power and technical competence than on democratic strategies and informal influence (Helwig 1968).

Democratic educational leadership rapidly lost ground during the 1970s to the view that leadership is a function of position in the organization and should be adaptable to fit the requirements of different situations. The increasing size and complexity of schools and school districts in the United States required supervisors to devote more time and attention to organizational goals, long-range planning, and change strategies (Ogletree 1972; Alfonso, Firth, and Neville 1975; Campbell 1975). Theories of leadership styles from business management and industrial psychology, such as McGregor's Theory X and Theory Y, Blake and Mouton's Managerial Grid, and Reddin's 3–D Theory, became prominent in supervision textbooks (e.g., Sergiovanni and Starratt 1979). Writers urged supervisors to select a leadership approach based on utilitarian "contingencies" instead of philosophical conviction. Several texts defined supervision and leadership in terms of "behaviors" (Harris 1975, Wiles and Lovell 1975, Sergiovanni and Starratt 1979). Others suggested that effectiveness was enhanced by organizationally conferred status and recommended that supervisors should lead others in a direction determined by the supervisor (Alfonso et al. 1975). Although clinical supervision, in a sense, preserved the spirit of democratic leadership, it focused cooperative problem solving and the methods of action research around classroom events and processes (Goldhammer, R. 1969, Cogan 1973) and away from curriculum development and schoolwide concerns.

The Corporate Visionary

During the 1980s, the term *leadership* probably appeared in the education literature more often than in any preceding decade; and writers paid especially close attention to the school principal's role as an instructional leader. Research on characteristics of what were termed "effective schools" in the late 1970s pointed to the principal as a key factor in determining school success (Brookover, Beady, Flood, Schweiter, and Wisenbaker 1979; Edmonds 1979; Rutter, Maughan, Mortimore, Ouston, and Smith 1979). A body of literature soon followed that sought to explain how principals contributed to instructional and curricular improvement and student achievement (Blumberg and Greenfield 1979, rev. ed. 1986; Bossert, Dwyer, Rowan, and Lee 1982; Sweeney 1982; Lightfoot 1983; Dwyer 1984; Little and Bird 1987).

Considerable discussion ensued as well over whether supervisory leadership was derived from an individual's expertise (Smyth 1980) or from managerial skills (Hoyle, English, and Steffy 1985). Reminiscent of Elliott's (1914) distinction between "administrative" and "supervisory efficiency" early in the century, several authors sought to differentiate school leadership from instructional leadership (Reilly 1984), institutional leadership from instructional leadership (Hoy and Forsyth 1986), and management from instructional leadership (Rallis and Highsmith 1986), viewing both elements of each pair as important but separate functions.

Beginning with the publication of *A Nation at Risk*, the 1980s became a decade of school reform. Many reports criticized schools for not keeping pace with changes in society and technology. Many states passed education-reform acts that included heavy doses of top-down management and tighter regulations. State officials expanded monitoring of local schools, and state agencies designed new programs to toughen processes of teacher certification and evaluation (Berry and Ginsburg 1990).

Business leaders' involvement in school reform at the state and local levels began to shape the agenda of schooling and educational leadership during the 1980s. During an extended period of economic growth, the mass media exalted chief executive officers of major corporations; and books on business management became best-sellers. By the late 1980s, an image of the successful educational leader as a "corporate visionary" was prominent. Some authors and practitioners drew direct analogies between schools and business (e.g., Schlechty 1990), encouraging educators to think of students as customers or workers, and to consider concepts like corporate strategy, market research, product development, and quality control.

By 1985, literature on leadership—in both business and education—focused heavily on four concepts: vision, culture, reflection, and transformation.

Vision

Foremost in the literature describing effective principals was the notion of vision, which successful principals were said to possess and unsuccessful principals were said to lack (Manasse 1982, Dwyer 1984, Bryman 1986, Wiles and Bondi 1986, Achilles 1987). Blumberg and Greenfield (1980) may have been the first to suggest that effective principals could "see" what their schools could and should be. The central importance of vision as a quality of leadership also received extensive treatment among authors in business management (Bennis and Nanus 1985, Kouzes and Posner 1988, Peters 1988).

Culture

Related to vision was the concept of "organizational culture," which was associated with organizational effectiveness in both business (Deal and Kennedy 1982, Peters and Waterman 1982, Schein 1985) and education (Patterson, Purkey, and Parker 1986; Deal 1987). The concept of culture called attention to the symbolic and social reality of schools instead of their bureaucratic or technical aspects. For many authors, cultures in organizations represented shared understanding and expectations that give meaning to human action. Writers in the 1980s believed that the vision of effective leaders helped determine the character of organizational culture through symbols, rituals, and storytelling (Deal 1984, Sergiovanni 1984, Firestone and Wilson 1985, Deal 1987).

172

Reflection

A third concept that significantly influenced thinking about leadership during the 1980s was that of the "reflective practitioner." Schön (1983, 1987) noted that problems of professional practice do not usually present themselves as simple, well-formed issues with obvious solutions. He observed that professionals make sense of puzzling problems through a process referred to as a "reflective conversation with the situation" (1983, p. 95). Schön suggested that values, attitudes, and prior understandings provide a sense of direction, goals, purposes, and standards for successful practitioners as they test tentative solutions that inform them about the nature of the problem they are facing. Professionals then adjust their subsequent actions accordingly, based on the new information (Schön 1983, 1987). Schön viewed this process, which he called "reflection-in-action," as guiding the manager's behavior and contributing to the "learning system" of the organization (1983, p. 242).

Transformation

Toward the end of the 1980s, James MacGregor Burns' (1978) conception of "transformational leadership" gained considerable popularity among authors in business (Bass 1985, Bennis and Nanus 1985) and educational leadership (Pajak 1989, Leithwood and Jantzi 1990, Sergiovanni 1990). With transforming leadership, the purposes of leaders and group members become closely joined as they pursue mutual goals and purposes that are related to higher levels of need and moral value (Burns 1978). Authors writing from a business management perspective highlighted the inspirational function of the transformational leader in mobilizing followers to work toward organizational goals. Bennis and Nanus (1985), for example, viewed Lee Iacocca as the prototype of a transformational leader. In contrast, authors in education emphasized that Burns' conception of leadership was grounded in values and morality, which made it particularly well suited for understanding the dynamics of leadership in education (e.g., Pajak 1989, Sergiovanni 1990).

The Leader as Teacher

"The most successful corporation of the 1990s," the magazine *Fortune* recently predicted, "will be something called a learning organization" that is capable of adapting quickly in a rapidly changing environment (Dumaine 1989). Although this maximally adaptive organization is still an ideal, many businesses are already using fluid, problem-focused teams to improve their performance (Dumaine 1991). Many school districts have also moved toward less bureaucratic, decentralized structures (Hill and Bonan 1991). Highly adaptive organizations are expected to become more common in business and education as technology makes society even less stable and predictable than it is now.

Peter Senge, of MIT's Sloan School of Management, points out that responsiveness through structural change is only a first step toward becoming a learning organization (1990a, b). He notes that learning is more than simply taking in information. As educators already know, learning is an organic process of growth that involves the stimulation of higher levels of thinking and creative expression. Because information is the coordinating principle of life, organizations are beginning to resemble organic systems more than mechanical ones. A challenge facing education in the 1990s and beyond is how to facilitate collective learning in classrooms and schools so that new knowledge and creative innovations are generated (Cohen, Lotan, and Leechor 1989; Schlechty 1990; Barth 1991; Fullan and Steigelbauer 1991; Garmston 1991).

Schools are *teaching* organizations by definition, but are not necessarily *learning* organizations. Most schools are designed primarily to transmit information; in other words, they are not designed to generate or invent it. Even schools that teach well may learn poorly if good practice is not constantly improved and internalized through continuous experimentation and feedback. The 1980s focused on getting schools to *teach* better. The future will require that schools *learn* better, as well. Self-disciplined individuals who recognize their responsibility for maintaining relationships and open communication with others are needed to make such an arrangement successful (Drucker 1989). Instead of emanating solely from a formal position in the organization, leadership is expected to emerge from short-term, problem-focused groups, as needed.

Senge (1990a, 1990b) proposes that popular images of leaders as heroes, and presumably scapegoats as well, are products of nonsystemic thinking. In contrast, he suggests, leaders in learning organizations recognize that they are part of a highly interrelated and interactive system; and they devote their time and energies to the comparatively less glamorous roles of designer, steward, and teacher. The role of designer requires a systemic sense of vision and core values, according to Senge, and a nurturance of effective learning processes. The role of steward implies a commitment of service to the mission of the organization and to the people within it. But it is the leadership role of teacher, Senge insists, that is most central to the fundamental process of learning as an organization:

> Leaders as teachers help people *restructure their views of reality* to see beyond the superficial conditions and events into the underlying causes of problems—and therefore to see new possibilities for shaping the future (1990b, p. 12).

Burns (1978) suggested that transformational leaders come very close to being great teachers. Thus, one might conclude that leaders in politics, business, and education must become more like teachers if they aspire to the leadership that Burns describes as transformational. Giroux, in fact, combines the role of teacher with that of transformational leader (1989, 1991). He calls for administrators and teachers to exercise leadership by becoming "transformative intellectuals" who think about and act on powerful ideas, instead of simply clerks and technicians who do as they are told. Giroux describes transformative intellectuals as:

> professionals who reflect on the ideological principles that inform their practice, connect pedagogical theory and practice to wider social issues, and work together to share ideas, exercise power over the conditions of their labor, and embody in their teaching a vision of a better and more humane life (1989, p. 729).

Senge's definition of the leader as teacher and Giroux's definition of the transformative intellectual have much in common—and they both reflect the view of leadership as a democratic, educational force that was prominent in the educational supervision literature of the 1940s and 1950s. Senge and Giroux agree that the *educational function* of leadership is most appropriate for today's emerging reality. In fact, the elements they include in their images of the leader overlap substantially: (1) an empowerment of self and others through cooperative effort, (2) an intellectual activity that helps group members transcend superficial understanding, (3) the collective application of knowledge to practical problems, and (4) a commitment to making the future somehow better than the present. These four common elements can be used to identify ways that educational leaders can encourage and facilitate organizational learning in their schools.

Element 1—Empowering Self and Others

Democratic leadership declined during the 1970s and 1980s, in part, because it appeared inefficient. As recent world events have demonstrated, however, democracy is an efficient form of organization, especially under conditions of change. Supervision in education has long been associated with democratic principles, and no potent educational leadership in modern society is possible without democracy as a central tenet. Without a common philosophical basis, the supervisory tasks of classroom observation, curriculum development, and staff development are insufficient because separately these tasks lack the capacity to transform schools into learning organizations, no matter how highly refined the techniques. Democracy in a school that is a learning organization goes beyond representative governance. Rather, democracy is action oriented with direct participation by all on problem-focused teams. Important decisions are based on group consensus achieved through dialogue, not majority rule (see Heslep 1989, pp. 195–220).

Allowing people time to discuss common concerns and goals is itself empowering to some degree. Teachers, administrators, and others need opportunities to engage in conversations to begin transforming the social reality of schools. Because they have worked so long in isolation, however, most administrators and teachers are likely to need training and practice in working cooperatively with colleagues, members of the community, and students.

Element 2—Transcending Superficial Understanding

Educational leaders have traditionally been taught and encouraged to break problems down into smaller and smaller pieces to make them more manageable. A difficulty with this approach is that smaller problems get solved while larger and more pressing problems get worse. Social systems theory, popular in the supervision literature during the 1960s, as well as narrative understanding (Bruner 1986), can help participants in an organization to see the "big picture" and understand how the elements composing the whole are related and interconnected.

A holistic and integrated perspective is necessary to determine and address the underlying systemic causes of problems. The most obvious solutions to problems are often temporarily effective because only the symptoms of the problem get treated. A holistic understanding reveals that the solutions to problems facing students, families, local communities, and schools today will not be found in the classroom alone. Systemic solutions must include institutions that make up the organizational environment of schools, such as business and local government. But schools should also be linked, through administrators, teachers, and students, to organizations like the Girl Scouts and Boy Scouts, Big Brothers and Big Sisters, the Lions Club, the American Red

Cross, and other volunteer groups. A difficulty with many business-school partnerships is that they tend to be patronizing. Partnerships with volunteer groups can and should be reciprocal and mutually beneficial, not just one-way.

Teacher unions are another important part of the "big picture" that must be included if effective and long-lasting solutions are being sought. Efforts by unions in some districts to assume responsibility for professional development and school success represent a promising trend (Hill and Bonan 1991).

Element 3—Applying Knowledge to Practical Problems

Culture serves two major functions in an organization (Schein 1985). First, it reduces anxiety by providing people with familiarity and predictability. Rituals and myths can be powerful tools for gaining compliance because such cultural symbols allay unconscious fears and make people feel secure.

Second, culture functions as a learning tool for processing new data and generating new knowledge and understandings. This learning function is especially important for helping the organization survive and succeed when adapting to a rapidly changing and unpredictable environment (Schein 1985). Rationality has a bad name among some authors in education because of its overzealous misapplication. As Callahan (1962) pointed out, what makes rational sense for business is not always reasonable for schools. Yet rational thinking is essential for making conscious choices about the realities we construct. Encouraging rational thinking is the educator's stock in trade. Rationality becomes offensive only when it is used to control people rather than to solve problems.

A weakness in relying on the leader alone as a reflective practitioner is that one person often cannot directly observe the consequences of choices in a complex organization, either because the consequences take place in another location or because the consequences are delayed and not identified with the original choice (Senge 1990a). In "loosely coupled" systems like schools, the link between intentions and actions—as well as between actions and outcomes—is especially imprecise (Weick 1982). Dewey's *cooperative*, action-oriented inquiry (Torbert 1990), which incorporates multiple and diverse perspectives, remains a most promising alternative for generating new knowledge and creative innovations (Westbrook 1991).

Element 4—Making the Future Better Than the Present

History is full of examples of people who conceived of a better future and convinced others to believe in their vision. In an information-rich environment, however, no single individual is likely to have all the pieces of the puzzle needed to make sense of the situation. Furthermore, hero-worship and the manipulation of symbols and rituals to gain compliance represent a retreat from democracy and come dangerously close to sanctioning a totalitarian impulse. Vision might better be thought of as a social phenomenon, something constructed collectively by the members of a group.

Not every collective vision is moral, however, even if arrived at democratically. A collective vision in a democracy is moral to the extent that it expresses, maintains, and extends the principles of justice, freedom, equality, and responsibility. Sometime during the 1970s, educational leadership lost its moral compass. The emphasis during the 1980s shifted away from "what's right" to "what works" in the short run. Contemporary thinking about leadership calls attention to the issues of value and meaning, which have special significance today, both nationally and internationally. Our ethical responsibilities as leaders must keep pace with our ability to accomplish change in schools. Educational supervision as a specialized area of practice and study must renew its traditional dialogue about the social and political responsibilities of educational leadership in a democratic society and, especially, the implications of those responsibilities for curriculum and instruction.

* * *

The world recently crossed the threshold of an era that is as disruptive and full of promise as the Industrial Revolution. Schools are at the forefront of these changes, and schools in the western democracies are among the first to be affected. New technologies are not only reshaping curriculum and instruction; they are also changing the social, economic, and political context of schooling throughout the world. At the moment, some of these changes seem to be for the worse.

As if preparing workers for the information age were not sufficiently challenging, educational leadership must somehow address the more pressing fact that many families and communities can no longer be depended on to provide the kind of environment that students need for personal and academic growth (Cunningham 1990). Large numbers of students come to school today alienated, chemically dependent, abused, pregnant, hungry, malnourished, diseased, chronically depressed, poor, homeless, and often violent. The learning capacities of many of them are diminished, even before they are born, as a result of inadequate maternal diets and prenatal drug and alcohol consumption (Kirst, McLaughlin, and Massell 1990). Schools have early received the full force of these problems, but the growing disintegration of families and communities spawning these problems now poses a new, major threat to the survival of democracy itself. Unfortunately, traditional, government-sponsored programs to alleviate these conditions seem impotent. Practitioner-led research and action are needed at the local level, instead of centralized social engineering, to improve schools and the environments that students inhabit.

Educational leadership must define its responsibility to include attention to the social conditions that affect the learning of children. But poverty, homelessness, child abuse, discrimination, sexual promiscuity, and drug and alcohol abuse are such serious social problems that schools cannot be expected to solve them alone. Both educators and the public must develop mechanisms that enable broader participation and encourage wider responsibility for student success (Hodgkinson 1991, Welker 1991).

Today's educational leaders face another complicated challenge: students are extraordinarily diverse in their cultural backgrounds, languages, and past experiences. Democratic values must be shared by members of diverse groups while simultaneously allowing and encouraging them to maintain their cultures and lifestyles. Although cultural assimilation may not be entirely possible, *political* assimilation is essential (Giroux 1991). Educators need to understand that education is potentially more than a system for transferring knowledge, skills, and even culture from one generation to the next. Education can and will be a system for *inventing* knowledge, skills, and culture.

A major component of almost every plan to improve education calls for the better use of new and emerging technologies. Students will need more than technical skills, however, to survive in tomorrow's technologically sophisticated world. Curriculum must address the social origins of technology and the influence that technology has on society. Students need to confront pressing issues such as: What are the consequences of new and emerging technology for life in a democracy? How does technology affect the manner in which people relate to one another? How does technology affect the manner in which people relate to their government, and the way their government relates to them (Hooghoff 1989)?

We must also prepare and encourage students to accept the social and political responsibilities of citizenship at local, state, national, and international levels. Students must especially learn that the responsibilities of citizenship extend beyond military service. As democratic citizens in a technologically advanced society, students need to be producers as well as consumers. Not only must they be economically productive and technologically inventive, they must also reproduce and reinvent democratic political and social structures. Their generation must answer these questions: What will hold together this pluralistic, multicultural, multiethnic, multiracial society? How can the imbalance between rich nations and poor nations be corrected? What will be done about the pollution of the land, water, and air? About world hunger? About new and horrifying diseases? For all our sakes, we hope that in answering these questions, the next generation will create a "new world order" that is democratic to its core.

Liberty and freedom can be lost more easily by failing to exercise them than by someone else taking them away. Because democracy takes time, energy, effort, and commitment, the process loses advocates in a society and a profession that have come to prefer quick fixes, easy solutions, and ready-made answers to problems. Part of this tendency is to look to others for leadership instead of recognizing that it lies within ourselves. Business corporations may indeed find a way to "thrive on chaos," but children cannot. Educational leaders, whether administrators, supervisors, or teachers, must recommit themselves to the value of democracy. As a moral imperative, democracy can provide the direction, goals, purposes, and standards of conduct that our profession and society desperately need.

References

Achilles, C.M. (1987). "A Vision of Better Schools." In *Instructional Leadership*, edited by W. Greenfield. Boston: Allyn and Bacon.

Alfonso, R.J., G.R. Firth, and R.F. Neville. (1975). *Instructional Supervision: A Behavior System*. Boston: Allyn and Bacon.

Anderson, C.J., A.S. Barr, and M.G. Bush. (1925). *Visiting the Teacher at Work*. New York: D. Appleton-Century.

Anderson, R.H. (1986). "The Genesis of Clinical Supervision." In *Learning About Teaching Through Clinical Supervision*, edited by W. John Smyth. London: Croom Helm.

Association for Supervision and Curriculum Development. (1946). *Leadership Through Supervision*, 1946 Yearbook. Washington, D.C.: ASCD, National Educational Association.

Association for Supervision and Curriculum Development. (1948). *Group Processes in Supervision*. Washington, D.C.: ASCD, National Education Association.

Association for Supervision and Curriculum Development. (1951). *Instructional Leadership in Small Schools*. Washington, D.C.: ASCD, National Education Association.

Association for Supervision and Curriculum Development. (1960). *Leadership for Improving Instruction*, 1960 Yearbook. Washington, D.C.: ASCD.

Ayer, F.C., and A.S. Barr. (1928). *The Organization of Supervision: An Analysis of the Organization and Administration of Supervision in City School Systems*. New York: Appleton.

Babcock, C.D. (1965). "The Emerging Role of the Curriculum Leader." In *Role of Supervisor and Curriculum Director in a Climate of Change*, 1965 ASCD Yearbook. Washington, D.C.: ASCD.

Bagby, G. (1972). "Help Wanted: Instructional Leadership." *NASSP Bulletin* 57: 40–46.

Barr, A.S., and W.H. Burton. (1926). *The Supervision of Instruction*. New York: D. Appleton.

Barr, A.S., W.H. Burton, and L.J. Brueckner. (1938). *Supervision: Principles and Practices in the Improvement of Instruction*. New York: D. Appleton-Century.

Barth, R.S. (1991). *Improving Schools from Within*. San Francisco: Jossey-Bass.

Bass, B.M. (1985). *Leadership and Performance Beyond Expectations*. New York: The Free Press.

Benne, K.D. (1949). "Democratic Ethics in Social Engineering." *Progressive Education* 26, 7: 201–207.

Bennis, W., and B. Nanus. (1985). *Leaders: The Strategies for Taking Charge*. New York: Harper and Row.

Berry, B., and R. Ginsburg. (1990). "Effective Schools, Teachers, and Principals: Today's Evidence, Tomorrow's Prospects." In *Educational Leadership and Changing Contexts of Families, Communities, and Schools*, Eighty-ninth Yearbook of the National Society for the Study of Education, Part II, edited by B. Mitchell and L.L. Cunningham. Chicago: University of Chicago.

Blumberg, A., and W. Greenfield. (1979, 1986). *The Effective Principal: Perspectives on School Leadership*. Boston: Allyn and Bacon.

Bobbitt, F. (1913). *The Supervision of City Schools*, The Twelfth Yearbook, Part I, National Society for the Study of Education. Chicago: University of Chicago Press.

Bolin, F.S. (1987). "On Defining Supervision." *Journal of Curriculum and Supervision* 2, 4: 368–380.

Bossert, S., D. Dwyer, B. Rowan, and G. Lee. (1982). "The Instructional Management Role of the Principal." *Educational Administration Quarterly* 18, 3: 34–64.

Brookover, W., C. Beady, P. Flood, J. Schweiter, and J. Wisenbaker. (1979). *School Social Systems and Student Achievement. Schools Can Make a Difference*. New York: Praeger.

Bruner, J. (1986). *Actual Minds, Possible Worlds*. Cambridge, Mass.: Harvard University Press.

Bryman, A. (1986). *Leadership and Organizations*. London: Routledge and Kegan Paul.

Burns, J.M. (1978). *Leadership*. New York: Harper and Row.

Burton, W.H. (1927). *Supervision and the Improvement of Teaching*. New York: D. Appleton.

Burton, W.H., and L.J. Brueckner. (1955). *Supervision, a Social Process*. New York: Appleton-Century-Crofts.

Callahan, R. (1962). *Education and the Cult of Efficiency*. Chicago: University of Chicago Press.

Callahan, R.E., and H.W. Button. (1964). "Historical Change of the Role of the Man in the Organization: 1865–1950." In *Behavioral Science and Educa-

tional Administration, The 63rd Yearbook of the National Society for the Study of Education, edited by D.E. Griffiths. Chicago: University of Chicago Press.

Campbell, A. (1977). "Are Instructional Leaders Still Needed?" *Educational Leadership* 35, 3: 11–14.

Cogan, M.L. (1973). *Clinical Supervision*. Boston: Houghton Mifflin.

Cohen, E.G., R.A. Lotan, and C. Leechor. (April 1989). "Can Classrooms Learn?" *Sociology of Education* 62: 75–94.

Counts, G.S. (1954). *Decision Making and American Values in School Administration*. New York: Cooperative Program in Educational Administration.

Culbertson, J.A. (1988). "A Century's Quest for a Knowledge Base." In *Handbook of Research on Educational Administration*, edited by Norman J. Boyan. New York: Longman.

Cunningham, L.L. (1963). "Effecting Change Through Leadership" *Educational Leadership* 21, 2: 75–79.

Cunningham, L.L. (1990). "Educational Leadership and Administration: Retrospective and Prospective Views." In *Educational Leadership and Changing Contexts of Families, Communities, and Schools*, Eighty-ninth Yearbook of the National Society for the Study of Education, edited by B. Mitchell and L.L. Cunningham. Chicago: University of Chicago Press.

Deal, T.E. (1984). "Searching for the Wizard: The Quest for Excellence in Education." *Issues in Education* 2, 1: 56–57.

Deal, T.E. (1987). "The Culture of Schools." In *Leadership: Examining the Elusive*, edited by L.T. Sheive and M. B. Schoenheit. Alexandria, Va.: ASCD.

Deal, T.E., and A.A. Kennedy. (1982). *Corporate Cultures*. Reading, Mass.: Addison-Wesley.

Department of Supervisors and Directors of Instruction. (1932). *Supervision and the Creative Teacher*, Fifth Yearbook of the Department of Supervisors and Directors of Instruction. New York: Teachers College, Columbia University.

Department of Supervisors and Directors of Instruction. (1933). *Effective Instructional Leadership*, Sixth Yearbook of the Department of Supervisors and Directors of Instruction. New York: Teachers College, Columbia University.

Department of Supervisors and Directors of Instruction. (1934). *Scientific Method in Supervisory Programs*, Seventh Yearbook of the Department of Supervisors and Directors of Instruction. New York: Teachers College, Columbia University.

Department of Supervisors and Directors of Instruction (1943). *Leadership at Work*. Washington, D.C.: Department of Supervisors and Directors of Instruction, National Education Association.

Dewey, J. (1910). *How We Think*. Boston: D.C. Heath.

Dewey, J. (1916). *Democracy and Education*. New York: Macmillan.

Dewey, J. (1927). *The Public and Its Problems*. New York: Henry Holt.

Dewey, J. (1929). *The Sources of a Science of Education*. New York: Horace Liveright.

Drucker, P.F. (1989). *The New Realities*. New York: Perennial Library.

Drummond, H.D. (1964). "Leadership for Human Change." *Educational Leadership* 22, 3: 147–148.

Dumaine, B. (1989). "What Leaders of Tomorrow See." *Fortune* 120, 1: 48–62.

Dumaine, B. (1991). "The Bureaucracy Busters." *Fortune* 123, 13: 36–38.

Dwyer, D.C. (1984). "The Search for Instructional Leadership: Routines and Subtleties in the Principal's Role." *Educational Leadership* 41, 5: 32–37.

Edmonds, R. (1979). "Effective Schools for the Urban Poor." *Educational Leadership* 37, 1: 15–24.

Elliott, E.C. (1914). *City School Supervision*. New York: World Book.

Firestone, W.A., and B.L. Wilson. (1985). "Using Bureaucratic and Cultural Linkages to Improve Instruction: The Principal's Contribution." *Educational Administration Quarterly* 21, 2: 7–30.

Firth, G.R. (1976). "Theories of Leadership: Where Do We Stand?" *Educational Leadership* 33, 5: 327–331.

Foster, R.L. (1964). "Poise Under Pressure." *Educational Leadership* 22, 3: 149–154.

Franseth, J. (1955). *Supervision in Rural Schools*. Bulletin 1955 No. 11. Washington, D.C.: U.S. Department of Health, Education and Welfare, Office of Education.

Fullan, M.G., with S. Steigelbauer. (1991). *The New Meaning of Educational Change*. New York: Teachers College Press.

Garmston, R. (1991). "Staff Developers as Social Architects." *Educational Leadership* 49, 3: 64–65.

Giroux, H.A. (1989). "Rethinking Education Reform in the Age of George Bush." *Phi Delta Kappan* 70, 9: 728–730.

Giroux, H.A. (1991). *Postmodernism, Feminism, and Cultural Politics: Redefining Educational Boundaries*. Albany: State University of New York Press.

Gitlin, A., and J. Smyth. (1989). *Teacher Education: Educative Alternatives*. Philadelphia: The Falmer Press.

Glanz, J. (1977). "Ahistoricism and School Supervision: Notes Toward a History." *Educational Leadership* 35, 2: 149–154.

Goldhammer, K., J.E. Suttle, W.D. Aldridge, and G.L. Becker. (1967). *Issues and Problems in Contemporary Educational Administration*. Eugene, Ore.: The Center for the Advanced Study of Educational Administration, University of Oregon.

Goldhammer, R. (1969). *Clinical Supervision*. New York: Holt, Rinehart, and Winston.

Harris, B.M. (1966). "Strategies for Instructional Change: Promising Ideas and Perplexing Problems." In *The Supervisor: Agent for Change in Teaching*, edited by J. Raths and R.R. Leeper. Washington, D.C.: ASCD, National Education Association.

Harris, B.M. (1969). "New Leadership and New Responsibilities for Human Involvement." *Educational Leadership* 26, 8: 739–742.

Harris, B.M. (1975). *Supervisory Behavior in Education*, 2nd edition. Englewood Cliffs, N.J.: Prentice-Hall.

Heffernan, H., and L.J. Bishop. (1965). "The Supervisor and Curriculum Director at Work." In *Role of Supervisor and Curriculum Director in a Climate of Change*, 1965 Yearbook, edited by R.R. Leeper. Washington, D.C.: ASCD.

Helwig, C. (1968). *Democratic Supervision and Creative Supervision: Are They Misnomers?* (Report No. EA-003-661). U.S. Department of Health, Education, and Welfare, Office of Education. ERIC Document No. ED 055324.

Heslep, R.D. (1989). *Education in Democracy: Education's Moral Role in the Democratic State*. Ames: Iowa State University Press.

Hill, P.T., and J. Bonan. (1991). *Decentralization and Accountability in Public Education*. Santa Monica, Calif.: Rand.

Hodgkinson, H. (1991). "Reform Versus Reality." *Phi Delta Kappan* 73, 1: pp. 9–16.

Holmes, G.W., and W.H. Seawell. (1965). "Further Studies for Administrators and Supervisors—Purpose and Scope." *High School Journal* 48: 242–249.

Hooghoff, H. (1989). *The Netherlands, A Multi-Ethnic Society*. Enschede, Netherlands: National Institute for Curriculum Development.

Hoy, W.K., and P.B. Forsyth. (1986). *Effective Supervision*. New York: Random House.

Hosic, J.F. (1920). "The Democratization of Supervision." *School and Society* 11: 331–336.

Hoyle, J.R., F.W. English, and B.E. Steffy. (1985). *Skills for Successful School Leaders*. Arlington, Va.: American Association of School Administrators.

Hughes, L.W., and C.H. Achilles. (1971). "The Supervisor as a Change Agent." *Educational Leadership* 28, 3: 840–843.

Karier, C. (1982). "Supervision in Historic Perspective." In *Supervision of Teaching*, 1982 ASCD Yearbook, edited by T.J. Sergiovanni. Alexandria, Va.: ASCD.

Kinsella, B.W., G.J. Klopf, H.T. Shafer, and W.T. Young. (1969). *The Supervisor's Role in Negotiation*. Washington, D.C.: ASCD.

Kirst, M.W., M. McLaughlin, and D. Massell. (1990). "Rethinking Policy for Children: Implications for Educational Administration." In *Educational Leadership and Changing Contexts of Families, Communities, and Schools*, Eighty-ninth Yearbook of the National Society for the Study of Education, Part II, edited by B. Mitchell and L.L. Cunningham. Chicago: University of Chicago Press.

Klohr, P.R. (1965). "Looking Ahead in a Climate of Change." In *Role of Supervisor and Curriculum Director in a Climate of Change*, 1965 Yearbook. Washington, D.C.: ASCD.

Kouzes, J.M., and B.Z. Posner. (1988). *How to Get Extraordinary Things Done in Organizations*. San Francisco: Jossey-Bass.

Leithwood, K., and D. Jantzi. (April 1990). "Transformational Leadership: How Principals Can Help Reform School Cultures." Paper presented at the annual meeting of the American Educational Research Association, Boston.

Lightfoot, S.L. (1983). *The Good High School*. New York: Basic Books.

Little, J.W., and T. Bird. (1987). "Instructional Leadership 'Close to the Classroom' in Secondary Schools." In *Instructional Leadership: Concepts, Issues, and Controversies*, edited by W. Greenfield. Boston: Allyn and Bacon.

Lucio, W.H., and J.D. McNeil. (1962). *Supervision: A Synthesis of Thought and Action*. New York: McGraw-Hill.

Lucio, W.H., and J.D. McNeil. (1979). *Supervision in Thought and Action*, 3rd ed. New York: McGraw-Hill.

Lucio, W.H. (1967). "The Supervisory Function: Overview, Analysis, Propositions." In *Supervision: Perspectives and Propositions*, edited by W.H. Lucio. Washington, D.C.: ASCD.

Lyotard, J.F. (1984). *The Postmodern Condition: A Report on Knowledge*. Minneapolis: University of Minnesota Press.

Manasse, A.L. (1982). "Effective Principals: Effective at What?" *Principal* 61, 4: 10–25.

MacDonald, J.B. (1966). "Helping Teachers Change." In *The Supervisor: Agent for Change in Teaching*, edited by J. Raths and R.R. Leeper. Washington, D.C.: ASCD, National Education Association.

McCoy, R.F. (1961). *American School Administration*. New York: McGraw-Hill.

McKernan, J. (1987). "Action Research and Curriculum Development." *Peabody Journal of Education* 64, 2: 6–19.

McNeil, J.D. (1982). "A Scientific Approach to Supervision." In *Supervision of Teaching*, 1982 Yearbook, edited by T.J. Sergiovanni. Alexandria, Va.: ASCD.

Mitchell, B. (1990). "Children, Youth, and Restructured Schools: Views from the Field." In *Educational Leadership and Changing Contexts of Families, Communities, and Schools*, Eighty-ninth Yearbook of the National Society for the Study of Education, Part II, edited by B. Mitchell and L.L. Cunningham. Chicago: University of Chicago Press.

Morris, R.B. (1976). *Encyclopedia of American History*. New York: Harper and Row.
Mosher, R.L., and D.E. Purpel. (1972). *Supervision: The Reluctant Profession*. Boston: Houghton Mifflin.
Neagley, R.L., and N.D. Evans. (1964). *Handbook for Effective Supervision*. Englewood Cliffs, N.J.: Prentice-Hall.
Ogletree, J.R. (1972). "Changing Supervision in a Changing Era." *Educational Leadership* 29, 6: 507–510.
Pajak, E. (1989). *The Central Office Supervisor of Curriculum and Instruction: Setting the Stage for Success*. Needham Heights, Mass.: Allyn and Bacon.
Patterson, J.L., S.C. Purkey, and J.V. Parker. (1986). *Productive School Systems for a Nonrational World*. Alexandria, Va.: ASCD.
Payne, W.H. (1875). *Chapters on School Supervision*. New York: Wilson, Hinkle.
Peters, T. (1988). *Thriving on Chaos: A Handbook for a Management Revolution*. New York: Alfred A. Knopf.
Peters, T., and R.H. Waterman. (1982). *In Search of Excellence: Lessons from America's Best-Run Companies*. New York: Harper and Row.
Rallis, S.F., and M.C. Highsmith. (1986). "The Myth of the 'Great Principal': Questions of School Management and Instructional Leadership." *Phi Delta Kappan* 68: 300–304.
Reilly, D.H. (1984). "The Principalship: The Need for a New Approach." *Education* 104, 3: 242–247.
Rutter, M., B. Maughan, P. Mortimore, J. Outson, and A. Smith. (1979). *Fifteen Thousand Hours: Secondary Schools and Their Effects on Children*. Cambridge, Mass.: Harvard University Press.
Schein, E.H. (1985). *Organizational Culture and Leadership*. San Francisco: Jossey-Bass.
Scheive, L.T., and M.B. Schoenheit, eds. (1987). *Leadership: Examining the Elusive*, 187 ASCD Yearbook. Alexandria, Va.: ASCD.
Schlechty, P.C. (1990). *Schools for the 21st Century*. San Francisco: Jossey-Bass.
Schön, D.A. (1983). *The Reflective Practitioner*. New York: Basic Books.
Schön, D.A. (1987). *Educating the Reflective Practitioner*. San Francisco: Jossey-Bass.
Senge, P.M. (1990a). *The Fifth Discipline: The Art and Practice of the Learning Organization*. New York: Doubleday/Currency.
Senge, P.M. (Fall 1990b). "The Leader's New Work: Building Learning Organizations." *Sloan Management Review*, pp. 7–23.
Sergiovanni, T.J. (1975). "Beyond Human Relations." In *Professional Supervision for Professional Teachers*, edited by T.J. Sergiovanni. Washington, D.C.: ASCD.
Sergiovanni, T.J. (1984a). "Cultural and Competing Perspectives in Administrative Theory and Practice." In *Leadership and Organizational Culture*, edited by T.J. Sergiovanni and J.E. Corbally. Urbana, Ill.: University of Illinois Press.
Sergiovanni, T.J. (1984b). "Leadership and Excellence in Schooling." *Educational Leadership* 41: 4–13.
Sergiovanni, T.J. (1990). *Value-Added Leadership: How to Get Extraordinary Performance in Schools*. San Diego: Harcourt Brace Jovanovich.
Sergiovanni, T.J., and R.J. Starratt. (1979). *Supervision: Human Perspectives*, 2nd ed. New York: McGraw-Hill.
Smyth, J. (1980). "The Principal as Instructional Leader: To Be or Not to Be?" *The Australian Administrator* 1, 1.
Sommerville, J.C. (1971). "Leadership That 'Rocks the Boat,' a Boat that Needs Rocking!" *Educational Leadership* 29, 1: 45–49.
Stone, C.R. (1929). *Supervision of the Elementary School*. Boston: Houghton-Mifflin.

Stoops, R.O. (1918). "Leadership in Instruction." *Addresses and Proceedings of the Fifty-sixth Annual Meeting of the National Education Association of the United States*, 56, Washington D.C.: National Education Association.

Sweeney, J. (1982). "Highlights From Research on Effective School Leadership," *Educational Leadership* 39, 5: p. 349.

Taylor, F.W. (1911). *Principles of Scientific Management*. New York: Harper and Row.

Toepfer, C.F. (1973). "The Supervisor's Responsibility for Innovation." *Educational Leadership* 30, 8: 740–743.

Torbert, W.R. (1990). "Reform From the Center." In *Educational Leadership and Changing Contexts of Families, Communities, and Schools*, Eighty-ninth Yearbook of the National Society for the Study of Education, Part II, edited by B. Mitchell and L.L. Cunningham. Chicago: University of Chicago.

Tyack, D. (1974). *The One Best System: A History of American Urban Education*. Cambridge, Mass.: Harvard University Press.

Van Til, W. (1946). "Exploring Educational Frontiers." In *Leadership Through Supervision*, 1946 Yearbook. Washington, D.C.: ASCD.

Weick, K.E. (1982). "Administering Education in Loosely Coupled Schools." *Phi Delta Kappan* 63, 10: 673–676.

Welker, R. (Spring 1991). "Expertise and the Teacher as Expert: Rethinking a Questionable Metaphor." *American Educational Research Journal* 28, 1: 19–35.

Westbrook, R.B. (1991). *The Radicalism of a Liberal*. Ithaca, N.Y.: Cornell University Press.

Wiles, K. (1950). *Supervision for Better Schools*. New York: Prentice-Hall.

Wiles, K. (1955). *Supervision for Better Schools*, 2nd ed. New York: Prentice-Hall.

Wiles, J., and J. Bondi. (1986). *Supervision: A Guide to Practice*, 2nd ed. Columbus, Ohio: Charles E. Merrill.

Wiles, K., and J.T. Lovell. (1975). *Supervision for Better Schools*, 4th ed. Englewood Cliffs, N.J.: Prentice-Hall.

Young, W.F. (1969). "Influencing Professional Negotiation." In *The Supervisor: New Demands, New Dimensions*, edited by W.H. Lucio. Washington, D.C.: ASCD.

8

Important Education-Related U.S. Supreme Court Decisions (1943–1992)

Cheryl D. Mills

Over the years, courts have played a critical role in the development of the elementary and secondary education system we know today, and the U.S. Supreme Court has had a pivotal role in a number of issues. It has not only influenced education policy, but in some instances has defined the school's and the community's obligations in educating their children, as well as students' and teachers' rights in the schoolhouse. Supreme Court decisions have fostered integration, quality education programs, and educational opportunities for students with physical and mental disabilities. The Court has also decided cases addressing students' rights with respect to free speech, due process, and free exercise of religion, in addition to rendering decisions that have affected teachers' authority in the school building. This chapter briefly describes some of the more important Supreme Court decisions affecting the primary and secondary education system in the last five decades.

Diversifying the Classroom

Three Supreme Court decisions, *Brown v. Board of Education of Topeka, Kansas*, 74 S. Ct. 686, 347 U.S. 483 (1954); *Green v. County School Board of New Kent County*, 88 S. Ct. 1689, 391 U.S. 430 (1968); and *Swann v. Charlotte-Mecklenburg Board of Education*, 91 S. Ct. 1267,

---

Editor's Note: The source of many fundamental policy shifts in education usually does not emanate from educators themselves, but from forces outside the school. Perhaps the most powerful such force is the courts. To record the major policy shifts in supervision and curriculum occasioned by decisions of the U.S. Supreme Court, I asked Attorney Cheryl Mills to synthesize what the most significant education-related supervision and curriculum decisions were and how they affected practice in the schools.

402 U.S. 1 (1971), fundamentally changed the racial and ethnic composition of the classroom. In *Brown*, the Court overturned the doctrine of "separate but equal" in public school education, finding that separate (by race) educational facilities are inherently unequal. The Court found that segregating children in public schools solely on the basis of race, even where the physical facilities and other tangible factors may be equal, deprives minority children of equal educational opportunities in violation of the Equal Protection Clause of the Fourteenth Amendment to the Constitution. *Brown*'s holding that separate classrooms or schools for children of color were unconstitutional was the necessary prerequisite for the multicultural classrooms we enjoy in America today.

In *Green*, the Court found that Virginia's "freedom of choice" plan to desegregate its schools (white students could "choose" to go to black schools, and black students could "choose" to go to white schools) was not adequate compliance with the school board's responsibility to remove the vestiges of state-imposed segregation because it did not work. School officials must design and implement an effective desegregation plan and take whatever action necessary to create a unitary, nonracial school system; thus, *Green* held that school officials have an affirmative duty to dismantle segregation in the public school system. *Green* therefore established that integrated classrooms in previously intentionally segregated school systems were not an option, but a requirement.

Finally, in *Swann*, the Court ruled that if school authorities do not fulfill their affirmative obligation to eliminate racial discrimination, district courts have broad equitable powers to fashion remedies to bring about a unitary, or desegregated, school system. Such remedies could include redrawing school-attendance boundaries and busing students. *Swann* also affected the composition of the classroom—however, not solely along racial lines. With the advent of busing, more and more students attending each school came from different communities, rather than from the immediately surrounding neighborhood. Thus, *Brown*, *Green*, and *Swann* ushered in a new era of racial, cultural, and community diversity in the student body of each classroom.

Remedying the Past, Magnetizing the Future

Milliken v. Bradley, 97 S. Ct. 2749, 433 U.S. 267 (1977) ("Milliken II"), was instrumental in changing the way many Americans view education. In *Milliken II*, the Supreme Court ruled that matters other than student assignments, such as compensatory or remedial educational programs (e.g., reading, inservice teacher training, testing, and counseling), may be addressed by the federal courts to eliminate the effects of prior segregation. This decision helped publicize the fact, which was first stated in *Brown*, that the harm to the victims of segregation was not limited to the substandard facilities. Indeed, the larger harm may well be the often limited educational exposure and opportunities available to students of color. *Milliken II* gave teachers the chance to play a vital remedial educational role in correcting the wrongs of segregation and eliminating its lasting effects. It ensured funding for teachers in desegregating school districts to explore new methods of teaching, testing, and counseling. Most significantly, *Milliken II* recognized that an equally important goal of desegregation must be quality education for all students.

Educational Opportunities for Students with Disabilities

In *Honig v. Doe*, 108 S. Ct. 592, 484 U.S. 305 (1988), the Court upheld the provision of the Education of the Handicapped Act requiring school officials to obtain parental consent prior to removing a disruptive, disabled student from his or her current educational placement before all complaint proceedings against the child have been completed. The Education of the Handicapped Act gives students with disabilities an enforceable, substantive right to public education in participating states and stipulates that federal financial assistance depends on state compliance with the Act.

The Court limited the authority of school officials by reaffirming the statute's mandate that disruptive students with disabilities cannot be removed from their current educational program or placement by the unilateral decision of school officials. Perhaps the most important decision for disabled students, *Honig* ensured that each student with a physical or mental disability had a meaningful opportunity to secure an education, according to the Education of the Handicapped Act. It mandated that disabled students, according to the Act, learn in the same classroom with other children to the greatest extent possible.

This decision gave important support to an Act intended to increase diversity in the classroom by offering all students the chance to interact daily and appreciate varying levels of physical and mental disabilities in the classroom. *Honig v. Doe* safeguarded even disruptive students' rights under the Act by upholding the requirement that parents and school officials seek consensus on the best educational placement or program for a student with a disability.

The First Amendment

Two Supreme Court decisions, *West Virginia Board of Education v. Barnette*, 63 S. Ct. 1178, 319 U.S. 624 (1943), and *Epperson v. State of Arkansas*, 89 S. Ct. 266, 393 U.S. 97 (1968), announced that the First Amendment had bite in the classroom. In *Barnette*, the Court held that local authorities (teachers, school boards, and legislatures) could not compel students to salute the flag and recite the Pledge of Allegiance, because such compulsion violates the First Amendment of the Constitution. And in *Epperson*, the Court found Arkansas statutes prohibiting the teaching of evolution in publicly funded schools, colleges, and universities to violate both the First and Fourteenth Amendments to the Constitution.

Both *Barnette* and *Epperson* illustrated the importance of freedom of expression in schools and laid the foundation for many of the free-speech rights that students and educational institutions enjoy today.

Extending Student Freedoms

Two cases, *Tinker v. Des Moines Independent Community School District*, 89 S. Ct. 733, 393 U.S. 503 (1969), and *Goss v. Lopez*, 95 S. Ct. 729, 419 U.S. 565 (1977), extended students' rights in the school building. Each case contributed to the move away from the strictures of classrooms of yesterday, where students learned in awe of the authority of teachers and the administration. In *Tinker*, the Court held that where the exercise of a forbidden (by the school) right of expression of opinion does not materially and substantially interfere with the requirements of appropriate discipline in the schools, prohibiting that expression violates the First Amendment of the Constitution.

In *Goss*, the Court found that where a state has chosen to extend the right of free education to all residents between six and twenty-one years of age, it cannot withdraw that right (expel students) for misconduct without fundamentally fair procedures (due process) to determine whether misconduct actually occurred. Both the right to free political expression and the right to fair process (to be heard where appropriate) prior to expulsion, balanced the power relationship between teacher and student in the classroom.

The Expansion of Teacher Authority

However, just as more rights were recognized on behalf of students, the Court gave teachers more legal authority in the school building. In *New Jersey v. T.L.O.*, 105 S. Ct. 733, 469 U.S. 325 (1985), the Court found that the Fourth Amendment prohibition against unreasonable searches and seizures applies to searches of students conducted by school officials. However, it held that under ordinary circumstances, a search of a student by a teacher (or other school official) is justified when there are reasonable grounds for suspecting that the search will turn up evidence that a student has violated, or is violating, either the law or the rules of the school. Therefore, a search of students' purses for cigarettes—in violation of the school's no-smoking rule—was found to be justified. *T.L.O.* gave teachers the power to conduct legally justifiable searches of a student's person, without the aid of a police officer or a warrant. Thus, teachers today enjoy considerable authority to enforce the rules of their environment.

Bethel School Dist. No. 403 v. Fraser, 106 S. Ct. 3159, 478 U.S. 675 (1986), established that students' First Amendment rights, as explicated in *Tinker*, were limited. In *Bethel*, the Court ruled that school officials could prohibit, without violating the First Amendment, the use of vulgar and offensive terms in public discourse (school assembly) as an appropriate function of public school education. Thus, teachers properly can prohibit the use of vulgar terms in school-sponsored activities.

Finally, in *Hazelwood School Dist. v. Kuhlmeier*, 108 S. Ct. 562, 484 U.S. 260 (1988), the Court found that a high school newspaper, published by journalism students who received academic credit and grades for their performance, was not a "public forum" entitled to the full protection of the First Amendment. In this case, a journalism teacher supervised the students' work on the newspaper and retained final authority over virtually every aspect of production and publication.

The Court, in *Hazelwood*, ruled that school officials had the right to impose reasonable restrictions on what was printed in the newspaper. Thus, the principal's decision to excise two pages from the newspaper on the grounds that the material unduly impinged on the privacy interests of two students, did not unreasonably interfere with the students' free speech rights. *Hazelwood* therefore gave teachers the authority to limit the content of school-sponsored newspapers without fear of treading on students' First Amendment rights.

Religion in the Schoolhouse

Although religion often is said to have no place in the classroom, the Court's decisions in *Wisconsin v. Yoder*, 92 S. Ct. 1526, 406 U.S. 205 (1972) and *Board of Education of Westside Community Schools v. Mergens*, 110 S. Ct. 2356 (1990), paid heed to religion. In *Yoder*, the Court ruled that a state cannot compel school attendance beyond the 8th grade when parents make a First Amendment claim that such attendance interferes with the practice of a legitimate religious belief. The state *can* compel attendance, however, if: (1) the state does not deny the free exercise of the religious beliefs by this requirement or (2) the state's interest is compelling enough to override the claim of First Amendment protection. In this case, Amish parents demonstrated that any formal education after 8th grade would seriously endanger the free exercise of their religious beliefs. Today, when the curriculum is found to harm the religious training and education of a particular student, parents now have the option to remove their child from formal education.

In *Mergens*, the Court ruled on whether allowing student religious groups to hold meetings before or after classes on school premises violated the Establishment Clause of the Constitution. The Court held that the Equal Access Act, which stated that if schools create a limited public forum for noncurriculum-related student groups (e.g., by allowing at least one such group to meet at school during noninstructional time), required school officials to provide equal access to student religious groups and that such access does not violate the Establishment Clause of the First Amendment. Thus, for students seeking to hold religious group meetings in the school building, the Court guaranteed that they too could use the classroom to further their activities without violating the constitutional requirement to separate church and state.

The Court's decision in *Mueller v. Allen*, 463 U.S. 388, 105 S. Ct. 3062 (1983), however, has perhaps the most far-reaching effects. In *Mueller*, the Court upheld a Minnesota statute that allowed taxpayers to take state tax deductions for expenses (tuition, textbooks, and transportation) related to their children's school attendance at any elementary or secondary school. In many instances, this statute benefitted parents with children attending parochial schools. The Court held that such deductions did not violate the Establishment Clause of the Constitution. By upholding state tax deductions for the costs of tuition, textbooks, and transportation for parents with children attending nonpublic (including sectarian) schools, the Court provided an avenue of support for the current "free choice" and voucher program discussions today.

Conclusion:
The Search for a System

Gordon Cawelti

This yearbook was conceived of as an attempt to record the continuing efforts to improve the educational system in the United
States during the half century of ASCD's existence. Eight distinguished
authors and their colleagues have drawn on their research and experience to probe for meaning in several of the key elements of any
educational system—no small task in an era of substantial change both
in society and in the technology of education. Today we have some of
the best schools in the world, but many schools continue to fail in
educating substantial numbers of their students. Work must continue
with all of the elements described in this yearbook, and it is hoped that
our understanding of the complexities involved will be illuminated by
the work of these invited authors.

ASCD was formed in Chicago in 1943 in the midst of World War II;
its first elected president, Hollis Caswell, was one of the giants of the
curriculum field. In the five decades that have followed, the Association
has played a key role in many developments occurring in curriculum,
instruction, and supervision. However, this yearbook made no attempt
to interpret the role the Association played during these years, but did
record the authors' interpretations of developments in their particular
area of expertise.

In this conclusion, I seek to interpret how the important elements
discussed by my colleagues fit into current efforts to reform the U.S.
system of education. That these elements are "loosely coupled" is an
understatement, but the American public and the education profession
have always resisted a more centralized kind of system. Perhaps this
ought not to be lamented: Fullan has pointed out that the really important things cannot be mandated, and neither centralization nor decentralization works in and of itself. The problem of the knowledge base
from which the teaching profession operates remains a serious one. In
many respects, our knowledge base in education has advanced a great
deal during the past fifty years, but such advances remain terribly slow
in finding their way into classroom practice.

School reform has been a topic of vital interest during this period, starting with influential books in the 1950s by Arthur Bestor and Rudolph Flesch citing data showing poor achievement by American students. Student performance has remained the centerpiece of the calls for reform. The 1960s saw substantial funds authorized by the U.S. Congress to help students catch up in mathematics and science, and the "age of innovation" became almost a cult among some school leaders. However, it was often innovation for its own sake rather than directly intervening to improve student performance. Changes became somewhat more focused on performance in the 1970s, as Head Start and Title I funds were spent to help students overcome conditions making them fall behind in school.

In the next decade, the now famous report *A Nation at Risk* showed that despite a substantial investment of federal funds, serious learning deficits still existed among many U.S. students. Although a number of reforms were already underway, they were accelerated or sustained by this report, which had been authorized by Secretary of Education Terrell Bell. There are few signs, early in the 1990s, of any letup in attempts to improve schools across the land.

One of the major constraints to real school reform is the lack of consensus about why reform is badly needed and what changes are most central. Various phases of reform have always been responses to social and political conditions, ranging from catching up technologically with the Russians in the 1950s to a broad concern today in the corporate sector for producing a better educated work force to enable the United States to retain a leadership role in the international trade arena. Politicians also believe economic competitiveness is the major reason for reform; thus many of the nation's governors have become much more deeply involved in education than in previous years. On the other hand, most educators have never considered preparation for work as a major mission of the schools—but they have not strongly resisted academic reforms (higher standards, more rigorous content, etc.) such as those recommended by former Secretary of Education William Bennett. Still other educators believe that the school's mission must center around developing thinking, caring citizens who will be devoted to the civic good. There is perhaps even less consensus about the need for restructuring of teaching and learning conditions. The great diversity of the U.S. school system virtually defies anyone to seek such consensus; and each wave of leaders tends to pursue its own reform agendas while largely ignoring questions of purpose and doing little to help clarify the central role of schooling in the lives of our nation's youth.

Comparing Student Performance with Earlier Times

Let us first address the question of just how much progress the schools have made in educating the nation's youth during the past half century. As Madaus and Tan observe in chapter 3, there has been tremendous growth in both the amount of testing and in the technology of testing, which has heightened the importance of this element of the U.S. school system. Clearly, many educators believe that repeated revelations of data about the performance of U.S. schools are useful in galvanizing leaders into action—even though by now this must be exposed as a highly dubious assumption. Nonetheless, the public has been led to believe—through annual reporting of the Scholastic Aptitude Test (SAT) results, national assessment achievement testing data, and other reports—that *U.S. schools and students perform less well today than in earlier years*. The SAT test scores are the most prominent of these, but they are said to be symptomatic of this alleged decline. Though it is also a dubious assumption, in my view, some believe this repeated criticism of schools is part of some sort of conspiracy to destroy public education in the attempt to make a case for privatizing public schools.

During the past two years, more careful probing by several competent analysts has strongly suggested that the long-term picture of student performance is not so grim and that, in fact, *U.S. students are doing as well or better than they ever did*. These analyses have been conducted by such people as David Berliner, Harold Hodgkinson, Gerald Bracey, Iris Rotberg, and scientists at the Sandia National Laboratory. Here are some of their conclusions, which contradict earlier findings.

The current retention rate for U.S. schools remains at about 75 percent of the 17–18-year-olds, which is among the highest rates in the world. It has leveled out at this point since 1965 despite a large influx of immigrants since then, and the dropout rate has been declining for all minority groups except Hispanics.

The decline in SAT scores since 1965 is only 3.3 percent of the raw score totals, or five fewer correct items, in the past twenty-five years. Many analysts believe that the reason for this slight decline is that much greater numbers of students in the bottom 60 percent of their class have been taking the test since the 1960s. If one compares scores of a cohort of today's 17–18-year-olds who demographically match those of the students who took the test in 1975, the average score moves from about 900 to 925.

When examining the trend lines in achievement of U.S. students on tests of the National Assessment of Educational Progress, the Sandia National Laboratory scientists reported that U.S. student performance doesn't decline in any areas. Further, although it is true that U.S. students score somewhere between the midpoint and bottom of international comparisons in mathematics and science, analysts say these data are very misleading because of the very different samples of students used in the various countries. For example, in Europe approximately the top fourth of the age group attends high school; and data for these students are compared with scores of U.S. students, where three-fourths of the age group were sampled.

These analysts contend that U.S. education has not gotten worse over the past few decades, but, in fact, that schools are just as effective as they ever were. Few would dispute the large variations in performance as achievement scores are disaggregated by gender, region, or race. However, to conclude that schools are as good as ever largely begs the question of how appropriate the current curriculum is to the multiple roles students will play in their future lives, which is the more important question. The work of these scholars in more accurately interpreting existing data is worth this brief mention because the net effect of the repeated barrage of criticism has been to diminish public confidence in the schools. We ought to at least debate the right issue: What learning experiences will best equip students for life in the 21st century?

Thus, while much progress has been and continues to be made in the technology of testing, there has clearly been an overreliance on testing. Too much optimism still exists for a measurement-driven strategy to become a major element of reform, as proposed by President Bush in the call for national testing in America 2000.

Shifting to National Curriculum Standards

Another key element of any school system obviously is the curriculum itself. Here again, issues of purpose loom large, and there is little semblance of consensus. During the past decade, it is fair to say that what Shubert has called "intellectual traditionalists" have gained increasing prominence. Currently, national curriculum content standards are being developed in history, geography, mathematics, science, English, and the arts. These government-sponsored attempts to establish what all students should "know and be able to do" have grown out of the belief that we need greater agreement than now exists on this issue, and particularly that if there is to be national testing, such tests should be based on a common curriculum.

The mathematics standards were first to be developed; an accelerated schedule will see standards developed in most other fields by 1994. The effort to reach more consensus of what the content should be in the major fields is, in my view, a healthy undertaking if it will stimulate serious discussion on issues of what kind of curriculum students ought to have to prepare them for the future. If the standard development leads toward high-stakes national testing, it will have been a serious mistake. Thus far, school leaders are moving slowly to integrate the mathematics standards into their curriculum, but it remains to be seen whether the other content standards will be taken seriously if national tests are not a part of the "system."

School-Based Development of Learner Outcomes

In the meantime, the "social behaviorist" school of thought has been reflected in attempts to obtain greater clarity on school goals. The so-called behavioral objectives movement has come and gone because it tended to fragment the curriculum without having paid sufficient attention to the more important, larger outcomes which hopefully will be reflected in the national standards. More recently, many school districts have seriously undertaken Outcome Based Education (OBE), developing general learner outcomes to be expected of all students, along with a much more comprehensive assessment system. Because national standards, except for mathematics, did not exist at the time this movement began, such outcomes obviously do not necessarily reflect the consensus that is now being obtained on what students need to know and be able to do in the various disciplines.

General learner outcomes developed in several districts reflect the views of the faculty and parents, with much less involvement of scholars from the various disciplines. In deciding on these outcomes, school leaders have examined the consequences of major social issues, requirements of the workplace, predictors of adult happiness and success, and teacher views on the importance of the content in their field. The kinds of outcomes believed to be appropriate to the future tend to concentrate on a broader range of outcomes that are both important and more difficult to assess.

The following learner outcomes are representative of those being established at the local level; they are based on my examination of such outcomes from several districts across the United States:

- Developing thinking skills such as problem solving or critical thinking.
- Developing character, ethical conduct, or moral education.
- Developing interpersonal skills such as working cooperatively with others.
- Developing skills in selecting and using technology and understanding the societal effects of technological advances.
- Developing a better understanding of the value of diversity of people and an international perspective among students.

In addition, students are often being expected to develop a plan for lifetime learning or for maintaining physical and mental health. While many of these outcomes have been articulated before, those that are currently being developed and implemented are more likely to be seriously pursued because of the work being done simultaneously in the standards and assessment area at the local level. These schools have an excellent opportunity to put together two key elements of any education system—curriculum and assessment—even if they have pursued OBE without whatever benefit national standards might have provided. But their larger challenge may be in seeing whether interdisciplinary approaches among teachers in various departments can really accomplish these important outcomes.

Emerging Role of States in School Reform

It will take several years before national standards are reflected in instructional materials and the technology today's schools are using. But it must be apparent that such standard development reflects a major shift in policy at the federal level. However, today's schools are much more likely to be affected by growing involvement of state governments in education. Although relatively little has been accomplished by way of fundamental changes during the Reagan-Bush years, various governors and state departments of education have forged ahead with a variety of mandates affecting the schools.

The most comprehensive reform package has been enacted in Kentucky, but its elements are more and more prominent in other states. The key changes in Kentucky include reaching agreement on learner outcomes, a state-level assessment plan, and financial rewards and penalties to schools depending on how well they succeed on the outcomes. Several states have developed new curriculum frameworks that are being followed by the schools because assessment is a part of the "system" under which they are required to operate. Because education is largely left to the states under the U.S. Constitution, this stronger state role will likely continue. Clearly the policies and mandates in some states will be imminently more sensible than in others, and there will need to be a good bit of collaboration in developing assessment systems because of the complexity and costs involved in good assessment.

The Constructivist View of Learning

The most critical ingredient of successful schools is the teacher and the quality of teaching in the classroom. The work of behaviorists in the field of learning have dominated the literature during the past several decades. Research on effective teaching tended to be oriented to this perspective and produced many highly prescriptive approaches to learning. But as Peterson and Knapp point out in their chapter, there were other views all the while. They record the important work of the "constructivists," who are seeking to demonstrate how students must be helped to create their own meaning out of the learning experiences the school provides. For many teachers, this is a very different view of the nature of the learner, and a good deal of staff development work will be essential to make the transition.

Many studies have documented the passive role students now play in the classroom, and teachers are faced with many students who are poorly motivated and see little value in schooling. The need for more active learning is great; students do need to assume more responsibility for their own learning. The constructivist movement in learning will do much to help get students more involved, particularly if students can be helped to see that in adult life they will need to know what they are being asked to learn.

The Professionalization of Teaching and the Knowledge Base

Darling-Hammond and Goodwin report the changes that must be made in teacher education programs and what must be done in the area of licensure and certification if a true profession of teaching is to evolve.

Of all the elements of our system of schooling, the concept of "professionalizing" teaching is perhaps the most complex and will require years of diligent leadership. The work of organizations such as the National Council for the Accreditation of Teacher Education, the plan for national certification of teachers, and the states' role in teacher certification will determine the extent to which a more bona fide profession will emerge over the next decade or two. What is clear now is that the system responds to supply and demand issues by lowering standards, that the profession doesn't attract the best and the brightest students, and that the primary ingredient of a profession does not exist in education—agreement on a knowledge base from which to operate. Though full agreement is rare in most professions, education has a long way to go in getting to the point where, given students with a wide variety of aptitudes and attitudes toward learning, a group of teachers would have some medium of agreement on the instructional strategies most likely to enable the students to succeed.

In all the discussion about school reform, this issue of our knowledge base has received the least attention except for where provisions are made for staff development. But the first question is: Staff development for what? National leadership in developing this knowledge base is essential. Teacher education cannot be reformed without it, and Pajak's conception of the leader as teacher must center around what teachers must know and be able to do if the school is to become learner focused.

What form would a synthesis of this knowledge base about teaching and learning take? We have had handbooks produced by scholarly organizations and curriculum programs reportedly based on research about learning. Contrasted to these scholarly, albeit overwhelming, handbooks, more cookbook kinds of publications focusing on "what works" have also been tried over the years. Textbooks used in university education courses presumably carry a good bit of this knowledge base, but such books are of very uneven quality. A number of trainers and consultants conduct programs that presume to convey what is known about teaching and learning in a particular area. The long-term work of the National Board for Professional Teaching Standards will afford much direction on this issue and will have an impact if significant numbers of teachers seek such certification.

ASCD has made a remarkable contribution over the years in disseminating aspects of the knowledge base about teaching. Members were early made aware of the importance of strategies to develop student thinking skills, and later have been given opportunities to develop skills in such programs as "Dimensions of Learning," which is a large-scale synthesis of research on learning, derived from several existing training programs and research in this area. It helps teachers see where particular strategies "fit" in meeting classroom situations on a daily basis. ASCD conducts many other kinds of training programs for various purposes, but few are as comprehensive as the "Dimensions of Learning" program.

We need more of this kind of work, which represents a consensus on what research has shown about the efficacy of various teaching strategies and where each fits into a larger repertoire of those discipline-based skills needed by teachers in typical classrooms. Such programs would help deal with the problem of bias on the part of advocates of particular strategies, who would have one believe their approach is the solution to any student learning problem. In addition to this entry knowledge base, teachers in the future no doubt will need to specialize in particular strategies effective with certain students.

If we are to have a knowledge base constituting what teachers need to know and be able to do, we need to classify the advances made in research on teaching and learning over the past several decades. Moreover, we need to find ways to gauge and report the probability of success of particular strategies. Helping prospective and practicing teachers interpret and apply such a knowledge base with some consistency will be a major undertaking. It should be apparent by now that the absence of any such basis from which to operate means it has been ignored in reform efforts. Is it any wonder that we have a paucity of striking results thus far? All the "Break the Mold" schools will probably fail unless they produce a culture under which the teaching profession can diagnose and decide what teaching strategies will work best with any individual or group of students.

The role of teachers in local school reform has seen some progress in the past decade. Unionization has compelled greater participation of teachers in district policy-making issues, but these efforts have rarely focused on school reform as much as salaries and working conditions. Fullan has properly regretted that even under highly touted decentralization plans, the focus of committees has remained more on the decision-making process than on how to improve student performance. If schools are to truly move out into partnerships with many other community agencies in educating their youth, as McKenzie advocates, such "systemic" reforms will compel a different set of issues on the agenda for school-level teacher teams and a good bit more than good "process" skills.

* * *

The pressure for school reform will continue in the years ahead as the rate of change accelerates and we continue the struggle to serve all students more effectively and prepare them more appropriately for their futures. During the past several decades, the courts have rendered decisions that have compelled schools to make fuller provisions for the diversity of student needs, as Mills has discussed; and the globalization of our economy will keep expectations for student performance high. Schools today are more fair than they were fifty years ago, teachers are better prepared, and schools have begun to better model the democratic institutions they must be.

We continue to need leaders who will shape schools that respond much faster to social and technological change, people who can lead others in reaching consensus on issues of both purpose and procedure. This yearbook analyzes several important facets of the education enterprise in America and makes apparent the difficulty in orchestrating all the parts of the system in some coordinated fashion. In many respects, the school must increasingly become the center of learning for everyone in the community, including the staff, because without continuous learning, institutions will rapidly stagnate. Although some will argue for greater centralization to orchestrate the parts more efficiently, the very nature of schooling itself—along with political trends in recent history—makes the prospect of larger, bureaucratic organizations very unlikely.

About the Authors

Gordon Cawelti, the editor of *Challenges and Achievements of American Education*, served as Executive Director of ASCD from 1973 to 1992. The former Superintendent of Schools for Tulsa, Oklahoma, Cawelti serves as an international consultant on school restructuring.

Linda Darling-Hammond is Professor of Education at Teachers College, Columbia University, New York City.

Michael Fullan is Dean of the Faculty of Education at the University of Toronto, Ontario, Canada.

A. Lin Goodwin is Assistant Professor of Education at Teachers College, Columbia University, New York City.

Nancy F. Knapp is a doctoral candidate in educational psychology at the College of Education at Michigan State University in East Lansing.

George F. Madaus is Boisi Professor of Education and Public Policy at the Center for the Study of Testing, Evaluation and Educational Policy at Boston College, Chestnut Hill, Massachusetts.

Floretta Dukes McKenzie is President of The McKenzie Group, a limited partner of Hogan & Hartson, Washington, D.C. She is the former Superintendent of Schools for the District of Columbia.

Cheryl D. Mills is an Attorney at Law in the Education Group of Hogan & Hartson, Washington, D.C.

Edward Pajak is Professor and Head of the Department of Educational Leadership in the College of Education at the University of Georgia, Athens.

Penelope L. Peterson is Professor of Education and Co-Director of the Institute for Research on Teaching at the College of Education at Michigan State University in East Lansing.

William H. Schubert is Professor of Education and Chair of Curriculum, Instruction, and Evaluation at the University of Illinois at Chicago. He is president of the John Dewey Society and past president of the Society for the Study of Curriculum History.

Ann G.A. Tan is Research Assistant at the Center for the Study of Testing, Evaluation, and Educational Policy at Boston College, Chestnut Hill, Massachusetts.

ASCD 1992–93 Board of Directors

Elected Members as of November 1, 1992

Executive Council

President: Stephanie Pace Marshall, Executive Director, Illinois Math and Science Academy, Aurora

Immediate Past President: Corrine Hill, Director, Utah Education Consortium, University of Utah, Salt Lake City

President-Elect: Barbara Talbert Jackson, Executive Director, Grants Development Branch, District of Columbia Public Schools, Washington, D.C.

Thomas Budnik, Coordinator for Planning, Research and Evaluation, Heartland Area Education Agency #11, Johnston, Iowa

Robert Clark, Associate Superintendent, Marietta City Schools, Marietta, Georgia

Robert Garmston, Co-director of Institute for Intelligent Behavior, El Dorado Hills, California

Ruud Gorter, Director of the Association of Educational Advisory Centers, The Netherlands

Edith Jensen, Associate Superintendent for Instruction, Lexington County School District 5, Columbia, South Carolina

Frances Jones, Executive Director, Piedmont Triad Horizons Educational Consortium, University of North Carolina, Greensboro

Irving Ouellette, Director of Elementary Education, Portland Public Schools, Portland, Maine

David Robinson, Superintendent, Sheridan Public Schools, Sheridan, Arkansas

Arthur Steller, Superintendent, Oklahoma City Public Schools, Oklahoma City, Oklahoma

Sheila Wilson, Director of Staff Support, Township High School, District 214, Arlington Heights, Illinois

Review Council Members

Chair: Marcia Knoll, Assistant Superintendent, Valley Stream Central High School District, Valley Stream, New York

Mitsuo Adachi, Emeritus Professor, University of Hawaii, Honolulu

Carolyn H. Chapman, Associate Professor, College of Education, University of Nevada-Reno

Arthur Costa, Kalaheo, Kauai, Hawaii

Phil Robinson, Detroit, Michigan

Members- at- Large

Bonnie Benesh, Director of Curriculum and Instruction, Newton Community School District, Newton, Iowa

Marguerite Bloch, Superintendent of Schools, Butler District 53, Oak Brook, Illinois

Marguerite Cox, Director of Instruction, Glenbard Township High School, School District 87, Glen Ellyn, Illinois

Mary Francis, Superintendent, Petersburg City School District, Petersburg, Alaska

Esther Fusco, Principal, Babylon School District, Stony Brook, New York

Sandra Gray, Director, K–12 Laboratory School, Southwest Missouri State University, Springfield

Phyllis J. Hobson, Director, Parental Involvement Program, District of Columbia Public Schools, Washington, D.C.

David Jones, Jr., Director of Secondary Programs, Metropolitan Public Schools, Nashville, Tennessee

Joanna Kalbus, Superintendent, San CLASS Regional School District, San Bernadino County Schools, San Bernadino, California

Ina Logue, Director of Curriculum and Instruction, Allegheny Intermediate Unit, Pittsburgh, Pennsylvania

Alex Molnar, Professor, Department of Curriculum and Instruction, University of Wisconsin-Milwaukee

Lynn Murray,Principal, Williston Central School, Williston, Vermont

Annemarie Romagnoli, Principal, Little Tor Elementary School, New City, New York

Susan E. Spangler, Director of Elementary Curriculum, Millard Public Schools, Omaha, Nebraska

Judy Stevens, Director of Elementary Instruction, Springbranch I.S.D., Houston, Texas

Beverly M. Taylor, Director of Professional Growth, Curriculum Design for Excellence, Oak Brook, Illinois

Elizabeth C. Turpin, Principal, Lansing School District, Lansing, Michigan

Nancy Vance, Associate Director for Professional Development and the Beginning Teacher Assistance Program, Virginia Department of Education, Dinwiddie County

P.C. Wu, Professor of Educational Leadership and Director, University of West Florida, Pensacola

Donald Young, CRDG College of Education, Honolulu, Hawaii

Affiliate Presidents

Alabama: Peggy Collins, Director of Instruction, Tuscaloosa City Schools, Tuscaloosa

Alaska: Toni McDermott, Anchorage

Arizona: Kay Coleman, Director of Instruction, Deer Valley Unified School District, Phoenix

Arkansas: David Rainey, Principal, Dumas High School, Dumas

California: Ruben Ingram, District Superintendent, Fountain Valley School District, Fountain Valley

Colorado: Leslie Olson, McGraw Elementary School, Fort Collins

Connecticut: LeRoy Hay, Superintendent of Schools, Windsor Locks Public Schools, Windsor Locks

Delaware: Darlene Bolig, State Supervisor, Elementary Education, Dept. of Public Instruction, Dover

District of Columbia: Linda McKay, Patricia Roberts Harris School, Washington, D.C.

Florida: Jill Wilson, Riverland Elementary School, Ft. Lauderdale

Georgia: Ann Spears, Director of Instruction, Rome City Schools, Rome

Hawaii: Vivian Hee, Principal, Jefferson Elementary School, Honolulu

Idaho: Mary Ann Ranells, Director of Curriculum and Instruction, Nampa School District #131, Nampa

Illinois: Michael Palmisano, Director of Assessment and Research, Illinois Mathematics and Science Academy, Aurora

Indiana: Rebecca Libler, Indiana State University, School of Education, Terre Haute

Iowa: Patricia Robinson, Principal, Harrison Elementary School, Davenport

Kansas: Marlin Berry, Superintendent, Unified School District #400, Lindsborg

Kentucky: Bob Pettit, Daviess County Schools, Owensboro

Louisiana: Aurelia Orr, Instructional Specialist, New Orleans Public Schools, New Orleans

Maine: Leon Levesque, Asst. Superintendent, M.S.A.D. #52, Turner

Maryland: Michael Savarese, Columbia

Massachusetts: Lyn Huttunen, Superintendent of Schools, Randolph

Michigan: Larry Johnson, Elementary Principal, Grand Traverse Area Public Schools, Traverse City

Minnesota: Marilyn Lindquist, Bloomington Public Schools, Bloomington

Mississippi: Jim Moore, Asst. Superintendent, Jackson Public Schools, Jackson

Missouri: Joe Ketterlin, Jefferson City

Montana: Bill Bartholomew, Principal, East Middle School, Butte

Nebraska: Jed Johnston, Elementary Principal, Cottonwood Elementary, Omaha

Nevada: Francine Mayfield, Principal, Whitney Elementary School, Las Vegas

New Hampshire: Kendall Didsbury, Director of Studies, Tilton School, Tilton

New Jersey: Mary Jane Donnelly, Asst. Superintendent for Curriculum and Instruction, Randolph Township School District, Randolph

New Mexico: Andre Trottier, Los Alamos Middle School, Los Alamos

New York: Robert Schneider, Director, Human Growth and Development Network, Huntington

North Carolina: Ruth Spargo, Director of Instruction, Randolph County Schools, Asheboro

North Dakota: Chuck DeRemer, Dept. of Public Instruction, Bismarck

Ohio: Dixie Barnhart, Program Specialist, Wright State University, Dayton
Oklahoma: Terry James, Asst. Superintendent, McAlester Public Schools, McAlester
Oregon: Ardis Christensen, Director, Special Services, Salem
Pennsylvania: Elizabeth Matgouranis-Gensante, Superintendent, Richland School District, Johnstown
Puerto Rico: Elsa Torres, Catholic University of Puerto Rico, Ponce
Rhode Island: Mary Chirico, Director of Reading and Literacy, Johnston Public Schools, Johnston
South Carolina: Sharon Keesley, Associate Superintendent of Instruction, Edgefield
South Dakota: Bryan Monteith, Director of Curriculum, Watertown School District 14-4, Watertown
Tennessee: Kay Awalt, Principal, Moore Elementary School, Franklin
Texas: Charles Reavis, Professor, Texas Tech University, Lubbock
Utah: Briant Farnsworth, Asst. Superintendent-Curriculum, Salt Lake City
Vermont: Darlene Worth, Director of Instruction and Curriculum, South Burlington School District, South Burlington
Virginia: Jan Adkisson, Staff Development/Early Childhood Supervisor, Arlington County Public Schools, Arlington
Virgin Islands: Migdalia Arthurton, St. Thomas
Washington: Phil Sorensen, Shoreline Public Schools, Seattle
West Virginia: Judy Szymialis, Wheeling Park High School, Wheeling
Wisconsin: Bruce Connolly, Superintendent of Schools, Merton School District, Merton
Wyoming: Bill Berube, Professor-Educational Administration, University of Wyoming, Laramie
Alberta, Canada: Michael Dzwiniel, Edmonton
British Columbia, Canada: Don Truscott, Asst. Superintendent, Mission
Germany: John Hunt, Hanau Middle School, Unit 20235, APO AE
Ontario, Canada: Evelyn Brown, Principal, Bracebridge and Muskoka Lakes Secondary School, Bracebridge
Singapore: Mok Choon Hoe, Director of Curriculum Planning, Ministry of Education
St. Maarten: Quincy Harrigan, Curriculum Coordinator, Island Dept. of Education, Philipsburg
The Netherlands: Martijn Dingemans, Bergen Op Zoom
Trinidad and Tobago: Annette Wiltshire, Diego Martin
United Kingdom: Elizabeth Dunham, Staff Development Specialist

ASCD Headquarters Staff

Gene Carter, *Executive Director*
Diane Berreth, *Deputy Executive Director*
Frank Betts, *Director, Curriculum/Technology Resource Center*
John Bralove, *Director, Administrative Services*
Ronald S. Brandt, *Executive Editor*
Helené Hodges, *Director, Research and Information*
Susan Nicklas, *Director, Field Services*
Michelle Terry, *Director, Professional Development*

Diana Allen
Teddy Atwara
René Bahrenfuss
Meleanie Bell
Vickie Bell
Kimber Bennett
Sandy Berdux
Jennifer Beun
Steven Blackwood
Gary Bloom
Maritza Bourque
Lorraine Bradshaw
Joan Brandt
Dorothy Brown
Kathy Browne
Robert Bryan
Colette Burgess
Edward Butler
Angela Caesar
Kathryn Carswell
Sally Chapman
John Checkley
RC Chernault
Eddie Chinn
Sandra Claxton
Lisa Manion Cline
Adrienne Corley
Christine Craun
Agnes Crawford
Sandy Cumberland
Elaine Cunningham
Brian Curry
Marcia D'Arcangelo
Keith Demmons
Becky DeRigge
Gloria Dugan
Shiela Ellison
Gillian Fitzpatrick
Frederick Fleming

Chris Fuscellaro
Sonja Gilreath
Regina Gussie
Nora Gyuk
Dorothy Haines
Vicki Hancock
Dwayne Hayes
Davene Holland
Julie Houtz
Angela Howard
Debbie Howerton
Harold Hutch
Arddie Hymes
Peter Inchauteguiz
Jo Ann Jones
Mary Jones
Teola Jones
Stephanie Kenworthy
Leslie Kiernan
Shelly Kosloski
Ana Larson
Diane MacDonald
John Mackie
Indu Madan
Lynn Malarz
Larry Mann
Jan McCool
Clara Meredith
Susan Merriman
Ron Miletta
Ginger Miller
Frances Mindel
Nancy Modrak
Cerylle Moffett
Karen Monaco
Dina Murray
Margaret Murphy
Peter Neal
Mary Beth Nielsen

Jonathan Nobles
John O'Neil
Jayne Osgood
Millie Outten
Kelvin Parnell
Margini Patel
Carolyn Pool
Jackie Porter
Ruby Powell
Vernon Pretty
Pam Price
Lorraine Primeau
Gena Randall
Melody Ridgeway
Judy Rixey
Jay Robbins
Rita Roberts
Gayle Rockwell
Cordelia Roseboro
Carly Rothman
Marge Scherer
Beth Schweinefuss
Judy Seltz
Bob Shannon
Valerie Sprague
Lisa Street
Susan Thran
Judi Wagstaff
Judy Walter
Dave Warren
Milton Washington
Vivian West
Kay Whittington
Linda Wilkey
Pam Williams
Scott Willis
Carolyn Wojcik
Edward Yi
Sue Young

ASCD Networks and Facilitators, 1992–93

ASCD sponsors numerous networks that help members exchange ideas, share common interests, identify and solve problems, grow professionally, and establish collegial relationships. Contact ASCD Field Services Department for additional information about networks, or write or call one of the facilitators listed here.

Accelerated Learning and Teaching
Doug McPhee
1888 Montgomery Ave.
Cardiff, CA 92007
TEL (800) 660-9899
   (619) 633-1433
FAX (619) 632-1305

African-American Critical Issues
Peyton Williams, Associate State
   Superintendent
Georgia Dept. of Education
Office of Instructional Programs,
   Twin Towers East
Atlanta, GA 30334-5040
TEL (404) 656-4722
FAX (404) 651-8582

Brenda Benson-Burrell
Asst. Professor of Education
Glassboro State College
Robinson Bldg., 2nd Floor
Glassboro, NJ 08028-1752
TEL (609) 863-6071
FAX (609) 863-5018

Alliance to Enhance Teaching of Science
Mary Louise Ray, Director of
   Curriculum and Instruction
Altoona Area Schl. Dist.
1415 6th Ave.
Altoona, PA 16602
TEL (814) 946-8204

Arts in Education
Bernadette C. O'Brien
Exec. Director, BIFAE, Inc.
141 Ellsworth Terrace
Glen Rock, NJ 07452
TEL (201) 445-4359
FAX (201) 670-8011

Authentic Assessment
Kathleen Busick
Pacific Region Educational Lab
1164 Bishop St., Suite 1409
Honolulu, HI 96813
TEL (808) 532-1900
FAX (808) 532-1922

Character Education
Kevin Ryan, Prof./Director
Center for the Advancement of
   Ethics and Character
Boston Univ., School of Education
605 Commonwealth Ave., Room 356
Boston, MA 02215
TEL (617) 353-3262
FAX (617) 353-3924

Clearinghouse for Learning/ Teaching Styles and Brain Behavior
Jerry Wedlund
Princeton Public Schools
110 S. 6th Ave.
Princeton, MN 55371
TEL (612) 389-2422

Collaborative/Compensatory Service Models
Rebecca Robinson Yariott, Principal
Judith Hanson, Title VII
 Coordinator
Hale Elementary School
1220 East 54th St.
Minneapolis, MN 55417
TEL (612) 627-2387
FAX (612) 627-2394

Cooperative Learning
Harlan Rimmerman, Director
N. Kansas City Schl. Dist.
2000 N.E. 46th St.
Kansas City, MO 64116
TEL (816) 453-5050

Curriculum Teachers
Marcella Kysilka
Educational Foundations
Univ. of Central Florida
Orlando, FL 32816
TEL (407) 823-2000

Designing District Evaluation Instruments for Math and Science Process Skills
Shelley Lipowich
Math/Science Consultant
6321 North Canon del Pajaro
Tucson, AZ 85715
TEL (602) 299-9583
FAX (602) 886-2370*
*Specify name and phone no. on fax.

Developing Giftedness and Talent
Brian Reid
Asst. Professor
Univ. of Alabama-Birmingham
UAB Station
Birmingham, AL 35294-1250
TEL (205) 934-3440
FAX (205) 934-2921

Early Childhood Education
Shirle Moone Childs, Director of
 Curriculum, Instruction, and
 Evaluation
Windham Public Schools
322 Prospect St.
Willimantic, CT 06226
TEL (203) 423-8401
FAX (203) 456-0859

Educational Futurists
Barbara Vogl, Consultant
Change Mgmt. Systems
5300 Glen Haven Rd.
Soquel, CA 95073
TEL (408) 476-2905

Kathleen Maury
Mankato State Univ.
132 East Glencrest Dr.
Mankato, MN 56001
TEL (507) 389-5704

Equity Issues
Ann Converse Shelly
Chair, Curriculum and Instruction
Univ. of Alabama-Birmingham
210A Education Building
UAB-Station
Birmingham, AL 35294-1250
TEL (205) 934-5371
FAX (205) 934-4963

Judith Lucarelli
R.R. #1, Box 6
Deer Isle, ME 01960
TEL (207) 348-7777

Global Education
Marilyn McKnight, Teacher
Milwaukee Public Schools/Forest
 Home School
5225 W. Vliet St.
Milwaukee, WI 53208
TEL (414) 645-5200

High Schools Networking for Change
Gil James, Principal
Sprague High School
2373 Kuebler Rd. South
Salem, OR 97302-9404
TEL (503) 399-3261
FAX (503) 399-3407

Indigenous People Education
Gerlad L. (Jerry) Brown, Equity
 Specialist
Interface West, Inc.
4800 S.W. Griffith Dr., Suite 202
Beaverton, OR 97005
TEL (503) 644-5741
FAX (503) 626-2305

Instructional Supervision
J. McClain Smith, Coordinator of
University Programs
Hilliard City Schools
5323 Cemetery Rd.
Hilliard, OH 43026
TEL (614) 771-4273
FAX (614) 777-2424

Interdisciplinary Curriculum
Benjamin F. Ebersole
Department of Education
Univ. of Maryland,
Baltimore Co., Wilkens Ave.
Baltimore, MD 21228
TEL (301) 455-2378
FAX (301) 455-3213

Intergenerational/Family Literacy
Maryann E. Nuckolls
Tucson Unified Schl. Dist.
6951 S. Camino de la Tierra
Tucson, AZ 85746
TEL (602) 798-2708

Learning Community
F. James Clatworthy
School of Education
Oakland Univ.
Rochester, MI 48309-4401
TEL (313) 370-3052
FAX (313) 370-4202

**Lesbian, Gay, and Bisexual Issues
In Education**
Jan Goodman, Coordinator
Mathematics Educ. Program
Lawrence Hall of Science
Univ. of California
Berkeley, CA 94720
TEL (510) 642-732
FAX (510) 642-1055

Manipulative Mathematics
Rosemarie Dyer, Teacher
Black Elementary School
14100 Heritage
Sterling Heights, MI 48312
TEL (313) 825-2840
FAX (313) 825-2844

James Callaghan, Co-Facilitator
Angus Elementary School
3180 Hein
Sterling Heights, MI 48310
TEL (313) 825-2782

**Mentoring Leadership and
Resources**
Richard Lange, Director of Staff
Development
Prospect Heights Public Schools
834 Inverrary Lane
Deerfield, IL 60015
TEL (708) 870-3857
FAX (708) 870-3896

Middle Schools
Evelyn Maycumber, Middle
Grades/Reading Consultant
N.E. Florida Educational
Consortium
Rt. 1, Box 8500
Palatka, FL 32177
TEL (904) 329-3800
FAX (904) 329-3835

**Network and Clearinghouse for
the Columbian Quincentennial**
Delno C. West
Professor of History
Northern Arizona Univ.
Box 6023
Flagstaff, AZ 86011-6023
TEL (602) 523-4378
FAX (602) 523-2626

**Network for Restructured
Schools**
Richard Ackerman and
Chuck Christensen
Ctr. for Field Serv. and Studies
Univ. of Massachusetts-Lowell
1 University Ave.
Lowell, MA 01854
TEL (508) 934-4633
FAX (508) 934-3002

**Quality Schools/Outcome-Based
Education**
Rick Scott
Chetwynd Secondary School, Schl.
Dist. #59
P.O. Box 447
Chetwynd, B.C.
CANADA V0C 1J0
TEL (604) 788-2267

Religion and Public Education
Austin Creel
Professor of Religion
Univ. of Florida
125 Dauer Hall
Gainesville, FL 32611
TEL (904) 392-1625
FAX (904) 392-3584

Rural and Small Schools
Raymond Francis, Coordinator
Science, Math, and Tech. Ctr.
Marion County Schools
c/o E. Dale Elementary School
Route 3
Fairmont, WV 26554
TEL (304) 367-2122
FAX (304) 366-2522

School-University Partnerships
Richard Kobliner, College Counselor
Benjamin Cardozo H.S.
57-00 223rd St.
Bayside, NY 11364
TEL (718) 631-7514
FAX (718) 631-6880

Science, Mathematics, and Technology Education
Dennis W. Cheek, Coordinator of Curriculum Development
NYSTEP, Rm. 232-M, EB
State Education Department
Albany, NY 12234
TEL (518) 473-1759
FAX (518) 473-0858

Staff Development
Rita Cook
Smokey Hill Central Kansas Education Service
3023 Canterbury, Suite 7
Salina, KS 67401
TEL (913) 825-9185
FAX (913) 827-5446

Vern Minor
Ponca ISD
613 E. Grand
Ponca, OK 74601
TEL (405) 767-8000

Strategic Planning Network: From Vision to Reality
Patricia R. Stelwagon
Principal Strategic Planning
Berryessa Union Schl. Dist.
1376 Piedmont Rd.
San Jose, CA 95132-2498
TEL (408) 923-1831
FAX (408) 259-3869

Teacher Leadership
Bonnie Konner
West Essex Regional Schl. Dist.
West Greenbrook Rd.
N. Caldwell, NJ 07006
TEL (201) 228-1200
FAX (201) 575-7847

Teaching for Multiple Intelligences
David G. Lazear
New Dimensions of Learning
4880 Marine Dr., No. 515
Chicago, IL 60640
TEL (312) 907-9588

Teaching Thinking
Esther Fusco
24 Hopewell Dr.
Stony Brook, NY 11790
TEL (516) 661-5820
FAX (516) 661-5886
*Call if sending fax.

Thinking Assessment
Sally Duff
Maryland Center for Thinking Studies
Coppin State College
2500 West North Ave.
Baltimore, MD 21216
TEL (410) 396-9362

TQM—Education
John Jay Bonstingl
Consultant in Quality Educ.
P.O. Box 810
Columbia, MD 21044
TEL (410) 997-7555
FAX (410) 997-7555

Understanding Educational Change
Michele Keenan
407 Enos Place
Ho-Ho-Kus, NJ 07423
TEL (201) 612-0950
FAX (201) 670-3833

Whole Language
Lenore Sandel
Professor of Reading
Hofstra Univ.
Room 102, Mason Hall
Hempstead, NY 11550
TEL (516) 463-5803
FAX (516) 564-4296

Wholistic Education
John Palladino
Associate Professor of Education
Long Island Univ.
C.W. Post Campus
Brookville, NY 11548
TEL (516) 299-2372, or -2374
FAX (516) 626-2476

ASCD Networks Program Liaison
Agnes Crawford
Asst. Director, Field Services
ASCD
1250 N. Pitt St.
Alexandria, VA 22314-1403
TEL (703) 549-9110 X506
FAX (703) 549-3891

We Want to Hear From You!

Please take a few minutes to answer some questions about yourself and about the 1993 ASCD Yearbook. Your comments are valuable to us as we plan for yearbooks in the future, as well as other ASCD publications. Please send your completed survey to: **ASCD 1993 Yearbook Survey, 1250 N. Pitt Street, Alexandria, VA 22314.** Or **FAX to (703) 549-3891**. We would like to receive all surveys by **June 1, 1993**.

____ 1. I am an ASCD member.

New ____   1–5 years ____   5–10 years ____   Over 10 years ____

____ 2. I am involved in the education profession. (If not, please list occupation under "Other.")

H.S. Principal ____   Elem. Principal ____   Superintendent ____   Other administrator ____

Curriculum Specialist ____   Other specialist or supervisor ____   Univ. faculty ____

H.S. teacher ____   Elem. teacher ____   School board member or officer ____   Parent ____

College or graduate student ____   Other student ____   Education editor or writer ____

Other ____

____ 3. Type of community I work in:

Urban ____   Rural ____   Suburban ____

Country: United States ____   Other country ____

_____ 4. On a scale of 1–5, I found the 1993 Yearbook to be helpful to me in my work with children and youth. *(Please list a number, from 1, not at all helpful, to 5, extremely helpful—or comment briefly. This survey will be read by humans.)*

_____ 5. On a scale of 1–5, I believe the 1993 Yearbook addressed topics I am interested in and involved with in my daily work with children and youth. *(List a number, as in question 4.)*

_____ 6. On a scale of 1–5, I believe the 1993 Yearbook is a valuable part of my ASCD membership (if you are a member) and represents thoughtful articulation of important educational issues.

_____ 7. On a scale of 1–5, the 1993 Yearbook is easy to read and comprehend.

_____ 8. On a scale of 1–5, the 1993 Yearbook is attractively designed and is well organized for easy access to information.

_____ 9. Please comment briefly on any specific chapter or issue discussed by yearbook authors.

_____ 10. Please comment briefly on topics you would like us to address in future yearbooks or other publications. Use extra paper if you wish. *We welcome your suggestions!*

768-7370